# The Habit Revolution

# Dr Gina Cleo

# The Habit Revolution

Simple steps to rewire your brain
for powerful habit change

**murdoch books**
Sydney | London

Published in 2024 by Murdoch Books, an imprint of Allen & Unwin

Murdoch Books Australia
Cammeraygal Country
83 Alexander Street, Crows Nest NSW 2065
Phone: +61 (0)2 8425 0100
murdochbooks.com.au
info@murdochbooks.com.au

Murdoch Books UK
Ormond House, 26–27 Boswell Street,
London WC1N 3JZ
Phone: +44 (0) 20 8785 5995
murdochbooks.co.uk
info@murdochbooks.co.uk

 A catalogue record for this book is available from the National Library of Australia

A catalogue record for this book is available from the British Library

ISBN 978 1 92261 665 4

Cover design by Julia Cornelius
Text design by Susanne Geppert
Typeset by Midland Typesetters
Printed and bound by CPI Group (UK) Ltd, Croydon CR0 4YY

DISCLAIMER: Some names and identifying details have been changed to protect the privacy of individuals.

DISCLAIMER: The purchaser of this book understands that the information contained within is not intended to replace one-to-one medical advice. It is understood that you will seek full medical clearance by a licensed physician before making any changes mentioned in this book. The author and publisher claim no responsibility to any person or entity for any liability, loss, or damage caused or alleged to be caused directly or indirectly as a result of the use, application, or interpretation of the material in this book.

Every reasonable effort has been made to trace the owners o f copyright materials in this book, but in some instances this has proven impossible. The author(s) and publisher will be glad to receive information leading to more complete acknowledgements in subsequent printings of the book and in the meantime extend their apologies for any omissions.

We acknowledge that we meet and work on the traditional lands of the Cammeraygal people of the Eora Nation and pay our respects to their elders past, present and future.

10 9 8 7 6 5 4 3 2

To you, my readers.
You are my guiding light and
inspiration, and it's with immense
gratitude that I dedicate this
book to you.

# CONTENTS

Introduction: The power of habits     1

1    What is a habit?     15

2    Why we form habits     37

3    Habits versus intentions     45

4    Habit triggers     57

5    How to create new habits     73

6    How to break old habits     87

7    The neuroscience of habits     105

8    Micro habits     117

9    Where is our self-control?     135

10    How long it really takes to change a habit     155

11    The recipe for change     179

12    Mastering motivation     191

13    Do something different     219

14    Goal-setting essentials and pitfalls     233

15    Dealing with setbacks     249

Conclusion     265

Appendix: The finer details of motivational theory     268

Acknowledgements     270

Notes     273

Index     286

## Introduction

# The power of habits

DO YOU REMEMBER YOUR VERY first driving lesson?

You probably fumbled around trying to find where the key goes, checked every mirror multiple times, made sure your foot was on the brake pedal and not the accelerator, then finally moved your foot and ever so slowly started to roll the car forward, making sure not to go even the tiniest bit above the speed limit.

Fast forward to now and you're probably arriving at places you drove to and thinking, 'How did I even get here? I don't remember the drive.' That's because driving is now an automatic action for you – a habit.

The task of driving, which once upon a time took a lot of mental energy and concentration, has now become subconscious, automatic, habitual. Your brain remembers how to drive a car because it's something you've done many times before. So instead of using up mental energy on a task that you already know how to do, your brain moves the familiar action of driving to the automatic part of your brain, so that driving becomes instinctive and subconscious.

You could also think of the time you were first learning to tie your shoelaces. I remember my parents teaching me a song that included something to do with bunny ears jumping into a hole and popping out the other side, beautiful and bold. I also remember tying my fingers in the shoelaces, which is not supposed to happen, doing some elaborate knot only to have it unravel as soon as I let it go, and making my parents late for our outing because I was so determined to tie my own laces. It took many practices, many failed attempts, and every brain cell I could recruit to successfully learn how to tie my own shoelaces. Now I tie my laces without giving it any thought. I'm usually planning my next move or looking around the room to locate my keys and wallet. Just as with driving a car, my brain has moved the familiar action of tying my shoelaces into the automatic part of my brain so that it's instinctive and subconscious; it's a habit.

Imagine living a life where you eat healthy meals, exercise regularly, get a good night's sleep and have a productive workday – and do it all without having to grind through it, because those things just happen automatically. That's the power of creating a life built around healthy habits. Once you understand the theory of habit change and learn how to implement it, you can apply it to any area of your life, be it health, wellbeing, mindset, finances, relationships or productivity.

If you've ever set a goal to start a new habit or break an old one and you fell off the wagon; if you've been in a cycle of yo-yo dieting, phone scrolling or alarm snoozing; or if you intend to do one thing but end up doing another, then you're in the right place. Changing your habits has the power to help you achieve and maintain your goals in the long term, but you've probably never been guided through the steps of how to successfully change your habits – until now, that is.

Growing up, I watched both my grandparents battle through mealtimes due to having type 2 diabetes. They would be served different meals from the rest of the family and at dessert time they would eat sugar-free jelly while the rest of us indulged in sugary pastries and ice cream. In my Egyptian culture, food is a pretty big deal. We celebrate just about everything with a feast. Food is basically its own love language. The attitude in my family is if we're not feasting, we're not really living, and the more the merrier. But my grandparents didn't get to enjoy this experience with us (I mean sugar-free jelly is okaaay, but it's got nothing on pastries and ice cream). It wasn't so much the feasting or even the food that I wished they could experience; I just wanted them to enjoy a better quality of life.

I wanted to help people like my grandparents, so I completed a bachelor's degree in biomedical science and went on to do a master's degree in nutrition and dietetics. As a dietitian, I had the privilege of helping people achieve their health goals and regain their confidence. I worked across various hospital settings and ran my own private practice. I loved my job, but I started noticing that my patients' results were only short-lived. Within just a few weeks or months they would be back in the clinic wanting to work on the goals we'd already worked so hard to achieve. Initially, I thought I must have been a terrible dietitian, that perhaps my love for food got in the way of my objective advice. Did other dietitians have this same issue? What could I be doing wrong?

I was determined to help my patients achieve long-term results, so I started to hunt for evidence-based strategies. I took a deep dive into the medical literature in search of answers and read something that changed the course of my life: in all types of attempts at goal attainment and behaviour change, there was an overwhelming fail rate. Whether the goal was to lose weight, get fit, drink more water, quit smoking, reduce drinking, get better sleep or spend less time using technology, most of the time, people fell back into their old patterns and old habits and did not successfully achieve their goal.

Everything I read reiterated the fact that we're very good at setting goals but not so great at maintaining those goals in the long term. I wasn't a terrible dietitian after all. This yo-yo life of bouncing between moving towards their goals and falling off the wagon wasn't just happening to my patients, it was happening to most people on this planet. In fact, the majority of people who lose weight end up regaining that weight over the following months or years.[1] In the same way, most New Year's resolutions are forgotten by February.

Not long after this discovery, I decided to put my private practice clinic on hold and embark on a research journey. I wanted answers, I wanted sustainable solutions and I wanted to be able to help people achieve long-term success. Over the next four years I completed a doctorate[2] in habit change and became a habit researcher.

I read every journal article about long-term change that I could get my hands on. I read hundreds of papers on behavioural theories, psychology, sociology, neuroscience, neuropsychology and public health interventions. All the successful strategies pointed in the same direction: habit change. Changing our habits is the only proven method for achieving our goals in the long term. This means that making consistent, achievable, bite-sized changes in our day-to-day life to alter our habits is the only scientifically backed system for achieving sustainable success. Talk about a light-bulb moment!

During my doctoral studies, my co-researchers and I designed and implemented our own clinical trials to really put this theory to the test. In one of our studies,[3] we focused on weight management, recruiting participants from the community who had unsuccessfully tried several diets before. They were randomly assigned to one of three interventions to see if habit change really did help them maintain their weight loss over time. The first group was given a habit-*forming* intervention – a list of 10 tips we asked them to repeat as often as they could, every day. The tips included things like eat mindfully, keep to a meal routine, and aim to walk 10,000 steps a day.

The second group was given a habit-*breaking* intervention – random tasks to do at random times and on random days. The tasks were things like drive a different way to work, listen to a new genre of music, or contact a long-lost friend – nothing to do with weight management.

The final group were on our waiting list, so we used them as our control, with no intervention, so that we could see what differences our interventions made to the other groups. After 12 weeks, our participants in both the habit-forming and habit-breaking groups lost similar amounts of weight – about 3 kilograms (6½ pounds). This weight loss is quite comparable to the amount achieved through conventional lifestyle programs, so there were no surprises there, but our focus was on how the participants *maintained* this weight loss. Usually, people start to regain weight as soon as their weight-loss program is over. We call this the Nike Swoosh of weight regain – the weight goes down, then back up again (often with interest). Whether people go on a strict diet and exercise regimen or take weight-loss medication, long-term weight regain is almost inevitable.

But much to our surprise (and absolute elation), the study participants in both the habit-forming and habit-breaking groups not only kept off the weight that they had lost during the study period, but continued to lose weight a full year after the study had finished.

**Changing habits led to lasting weight loss**

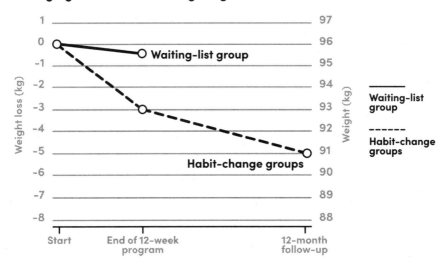

Despite the different underlying mechanisms of the habit-forming and habit-breaking interventions, participants in both groups achieved significant weight-loss maintenance. It was just as effective to introduce new, healthy habits as it was to break old habits. Whenever we form new habits, we're also simultaneously breaking old habits, and when we break old habits, we're also creating new ones in their place. Fundamentally, the participants achieved such a fantastic outcome because the study was focused on changing their habits and therefore changing their subconscious behaviours. It focused on creating consistency, promoting automaticity, increasing behavioural flexibility and improving self-regulatory skills – essential tools that we will unpack later in this book.

Never in the history of behavioural science had we seen results like this. Researchers get excited when weight-loss participants maintain their results after a study has finished, but to see these participants not only maintain weight loss but continue to lose weight long after the study had ended was a scientific breakthrough. I was dancing up and down the corridors of my very professional research centre. This was it. People no longer had to live in a constant cycle of yo-yo diets and failed attempts at reaching their goals.

I interviewed some of the study participants to get a better understanding of their experience on the habit-change programs.[4] What they shared with me would confirm everything I had read about the long-term nature of changing our habits. One participant after another told me that their new behaviours started to feel automatic, meaning they didn't even realise they were still doing the things we'd asked them to do during the study because those things had become habitual and therefore subconscious. The habit-forming group still ate mindfully, kept to a meal routine, and aimed to walk 10,000 steps a day after the study finished. And the habit-breaking group still changed their routines and practised doing random things they'd never done before. And the best part was they did all of this without using any mental energy or willpower; it was all subconscious.

Our study was published in a highly regarded medical journal and within hours of publication it was picked up by the media. Next minute, I was doing back-to-back media interviews with major news outlets around the world. To date, I've been interviewed by more than 200 media organisations. I'd finally found the answers I was looking for – the sustainable long-term solution that would revolutionise how people achieve their goals – and I was beyond excited to share them with the world.

I don't use the word 'revolutionise' lightly here. Learning to change your habits is an infallible way to revolutionise your life, which is why I've called this book *The Habit Revolution*. A revolution can be defined as a complete turn; a radical or complete change; the overthrow of a social order in favour of a new system; or a departure from the status quo and a move towards something new and different. All of these definitions apply here, and to making lasting changes to your life.

I've been a student of both the theory and practice of habit formation for many years, and have been privileged to witness the transformative results that habit change can have in many people's lives. Let me tell you about one of the most memorable times in my own life where the hard daily work of applying my knowledge of the science helped me recover from a major setback.

It was 2014 when I started formally researching habits. That spring, I met the 'man of my dreams'. My housemate and I had decided to rent out our spare room, so I posted an advertisement online that stated, 'Females only' (because we thought women would be less trouble). After several weeks of unsuccessful meet-and-greets with potential housemates, I received a phone call from a gentleman wishing to view the property. He had a kind and tender voice, and he turned out to be tall and handsome. He moved in that week.

There was instant chemistry between us, and we went from being housemates to friends to lovers in a fairly short space of time. Our love felt warm, electric and everything romantic poetry describes love to be. We eventually moved out of our shared house, bought a home together and got married in a beautiful ceremony overlooking the most stunning hinterland. We were 'living the dream', or so I thought.

Less than a year into our marriage, things didn't feel right. My husband seemed distant, both emotionally and physically. I describe it like he was a puff of smoke – I could see him there, but I couldn't connect with him. I didn't feel like he was accessible, responsive or emotionally available. On a particularly lonely Saturday afternoon, I unexpectedly learned of a devastating betrayal that led to the painful end of our relationship. I felt like the very tapestry of my life was unravelling in front of my eyes and there was nothing I could do to stop it. Nothing made sense, but then everything made sense at the same time. The more I discovered, the less I could breathe. I felt like I was going crazy. This couldn't be my life story, it just couldn't be.

It was one thing not to know how my future would unfold, but it was a whole other thing to question my entire past. Somehow there was a completely different story going on in the midst of a place where I thought I knew the plot intimately.

In her book *The State of Affairs*, psychotherapist Esther Perel writes that unfaithfulness is so unsettling because it attacks our memory of the past, which is one of the most important, seemingly dependable parts of our psyche.[5] If I couldn't trust what I once knew to be true, how could I trust what would happen tomorrow?

We are meaning-making creatures, and we rely on a coherent narrative to predict and regulate our future actions and feelings. Coherence creates a stable sense of self, and is a prerequisite for our habits because it's constant, steady and predictable – just as our habits are. Without this sense of coherence I felt estranged, not just from my husband but from myself.

Traumatic events[6] challenge our view of the world as a just, safe and predictable place. Trauma affects every facet of the body and mind, making the sufferer more likely to develop chronic diseases and other physical illnesses, mental illnesses and substance-related disorders. It also significantly impacts their capacity to connect and be vulnerable with others. Trauma impacts the brain by increasing the functioning of the amygdala, the 'emotional response' centre of the brain, causing greater fear responses. At the same time, it reduces activity of the prefrontal cortex, the brain region responsible for rational thinking and reasoning. And if that wasn't enough, trauma decreases the function of the hippocampus, the brain region associated primarily with memory and learning, which helps us differentiate between the past and the present. So my scrambled brain was more vulnerable to fear, it was less rational, and it was unable to determine the difference between the traumatic event and a later trigger … Gah, what a state!

---

## We are meaning-making creatures, and we rely on a coherent narrative to predict and regulate our future actions and feelings.

---

I experienced symptoms of PTSD,[7] the worst being flashbacks, nightmares, insomnia and intense fear. At first it felt like everything triggered my trauma responses. The sound the pebbles would make in the driveway when a car drove in (the poor delivery man must have seen me running to the back of the house every time he came to drop off a parcel); black cars; the smell of coffee … I felt like I couldn't escape the tormenting memories. I was equal parts on high alert like a deer in headlights, and absolutely terrified every second of every day like a lost child in the middle of the Pamplona bull run.

Because my mind felt so fractured, I had lost the ability to do anything, even basic things to look after myself. When you think of your morning routine, it might include a habit chain like getting out of bed, going to the bathroom, taking a shower, brushing your teeth, getting dressed, etc. And within those behaviours are many micro behaviours: getting out of bed might mean you turn your alarm off, fold the blankets back and place your feet on the floor. Drying yourself after a shower might mean grabbing a towel with a certain hand and drying yourself in a similar sequence each day. I had somehow lost all of that familiarity, and the very basics of my daily routine were no longer normal for me because nothing was normal, nothing was certain, nothing was safe.

In the past, understanding and changing my own habits had helped me get back on my feet and recover from a 10-year battle with an eating disorder (more about this later in the book). Now, my brain was in overdrive as I relearned the very basics of life's daily practices. It started with saying to myself, 'Gina, all you need to do today is brush your teeth, that's it,' and I'd find the mental energy to do that. But I now had to think my way through every step of the process. I'd feel completely exhausted after such a tedious task and crawl back into bed. Then the following day, I'd say to myself, 'Okay, today, you need to brush your teeth and have a shower, then you can sneak back into bed,' and I'd go through the process of relearning the sequence of showering. I noticed that brushing my teeth the second day was a little easier than the first day and it was easier again each day after that. My brain was relearning my basic daily routines and rebuilding my habits into my life once more.

I gradually reintroduced one habit at a time, until eventually I was able to cook myself a meal, get back into the gym and drive to work. The simple act of practising healthy habits daily helped me reshape my world during the most destabilising time of my life (as if I wasn't already a huge fan of creating healthy habits). I persistently practised physical and mental habit change. I had to reframe my fearful thoughts and calm my ruminating mind. I refused to let this crushing blow break me. I wanted to get to a place where I could love and trust and be truly vulnerable again. And by challenging and reshaping my habitual thought patterns (the ones I developed in a bid for self-preservation), I did just that.

Several years after this tornado, I met Mitch, the actual man of my dreams, and we eloped to Mexico. I wore a red lace dress and he wore a white Mexican suit topped with a sombrero. We were perched up on a hillside where the ocean meets the desert; it was magical in every way.

But it took more than just relearning my habits to get back on an even keel. My healing journey included a lot of therapy: trauma therapy, exposure therapy (wow, that was hard), psychotherapy – anything that ended in 'therapy' and included a psychologist, I did. I learned to sit with the discomfort, to physically feel the anxiety in my body until it dissipated. I learned how to shorten my trauma responses from several days to several seconds through breathing techniques and other strategies.

I applied foundational principles that I'd been teaching in my habit courses for years, and that are outlined in this book: principles such as finding motivation in action; creating cue–response associations; and making small, achievable changes rather than trying to make big changes (which for me, as an all-or-nothing thinker, sucked but was extremely effective). I am today a different woman from the one crippled with fear and anxiety. I'm not perfectly back to my pre-trauma self, but gosh I've come a long way. I have re-established my life, rebuilt myself and redefined my identity.

Because of my own journey and watching countless others transform their lives, I've found a passion for teaching people how to reach their highest potential through the power of habit change. I now fill my days speaking at corporate events and conferences, and running training courses for others to become certified habit coaches through my Habit Change Institute. I also run habit-change programs for people who are ready to live their life by design, not by default.

This book is not a self-help guide to recovering from trauma, although the principles outlined here can absolutely help you to rebuild your life and regain your confidence. This book is a practical, evidence-based manual for how to create a life that you desire, one habit at a time.

The truth is, most of the time what we do is what we do most of the time, and sometimes we do something different. The good news is, the future is not written yet and you have the power to change your habits to transform, restore and reclaim your self.

Consider this book your personal habit coach. Each chapter guides you through everything you need to know about changing your habits for good. You'll learn how to turn your goals into habits so that they're as seamless and automatic as driving a car. You'll understand why you do the things you do, why willpower fails us, what triggers your habits, and how to get and stay motivated to achieve the things you set out to achieve.

---

## Most of the time what we do is what we do most of the time, and sometimes we do something different.

---

The order of the chapters is designed to take you on a journey of change. We'll start with what habits are, why we form them and how they're different from behaviours. We'll then get into what triggers our habits, because once we understand our triggers, we can analyse our habits and change them for good. When we've covered these fundamentals, we'll move on to how to create new habits and break old ones in a meaningful way that you can implement straight away. We'll then go through the incredible processes that take place in our brain when we're changing our habits, and how you can use your brain power rather than your willpower to make lasting change. In the final chapters of the book, we'll cover how to master your motivation, how to set effective goals you can actually stick to, and what to do when you're faced with setbacks.

Everything laid out in the pages of this book is backed by science. The information comes not only from my life's work, but from the work of hundreds of researchers from around the world.

I encourage you to complete the activities that appear at the end of certain chapters. Some will help you learn more about yourself, some will help you reflect on the things you really want to achieve, and some will guide you through the process of changing your habits – whether that's creating new ones or breaking old ones. Doing the activities is an important step in the process of taking control of your life and creating the life you want to live.

I'm so excited that you're here. So let's get to it, shall we?

# Chapter 1

# What is a habit?

LET'S START BY DEFINING WHAT a habit is. Often the word 'habit' is preceded by the word 'bad' and has a negative connotation. It comes up when we talk about nail biting, smoking or scrolling too much on social media. But the reality is, habits have no intrinsic moral value. A habit is neither good nor bad, a habit is neutral. Some of our habits move us towards our goals – they're the ones we call 'good', like exercising regularly. Other habits pull us away from our goals – these are the ones we call 'bad', like not making space in our life for enough sleep. And other habits are neither 'good' nor 'bad', like opening the door with your right hand instead of your left (or vice versa) – these impartial habits pose no benefit or hindrance to our life, they simply make it a little more streamlined.

In the same way, what might be considered a 'good' habit for one person might be thought of as 'bad' for another. Take eating a piece of cake, for example, which becomes a positive or negative habit based on the context and our goals. For someone recovering from disordered eating, it might be considered a step forward, but not so much for someone with type 2 diabetes. A habit can take many forms, but it's simply a subconscious action or sequence of actions, or a mental response or even an emotional reaction or belief.

'Behaviour' is easily defined in one sentence: a behaviour is the way you act or conduct yourself. A behaviour is a conscious action. For example, mindfully (i.e. consciously) moving from one place to another, cooking a new meal, or conducting yourself in a meeting.

A habit, on the other hand, requires a little more explanation to define accurately.

Early writers, from the ancients to the 19th century, described a habit as an acquired *propensity*. Propensity can be described as an inclination, a tendency, a predisposition, a susceptibility or a readiness. Habits are formed through the process of classical conditioning, where a trigger that is initially neutral becomes associated with a particular response through repeated pairing. When we repeat an action in a consistent context (such as at the same time or place; or in response to a certain emotion, social situation or prior action), we create neural pathways in our brain between the action and the context. The more we repeat the action in the same context, the stronger the relevant neural pathways get, until eventually the context–action association becomes ingrained in our brain and the context triggers the associated habit.

'Habit' is therefore defined as the process by which exposure to a context activates an impulse to act, based on context–action associations we've learned through repeated performance. In other words, a habit is a repeated behaviour that has become automatic through frequent repetition in the same context.

Over time, the context alone can trigger the responding habit without conscious thought. 'Habitual behaviour' describes the actions that are generated by this process.

Stay with me as we look at a little more theory, and then I'll illustrate how this all plays out in our lives.

# THE HABIT LOOP

A habit requires three key ingredients: a *cue*, a *routine* and a *reward*. This is known as the *habit loop*.

- **The cue** is the context or trigger for the action you take. It's either the place you're in, the time of day, your emotional or social situation, or your preceding action. Habits are always triggered.
- **The routine** is the habit triggered by the cue; it's the action itself.
- **The reward** is the benefit you gain from performing the habit. The reward is often the reason you continue to repeat the habit. Positive rewards form a positive feedback loop that tells your brain, 'Next time you encounter this cue, do the same thing.'

Let's say, for example, that each time you get home in the evening you eat a cookie. You really enjoy the taste of these cookies (that's your reward). The first time you ate a cookie when you got home, a mental link was created between getting home (cue) and eating a cookie (routine). Each time you repeat this behaviour (eating a cookie in response to getting home), you reinforce the habit loop and the *getting home = eat a cookie* mental link strengthens to the point that getting home prompts you to eat a cookie automatically. A habit has been formed.

Eventually, just thinking of getting home automatically triggers the learned routine. Getting home means eating a cookie! This learned routine becomes the default action and alternative options become less accessible in your memory.

**The habit loop**

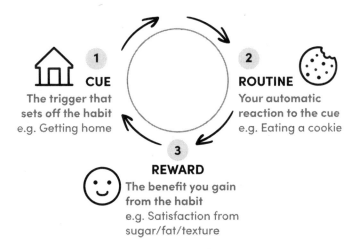

There's a common misconception that habits develop when we repeat a behaviour over and over again, but that's only half correct. Habits develop when we repeat a behaviour over and over again *in the same context*. A habit is only a habit if it includes the three key ingredients of the habit loop: cue, routine and reward.

You may not eat cookies every day, but you do have habits you unconsciously repeat every day – we all do. Perhaps you eat the same breakfast every day or dry yourself after a shower in the same sequence, or maybe you park in the same spot at the shops or the office. Philosopher and psychologist William James was a big believer in habits. In the 20th century, James enthusiastically assessed that 99 or 99.9 per cent of our actions are purely automatic and habitual, from the moment we wake up to the time we lie down each night.[1] More recent studies estimate that anywhere between 43 and 70 per cent of everything we do is habitual.[2] Hundreds of habits influence how we live our lives and guide how we act day to day: how we eat, sleep and talk to our loved ones; how we get dressed and drive our car; how we do business; and whether we exercise or have a glass of wine after work. How we unthinkingly spend our time, attention and money is predominantly habitual. Habits are the invisible blueprint for our everyday life.

## How habits start

You may be wondering why we all have different habits. Some people habitually exercise in the mornings, for example, while others prefer to sleep in; some people religiously have a coffee as soon as they wake up while others may have their first coffee mid-morning, or they may have tea, or maybe just water. The patterns of our habits intricately weave the narrative of our life's journey, revealing the chapters of our choices and priorities. Our habits tell a story about our life – not necessarily our life right now, but perhaps our life a few months or even a few years ago. Because once upon a time, most of our habits were intentional actions. They are things that we once chose to do – perhaps we were trying to achieve a goal or suppress an uncomfortable emotion or reach some kind of desired outcome, such as convenience, productivity or wellbeing.

Let me repeat that because it's important. Our habits – the things we do automatically day in, day out – were once upon a time intentional behaviours. They started in the reflective part of our brain and eventually moved across to the impulsive part of our brain.

Let's say, for example, you noticed you were feeling a little sluggish one morning, so you decided to make a coffee when you got to work. The coffee hit the spot and gave you the pick-me-up you were looking for. Your sluggishness subsided and you were able to concentrate and focus better. The next morning when you got to work, you decided

---

Our habits – the things we do automatically day in, day out – were once upon a time intentional behaviours.

---

to make a coffee again, and you did the same the following day, and the day after that, and the day after that. Your brain created a cue–response association, with the cue being getting to work and the response being making a coffee. The more you repeated this sequence, the stronger your cue–response association became, making your coffee-drinking habit stronger and more automatic.

This coffee-drinking habit started off with the intention of getting a boost of energy when you got to work, but it's now become an automatic habit. Eventually, just thinking of the context (in this case, getting to work) triggers the habit of making a coffee, and the goal of being more alert is no longer needed. This means that even when you're not feeling sluggish, you'll still habitually make a coffee when you get to work. In the same way, many people eat lunch at noon even when they're not necessarily hungry; it's just a programmed habit. Or they take a particular route to work when there could be a more efficient way.

Consider the process of cooking pasta. Most of us have been taught to boil a large pot of water, add salt, wait for it to reach a rolling boil, and then add the pasta, stirring occasionally until it's cooked to our preferred level of doneness. While cooking pasta like this is effective and has carried on for generations, alternative methods can be even better. Take the 'one-pot pasta' technique, for example, which involves cooking the pasta in a single pot along with the sauce and other ingredients. This can save time, energy and water, and the pasta absorbs the flavours of the sauce more readily. There's also the added bonus of using fewer dishes.

But many of us continue to use the traditional method. This resistance to change can be attributed to the comfort and familiarity of the old habit, as well as reluctance to try something new or deviate from what has worked in the past. We're accustomed to our existing routines and may not always see a compelling enough reason to change, even when it may have clear advantages.

We've got enough things to think about, so naturally we don't want to have to overthink what we're doing while fixing dinner – or life for that matter. We only have so much capacity for cognitive processing, so our brain functions on autopilot whenever it can.

## HABIT: THE BEST OF SERVANTS OR THE WORST OF MASTERS?

In habit science, we say that habit formation is a process by which behavioural control shifts from goal dependence to context dependence. The actions you once performed to achieve a goal, you now do in response to a trigger, without the need for the original goal. Habits develop through a process of context-dependent repetition, meaning when you perform a behaviour in a specific context, you reinforce the cue–response association in your memory. Performance of a habit therefore involves delegating behavioural control to that cue. The more we reinforce the cue–memory associations, the more ingrained the habit becomes. Our brains literally create new neural connections and pathways, and strengthen those connections the more we repeat the habit. The stronger the neural pathways in our brain, the more efficient, automatic and subconscious the habit will be.

Habit is not dichotomous: it's not the case that you either have a habit or don't have a habit. Rather, habits vary in strength on a continuum, so that they may be more or less strongly habitual. Essentially, the more you repeat a behaviour in a consistent context, the more hard-wired it will become in your life. This is also known in neuroscience as Hebbian learning.

Hebbian learning is based on the principle that if one neuron (brain cell) fires and then another neuron fires, the first will connect to the second, making them more likely to fire as a pair. This is how we learn. This learning theory explains why if you were bitten by a dog as a kid, you might have developed a fear of dogs – because your

# Neurons that fire together, wire together.

'dog' neuron fired, then your 'pain' neuron fired, and so dog became connected to pain. This theory, proposed by one of Canada's greatest neuropsychologists, Donald Hebb, is often summarised in one handy phrase: 'Neurons that fire together, wire together.'[3] Getting home is connected to eating a cookie, getting to work is connected to having a coffee. This is how habits are formed and strengthened in our life.

In the context of practising a skill, each time we execute the skill, neurons are firing together, and those connections get stronger and stronger. That's why it can be difficult to change a poor technique if we've been reinforcing those connections for some time. Practice doesn't necessarily make perfect; practice makes permanent. A permanent action is generally automatic because it's been repeated hundreds of times, and an automatic action can override intentions. So the more we repeat a behaviour, the less influence our intentions will have over our actions and the more our automatic brain system will take control.

Our habits prompt our actions automatically, and they do this in the absence of intention, motivation, conscious control or awareness, and with minimal cognitive effort. If you've ever been frustrated at yourself for repeating old, unwanted behaviours, ones that you specifically told yourself you would no longer do, you now understand that habits are automatic – they act like a knee-jerk reaction when they're triggered, and they override your good intentions. Habit is therefore either the best of servants or the worst of masters. Of course we can break habits; in fact, breaking unwanted habits is a really important life skill to have, which is why Chapter 6 is dedicated just to it.

The upside of habits making our actions automatic is that once we create healthy habits, they are likely to persist long-term, without the need for sustained motivation or self-control. You can become one of those people who wakes up early, exercises regularly and eats healthy meals without putting in too much effort.

# AUTOMATICITY

I recently walked into a car dealership to test drive one of their new cars. The consultant stood next to me at the front door of the building. I watched him press a button on his phone, which signalled this car to move itself from where it was positioned in the carpark and park perfectly in front of where we were standing. No one was in the car; it drove itself with the push of a button. I was trying to act cool, but inside I was like 'Oh my goodness, this is incredible!' I started thinking how I never had to worry about doing another parallel park or squeezing out of a tight parking spot.

Autopilot refers to a system that controls the operation of a vehicle or device without requiring constant manual input from a human operator. These systems are commonly used in aircrafts to maintain a stable flight path, adjust the altitude, and even land the plane in certain situations. Autopilot systems gather information about an aircraft or vehicle's position, speed and orientation, then process that information using an algorithm and pre-programmed instructions to adjust the controls and maintain a desired course or trajectory. With the press of a button, a driver or pilot can activate autopilot mode and leave it up to the pre-programmed system to do the work.

Autopilot works much like our habits. When we encounter a habit trigger, our brain draws on its memory of the learned response and activates the pre-programed neural pathways associated with activating the habit. The trigger is like the button and the habit is like autopilot mode.

That automatic nature of habit is termed automaticity. Habit automaticity is the degree to which a habit has become automatic or unconscious. You could think of automaticity as the fluency, ease or effortlessness of habitual behaviour. When you're performing a habit and it's effortless, like brushing your teeth, drying yourself after a shower, or tying your shoelaces – you are in a state of automaticity.

Over time, as we repeat behaviours in the same contexts, they become more automatic, and they require less cognitive effort to perform. Once a habit is formed, automaticity is a key pillar of that habit. But automaticity can be both beneficial and detrimental to our lives. On the one hand, healthy habits can help us live a positive and fulfilling life. We can eat well, exercise regularly, have a good sleep routine, be productive and have wonderful relationships, while still conserving cognitive resources for other tasks. On the other hand, unhealthy habits can lead to negative outcomes, such as health issues, poor mental wellbeing or procrastination.

Automaticity can also be both beneficial and detrimental for the same habit, such as driving a familiar route on your daily commute. Once you've driven the same route many times, you may find yourself arriving at your destination without much conscious thought or effort. This can be beneficial in that it frees up cognitive resources for other tasks, but it can also be risky if you become too complacent and fail to pay attention to potential hazards on the road.

The moment we're faced with a habit trigger, our brain directly retrieves the associated response from our memory – that's the cue–response association. Having automaticity for a certain habit means our brain doesn't need to exert any energy on calculating how to respond. This echoes the concept of a habit being a direct retrieval of a behaviour in response to a trigger, without reflection.

When our habits reach automaticity, the actions tend to be *goal-independent,* as they can operate without, or even contrary to, our intentions. They are *unconscious,* as they can operate without conscious awareness and may not even have access to awareness. They are *efficient*, as they do not require effortful attention or mental processing and they are generally enacted quickly. And, perhaps most importantly, they are *cue-driven*, as they can be triggered directly by the presence or the perception of certain elements in our environment.

## Developing or breaking automaticity

You know you've reached a level of automaticity with a certain habit when you're starting to do it unconsciously and effortlessly, and it would feel somewhat strange if you didn't do it. Imagine a phone ringing and you have to answer by saying 'Greetings' rather than your usual way. How you usually answer is likely an automatic habit you've developed over the years. Answering the phone with 'Greetings' would probably feel strange. Or think of holding a spoon with your non-dominant hand, or even wearing your watch on the opposite wrist. There's no flow in doing things differently. Our brain becomes conscious of the change. There's no automaticity.

Our aim, therefore, should be to develop automaticity for the habits we want in our lives and eliminate automaticity for the habits we want to break. We want our desired habits to be easy and natural; we want living a healthy lifestyle and being productive to be effortless. In the same way, we don't want our undesired habits to be easy and automatic, because the easier they are, the more likely they are to remain in our lives. We want habits like smoking, drinking too much alcohol or staying up too late to present a challenge and require effort and energy to be performed. We want to have a sense of control and intentionality over those undesired behaviours.

One study in the UK looked at the smoking habits of nearly 50 adult volunteers.[4] Two months before the study, the UK government introduced a smoking ban in pubs. Smokers who had a habit of smoking while drinking alcohol reported smoking in a pub despite intending to adhere to the ban. Several smokers described 'finding themselves' beginning to light up a cigarette while consuming alcohol. Habitual automaticity predicted the likelihood of these 'action slips', meaning the more automatic it was for the participants to smoke while drinking, or the stronger their smoking habit, the more likely they were to light up unintentionally. This demonstrates that habits can direct actions, despite conscious motivational intention.

Another interesting finding in this study, which was consistent with previous research, was that the smokers showed attentional bias to triggers associated with smoking cigarettes. Attentional bias refers to our tendency to prioritise the processing of certain types of stimuli over others. Attentional biases may explain our failure to consider alternative possibilities when engaged in an existing train of thought. If you've heard the term 'selective hearing', think of attentional bias as 'selective habit triggering'.

Just like a computer, your brain has a search function, and it finds the things that are relevant to you. It's programmed by what you focus on and, more importantly, what you identify with. It's why when we buy a new car, we suddenly see the same type of car on the road more often. It's why when we buy a new outfit, we start noticing other people wearing a similar outfit. And it's also why you might hear your name being called out in a noisy, crowded room.

To demonstrate how this filter works, wherever you are right now, scan your environment and focus on the colour red. If there's any red at all, you'll see it, even if it's only a tiny bit. Try it for yourself!

The smokers in the British study were subconsciously 'looking out' for triggers associated with their smoking. This finding tells us that the way we experience the triggers that prompt our daily habits, and therefore how strong our habits are, could be predicted by how much we 'look out' for cues. The saying, 'We attract what we focus on' sounds woo-woo, but the science proves it's true. To a reasonable extent, we absolutely do attract what we focus on.

# CHARACTERISTICS OF A HABIT

Habit researchers agree that there are three central characteristics of a habit:

1. a history of repetition
2. a high degree of automaticity
3. being triggered in stable contexts.[5]

Understanding these characteristics allows us to identify whether the actions we are taking are habits or behaviours. To change habits, we need different strategies from those we would use to change behaviours. Changing habits requires an understanding of the habit triggers and the habit rewards (which we'll look at later in this book), whereas changing behaviours can simply take an intentional decision to make a change. Once you know if your actions are habits or behaviours, you can implement the applicable strategies to change them.

## 1. Repetition

We never do something only once and think of it as a habit. Our habits are actions, thoughts or responses that we've done repeatedly before. We recognise them, they're familiar to us; we may even identify with them as part of who we are. For example, if you go for a run frequently, you might think of yourself as a runner, or if you spend a lot of time working, you might think of yourself as a workaholic. All your habits have a history of repetition.

There's an interesting nuance to note here. Despite the predictable cumulative effect that takes place in habit formation – the more you repeat an action in response to a specific cue in a stable context, the more automatic and habitual it becomes – there's a distinction to be made between frequency and repetition. A habit has a *history* of repetition, but it's not solely dependent on *frequency* of repetition.

Some of us have strong habits we might perform infrequently

because we only encounter the cue that triggers them infrequently. For example, some people have a habit of attending church at Christmastime, but since Christmas comes but once a year, they only perform this habit annually. It's still a habit, it still has a history of repetition, the person might feel strange if they didn't attend church at Christmastime, but it's not a frequently occurring habit. In this same context, another example is the habit of saying 'amen' at the conclusion of a prayer. Weekly churchgoers will say amen on a weekly basis, but those who attend church only at Christmastime will only say amen once a year. Saying amen is habitual and automatic in both instances, but its frequency differs considerably.

I have friends who like to go camping in the same spot every year. They've booked this particular campsite two to three years in advance and always at the same time of year, just to make sure they don't miss their beloved annual holiday. When they're there, they do similar activities – riding bikes around the park; and kayaking, fishing and swimming in the creek. They eat similar meals, so they pack similar food, and they spend a similar amount of time there each year. Although where my friends go and what they do on their holiday is very habitual (almost on autopilot), those habits don't occur very frequently at all – only once a year.

My theory here is that we can build strong habits even if we enact them infrequently, as long as we enact them each time we encounter their associated cue. So if you habitually go to yoga on Saturday mornings and, for whatever reason, you miss a week or two, your Saturday-morning yoga habit may get weaker because you missed an opportunity to habitually respond to the habit cue. The more we perform a habit in response to its trigger, the stronger it gets, and in the same way, the less we perform a habit in response to its trigger, the weaker the habit gets. So if you've repeated an action at the same time, or in the same place, more than once before, then it could become a habit (if it hasn't already).

## 2. Automaticity

I wrote earlier about automaticity, but I wanted to touch on it here because automaticity – the fluency of habitual behaviour – is a key characteristic of a habit. To recap, habit automaticity plays out when we perform actions with minimal awareness and lack of conscious intent, and those actions require little energy to perform.

In my late teens, I was obsessed with trying to lose weight. I say 'trying' because I was wildly unsuccessful in my dieting attempts. I wasn't overweight, but my body had rapidly changed when I hit puberty and I wasn't thrilled about my newly acquired wider hips and larger breasts. Curves are more accepted in modern society's beauty standards, but back then they weren't so much. In line with my view of the perfect body, I aspired to look more like a stick insect than a horse saddle. Like every good dieter, I would wait until Monday would roll around to start the next new fad diet. Most of the diets I tried were quite restrictive – the cabbage soup diet, the lemon detox diet (I'm ashamed to even admit that I've tried that), the keto diet, or the carb-lover's diet (which in my opinion is deceptively named given you're only allowed to eat carbs once a day).

I could confidently say that I've tried pretty much every diet out there. But very often, I would find myself halfway through a bag of crisps or finishing off a chocolate-chip cookie before I would realise that crisps and cookies were definitely not on the diet menu. I remember getting extremely frustrated with myself that I didn't have more awareness of my behaviour. I mean, I had to get up from wherever I was, seek out the crisps, find them in the cupboard, take the packet back to my seat, open it and start eating. It seemed like there were so many opportunities to have a mindful moment and think, 'Hang on, Gina, I definitely don't recall reading "crisps" on the foods allowed list,' but that didn't happen. I often became aware of what I was doing when I was either elbow-deep in the crisps packet, or when someone else walked in the room and asked me if I was off my diet. I felt like a total failure.

I now know that I was simply operating on autopilot. Grabbing an afternoon snack was something I did mindlessly, effortlessly and with a high degree of automaticity. It was a habit.

We know what it feels like to make a decision, to want something to happen and to control our actions to make it happen. But we can't be introspective about the mechanisms of our habits; we can observe the results of our habitual actions, but we're blind to their mechanisms because they occur largely outside our conscious awareness.

Here's a story of a person who was newly employed in an office job. On their first day, they were notified that the office doorknobs locked when turned clockwise. Despite the warning, the new employee haplessly turned the doorknob in a clockwise position and consequently locked one of their colleagues in the office for several hours. What a way to build a first impression! But there's more to the story. You see, this new employee had exactly the same type of doorknobs at home, but they would *open* when they were turned clockwise. When the other employees noted this, they were less inclined to judge the new employee for the error. Without the justification of having identical doorknobs at home that worked in the opposite direction, the new employee would have been held to greater account for their oversight. But we understand that habits can run off without thought or intention.

### 3. Being context-cued

The last key habit characteristic is that they are triggered in stable contexts. The first part of the habit loop is the cue, or the trigger, which is followed by the routine (the habit), then the reward. Habits are always triggered, as triggers are the precursor for habits. Without triggers, we don't have habits.

It's estimated that almost half of our daily behaviour happens in the same context, meaning we tend to do things at the same time, or in the same place, or after a certain action.[6] For example, we might eat our meals at a similar time of day or follow the same path on our daily walk. Our life is filled with cues that trigger both wanted and unwanted habits.

In the smoking study I mentioned earlier, the researchers wanted to know to what degree it was likely that the participants would unintentionally light up when they were in a pub. Essentially, they were measuring the strength of the cue–response association; the cue was being in the pub and the routine was smoking. The researchers found that the likelihood of a behavioural slip was determined not by the typical indicators of smoking dependence, such as the number of cigarettes usually smoked in a day, but by the strength of the habit association between drinking and smoking.

We learn from this study and others that we may have great goals and intentions, but those well-intended plans can be easily overruled by the automatic habit responses that are cued by the triggering environment. The stronger the cue–routine association, the more likely we are to perform the responding habit.

Don't be disheartened though; with enough awareness, a solid plan and strong intentions, you can break any unwanted habit.

## HOW TO IDENTIFY A HABIT

If you're wondering if something you do is habitual, ask yourself, 'Have I done this before?', 'Does it feel natural or automatic?' and 'Is it happening at the same time, or place or after I perform a certain action, or when I'm feeling a certain way?'

## Measuring habit strength

You can also measure your habit strength for each habit using a scale called the self-reported behavioural automaticity index (SRBAI).[7]

### Self-reported behavioural habit index

| Habit X is something ... | Strongly disagree | Disagree | Neither disagree nor agree | Agree | Strongly agree |
|---|---|---|---|---|---|
| | 1 | 2 | 3 | 4 | 5 |
| 1. I do automatically | | | | | |
| 2. I do without having to consciously remember | | | | | |
| 3. I do without thinking | | | | | |
| 4. I start doing before I realise I'm doing it | | | | | |

Answer each of these questions for each habit you want to measure. To calculate your average habit-strength score for each habit, divide the total score for that habit by 5. Your overall score will be between 1 and 5, and the higher the score, the stronger the strength of that habit. A score of 1 indicates no habit, 2 is a weak habit, 3 is a moderately strong habit, 4 is a strong habit and 5 is a very strong habit.

In the example opposite, the habit-strength score of 3.2 means that walking my dog is a moderately strong habit. This is a great way to measure how strong your habits are, especially as you work to create new habits and break old ones.

| Walking my dog is something ... | Strongly disagree | Disagree | Neither disagree nor agree | Agree | Strongly Agree |
|---|---|---|---|---|---|
| | 1 | 2 | 3 | 4 | 5 |
| 1. I do automatically | | | | ✓ | |
| 2. I do without having to consciously remember | | | | | ✓ |
| 3. I do without thinking | | | | ✓ | |
| 4. I start doing before I realise I'm doing it | | | ✓ | | |
| SCORE | | | 3 | 8 | 5 |

Total score = 3 + 8 + 5 = 16, then 16 ÷ 5 = **3.2**

## HABIT VERSUS ADDICTION

Habits and addictions are both regularly repeated patterns of behaviour, but they differ in terms of our level of control over them and their impact on our life.

As we now know, a habit is a behaviour that has been repeated so often in the same context that it becomes automatic, requiring little or no conscious thought or effort. An addiction, on the other hand, is a compulsive behaviour that a person feels unable to control, even if it has negative consequences in their life. Addictions can be physical or psychological, and can include behaviours such as substance abuse, gambling or compulsive shopping. While habits can be positive or negative, addictions are almost always negative and harmful to a person's life.

Dopamine is a neurotransmitter (a chemical messenger between nerve or brain cells) that is the communicating chemical in the reward centre of the brain. This reward system plays a key role in both habits and addictions, but the way it functions differs between the two.

In the context of habits, dopamine is released in the brain when we engage in a behaviour that we find rewarding or pleasurable. This reinforces the behaviour and makes it more likely that we will repeat it in the future. Over time, the brain begins to associate the behaviour with the release of dopamine, which feels good, leading to the behaviour becoming a habit.

In the context of addictions, dopamine plays a similar role, but with some important differences. When someone engages in a behaviour that they are addicted to, such as using drugs or gambling, dopamine is released in the brain at much higher levels than with a habit. This leads to a more intense feeling of pleasure or reward, which strongly reinforces the addictive behaviour, making it both something they really crave and something that's difficult to quit. We'll talk more about dopamine and the reward systems that drive our behaviour later in the book.

What you need to know now is that there are distinct differences between habits and addictions. Habits are not addictions and not all addictions are habits, although they embody some of the characteristics of a habit. You are not addicted to brushing your teeth; it's simply a daily habit.

# SUMMARY

» A habit is a repeated behaviour that has become automatic through consistent repetition in the same context.

» A habit requires three key ingredients: a *cue*, a *routine* and a *reward*. This is known as the habit loop.

» Habits are behaviours that were once initiated intentionally but then with repetition became automatic.

» There are three central characteristics of a habit: a history of repetition, a high degree of automaticity, and being triggered in stable contexts.

» You can measure how strong your habits are using the self-reported behavioural automaticity index (SRBAI).

» Habits and addictions are both patterns of behaviour that are repeated regularly, but they differ in terms of a person's level of control over them and their impact on that person's life.

---

**ACTIVITY**

# Your habits

Because your habits are automatic, you won't always be aware of them. To better understand your habits and bring them into your awareness, it's good to reflect on the things you do automatically and identify when or where you're doing them. Once you identify your habits and triggers, you can have much more control over your automatic actions.

Use a notebook or journal to respond to these prompts.

## Wanted habits

List three habits you currently have that you're happy with. Then identify the trigger for that habit. For example:

**Habit:** *I do 10 minutes of meditation*
**Trigger:** *When I get into bed at night*

## Unwanted habits

List three habits you currently have that you would like to break, and identify their triggers. For example:

**Habit:** *I snack when I'm not hungry*
**Trigger:** *When I'm feeling bored or lonely*

---

# Chapter 2

# Why we form habits

WE LIVE IN A VIBRANT, complex and transient world where we constantly face a barrage of information competing for our attention. To function in this environment, we rely on our senses – sight, smell, sound, taste and touch – to inform us of our surroundings and the things happening around us. This shapes how we perceive the world. Our senses are extraordinary. I remember the 20-year-old me crying tears of awe in a human biology lecture about sensory neurons and motor neurons. The human body's ability to function within itself and interact with the outside world is simply amazing.

For example, our eyes take in more than 1 megabyte of data every second, the equivalent of reading 500 pages of information or an entire encyclopedia every minute. We can hear someone shouting from 100 metres (300 feet) away or whispering from 10 metres (30 feet) away. As I'm writing this, I can hear the washing machine rumbling, the rain outside, birds and crickets, the tapping of my keyboard and, of course, the cute snoring of my dog, Macy, as she snoozes by my feet.

Just one whiff of a familiar smell can trigger a memory from childhood in less than a millisecond, and our skin contains more than 4 million receptors that provide us with important information about temperature, pressure, texture and pain. Because we simply cannot process all of the available information at once, our brain has developed efficient methods of filtering, interpreting and responding to the vast amount of information our senses provide. To a large degree, we form this filter ourselves by telling our brain (whether consciously or subconsciously) what's important to us, what we believe, what we fear and what we're focused on. Our brain then places emphasis on facts we already know or value; things we might find enjoyable or rewarding; things that are dangerous or could harm us; and things that are unusual, interesting or novel. This filtering system means that of the thousands of bits of information we receive through our senses every second, we can only consciously process three to four bits of information at any one time.[1]

Our brains are prone to information overload and as a result can overlook obvious pieces of information. The way we experience the world is through our perception and attention. Perception helps us become aware of the world around us; our attention then helps us focus on the most relevant and pertinent pieces of information. The information we don't need to focus on becomes peripheral to our attention or shifts into the subconscious, habitual part of our brain. We rely on habits to get us through our day efficiently. Grabbing your keys, backing the car out of the driveway, navigating to work – with repetition, your brain converts each of these actions into automatic habits and they become more fluid and less prone to error.

As the father of modern psychology, William James, suggested, we can use automaticity to our advantage. The more tasks we allow our unconscious mind to take over, the more we free up our conscious mind to focus on the things that are important to us. Someone for whom almost nothing is habitual is plagued by indecision because everything they do requires conscious thought and effort.

Habits are ways that our neural networks 'remember' recurring contexts, and are therefore triggered when we encounter those contexts.

We could see habits as a way nature deals with our world's inherent chaos and impermanence.

## HABITS PRESERVE ENERGY

As we know, when a habit is formed, it moves from being a conscious behaviour to being a subconscious behaviour. Our brain does this because we make more than 35,000 decisions every single day.[2] If we had to *consciously* think about each of those decisions, we would be totally exhausted. It would be impossible to really function in this world.

Let's take the simple action of sitting on a chair from a standing position. You probably don't give much thought to taking a seat, and that's perfectly normal. Because you've sat down so many times, your brain has moved the action of sitting over into the subconscious part of your brain. But unbeknown to you, your brain is making a myriad of decisions just to get your bum down on that seat. All you do is think, 'I'm going to sit down,' and your brain starts a cascade of decisions – including where to place your feet, where to hold the chair and which hand to hold it with if you hold it at all, the pace you'll use to sit down, perhaps even sitting more gracefully when in company and just plonking down when you're alone. Your brain thinks of how to adjust your body in the chair so you're comfortable, adjusting your posture to suit the setting, making sure you're not blocking anyone's view, and assessing whether you're sitting too close or too far away from others. And within all those decisions are many other micro decisions: where you place your feet before sitting down, for example, includes decisions such as the direction each foot will point in before you sit, the angle of your body as you sit, how much pressure to place on each toe, and many, many more.

If you had to think intentionally about every single decision needed to sit down, you would probably experience decision fatigue by the time your bottom reached the chair. Forming habits allows our brain to automate all the nuances of well-practised actions so that we don't need to think consciously about the tedious details.

Habits are our mind's shortcuts, allowing us to successfully engage in our regular daily life while reserving our reasoning and executive functioning capacities for other thoughts and actions. Forming habits is a natural process that contributes to energy preservation, as our brain doesn't have to think consciously about our habitual behaviour and is therefore free to consider other things, such as what to make for dinner, or where to go on our next holiday.

## HABITS CREATE A NATURAL FLOW

Imagine you've relocated to a completely new city. You have a new job and a new home. Everything has to be rediscovered: the best way to get around, the best place to shop for groceries, the layout of the neighbourhood supermarket, and who to socialise with. You are leading a life devoid of your usual habits, so getting through the day won't be as seamless as it used to be. Things that were once simple now require effort and deliberate thought. You might occasionally feel confused, worn out or even frustrated. After some time and plenty of trial and error, you eventually figure out the best way to get to work, you find your favourite coffee shop, you navigate your way directly to the produce section of the supermarket, and you meet a group of friends at your neighbourhood café. It feels good to form new habits as you figure out what works and what doesn't. Things start to feel 'normal' again, and life starts to flow as it used to.

Habits contribute significantly to our sense of continuity during our waking hours. You may experience habits as a natural flow of events, whereas in fact you're making thousands of small decisions all the time, such as where to sit, how to move, where to go, what to take, where to look or what to say.

When I'm making a cup of tea, I think of it as making a cup of tea – it's one clustered action. But it's actually turning the kettle on, grabbing a mug, placing a teabag inside the mug, pouring the boiling water in, and so on. And we can break down those actions even further. For example, I turn the kettle on with my left hand as my right hand reaches up to open the cupboard, my right hand then grabs a mug as my left hand closes the cupboard, and so on.

One habit feeds off another and they create a natural flow, so that all these intricate actions meld into one. As we experience habits as a natural flow of events, we get the benefit of making fewer conscious decisions.

This concept of natural flow is widely used among athletes. When an athlete mimics the same conditions during their training as they'd expect on game day, they start to create natural flow. This then allows their brain to focus on the game or event and not on what's going on around them.

Weightlifters will practise their walk up to the bar, they practise their stance once they get to the bar, they mimic the temperature and sounds they can expect on competition day, they even eat the same food and listen to the same music. Serena Williams would wear sandals to the tennis court, tie her shoelaces a specific way, and bounce the ball a specific number of times at specific moments during a match (five times before a first serve, twice before a second serve). This was all intentional and all designed to help her optimise her performance by removing distractions so that she could focus on the most important thing – winning.

Only when we face a new or important situation do we have to make deliberate choices. In those moments, we lose flow and we experience making a decision, which comes with focused attention and requires allocating mental resources to the task at hand. When habits are in place, there is no need for conscious attention.

## HABITS FACILITATE EFFICIENCY

French psychologist and philosopher Léon Dumont describes habits as imprints left in the nervous system, similar to when water running down a sand slope leaves imprints in the sand.[3] These imprints provide the pathways for later – more efficient – water streams. Forming habits, therefore, creates an efficiency to our behaviours and thoughts. This efficiency makes habits the easier, less laboursome option when we encounter the habit trigger, while taking a different action becomes effortful.

For example, if you want to change a habit of checking your phone as soon as you wake up (waking up is your trigger and checking your phone is your habitual response), you would have to create a barrier to checking your phone, otherwise you'd be likely to pick it up and start scrolling automatically. A barrier could be putting your phone in a different room or keeping it on flight mode until you're ready to check it. Because our habits are efficient, they're usually the easy, default option. In the same way, if you have a healthy habit of exercising every day, then exercising is your default behaviour, and you get ready and get moving efficiently.

A few years ago, I developed a habit of exercising first thing in the morning. I found that I was the most motivated at that time and there were fewer distractions. There was no risk of getting caught up in a meeting or feeling too exhausted to train. I now roll out of bed, walk over to my wardrobe and pick out a set of active wear completely mindlessly and efficiently; I could do it with my eyes closed. You too have countless habits that are more or less reflexive (i.e. occur as a reflex). You might make your morning coffee without having to think through the steps, or you might go about your usual morning routine with very little cognitive effort.

# SUMMARY

» We form habits to preserve energy, promote flow and facilitate efficiency. Without habits, we would require a heightened sense of focus and mental resources.

» Habits are the mind's shortcuts, allowing us to engage successfully in our regular daily life while reserving our reasoning and executive functioning capacities for other thoughts and actions.

# Chapter 3

# Habits versus intentions

Two forces govern our behaviour: intention and habit. You could say that we have two brain systems (dual processing systems), like a computer with two central processing units that work independently and simultaneously. Performing an action for the first time requires intention, attention and planning, even if the plans are made only moments before the action is performed. As behaviours are repeated in consistent contexts, they begin to proceed more efficiently and with less thought, as control of the behaviour transfers from intention to triggers that activate an automatic response: habit.

Intention is driven by our beliefs, attitudes, values, social context and affect (underlying emotions). It's our reflective brain – it requires us to reflect or think. Habit, on the other hand, is driven by past behaviours and learned cue–response associations. It's our impulsive brain.

Our reflective (intention) brain is our prefrontal cortex, which sits directly behind our eyes and forehead. More than any other part of the brain, the prefrontal cortex is responsible for making deliberate and logical decisions. It's the key to reasoning, problem-solving, comprehension, impulse control and perseverance. It affects behaviour via goal-driven decisions.[1] For example, our prefrontal cortex will tell our body to stop eating when we're starting to feel full, or to go to bed on time because sleep is important, or to move our body because we'll feel great afterwards. When we're learning a new skill or acquiring new knowledge, we will draw heavily on our reflective brain system to form new synaptic connections (connections between neurons) in our memory. This system requires energy and effort.

Our impulsive (habit) brain is made up of our basal ganglia, which sit in the centre of our brain. These form the brain system that plays a key role in the development of emotions, memories and pattern recognition. The impulsive system relies on cue–response associations and operates at a high degree of automaticity. It's impetuous, spontaneous and pleasure-seeking. For example, your basal ganglia might influence you to eat a whole box of cookies because they're delicious, or pick up takeaway on the way home from a hard day at work even though there's a healthy meal waiting for you at home, or spontaneously buy an expensive new television. This system requires no energy or cognitive effort, as it operates reflexively.

## FORCES OF BEHAVIOUR

When the influence of intention is strong, the force of habit is weak, and vice versa. So when we have strong intentions, our habit strength is weaker, and we are more likely to act out of intention rather than habit. And in the same way, when our intention of performing a certain behaviour is weak, our strength of habit is stronger and we're therefore more likely to act out of habit rather than intention. We call this the intention–behaviour gap. It occurs when we intend to do one thing but end up doing something else. It can sometimes feel frustrating. But the stronger our intention, the weaker the habit strength; and the weaker our intention, the stronger the habit strength.

This is partly why setting goals can be a powerful strategy when we want to make changes in our life. Goals by default prompt us to consider our intentions and reflect on why we want to achieve those goals – which further strengthens our intentions. New Year's resolutions, for example, are simply an act of listing our intentions for the year. Without intentions, our current habits will continue to dictate our behaviour, and our life will remain the same. Our routines will play out one day after another, leaving no room for innovation, development, improvement, that unique sparkle that comes from doing something different, or the sense of achievement we feel when we accomplish a goal. So just as it's important to develop healthy habits to preserve brain energy, create a natural flow and facilitate efficiency, it's important to have intentions, in order to continue improving our self and our life.

The stronger our intention,
the weaker the habit strength;
and the weaker our intention,
the stronger the habit strength.

If only it was as easy as placing healthy habits in the automatic part of our brain and intentions in the reflective part of our brain, and having the option to select which behaviour we want to put in each section. We'd put healthy eating, exercise, meditation, a great sleep routine and productivity in the automatic, habitual part; and we'd put things like strategic thinking, unique experiences, fun and play in the intentional, reflective part of our brain. In an ideal world, we would face a crossroads in every situation and press the desired brain button – left for habit and right for intention – and our behaviours would follow the chosen path. The reality is, however, that many factors influence whether we act out of habit or intention, and it's not always a conscious choice.

## The reflective brain

Past behaviour has a strong impact on future behaviour when it's been frequently performed (i.e. become habitual), whereas behavioural intentions, representing more deliberate processes, are the strongest predictors of infrequent behaviours. For example, when you find yourself in a new situation, perhaps a new city, or a new job, or a new restaurant, the weight of intention will be increased, and you're more likely to make conscious and deliberate decisions. The reflective brain system has limited capacity and does not deal well with distractions or extreme levels of arousal. Say you're reading an important document and the kids are making noise in the background. It becomes difficult to focus.

As I'm writing this book, I'm reading complex neuroscience literature and translating it into practical, digestible language. This process operates strongly from my reflective brain system and I've noticed that I'm extra sensitive to external noise. To find my flow, I have to turn off my email and phone notifications and sit in a room by myself. I'm even wearing soundproof headphones and listening to an audio of rain sounds, because it acts as white noise and drowns out other external distractions. Without doing this, I lose flow from the smallest noises that seem to take my brain to all sorts of irrelevant places. In the same way, I catch myself turning the music down in my car when I'm parking in a tight spot; this is my reflective brain removing distractions so that I can focus on parking.

## The impulsive brain

On the other hand, if we're under time pressure, or find ourselves in a familiar environment or repeating past behaviours, the weight of habit will increase, and we're likely to act automatically, impulsively and subconsciously. The impulsive brain system relies on already formed habits and operates even under suboptimal conditions. Things like alcohol, stress, fatigue, emotional or physical exhaustion, hunger, time pressure, lack of sleep and negative emotions (e.g. stress, depression, anxiety) decrease the ability of our reflective brain to function and increase our impulsive brain activity.

My friend Jamie recently got a new puppy. If you've ever had a puppy, or a baby, you know that the first few weeks (or months, for a baby) can be emotionally and physically taxing. You're not sleeping as well, and your routine is interrupted as you care and nurture for this new addition to the family. Jamie's puppy, although completely adorable, had a tiny bladder and needed to be let outside several times each night. For weeks, Jamie was in a constant state of exhaustion, and his sleeplessness caused his body to crave energy-dense, high-carbohydrate foods (pastries were his weapon of choice). He started developing a 'dad bod', as he called it. One day, Jamie was in the waiting room at his mechanic's workshop waiting for his car to get serviced. On the wall was a display of the latest handsfree Bluetooth hardware for playing music from a phone through a car's speakers. Without a second thought, Jamie purchased the most expensive handsfree system just to save himself from plugging his phone in to listen to his music. The irony of this story was that Jamie spent hours researching the most affordable mechanic in his neighbourhood but spent triple the price of the service on the handsfree kit (which he admits he didn't need). This impetuous purchase was driven by his impulsive brain system, which was dominating due to his state of tiredness.

You can probably relate in many ways. When we're in a rush, it's harder to keep our cool. When we're feeling exhausted or stressed, it's more challenging to make healthy choices. Our impulsive brain is in control and so we go back to our old familiar habits, or we act in a way that's pleasure-seeking.

Impulsivity may be useful, such as when we need to quickly come up with a solution to a recurrent problem, or when we're overloaded with tasks and need to preserve our cognitive energy for critical decisions. But impulsivity can also be unfavourable or even harmful. For example, in the case of treating a sore throat, clinical practice guidelines encourage doctors to advise patients that a sore throat can last about one week and that they should manage their symptoms with self-care rather than medication. A doctor's more habitual response, however, may be to prescribe an antibiotic, especially if that doctor is working under difficult conditions, such as time pressure or exhaustion, even though antibiotics have absolutely no effect on a cold.

Studies of healthcare professionals have shown that many factors influence their decisions and whether they are operating from their impulsive or reflective brain system.[2] Factors such as long working hours, lack of staff, patients with difficult problems, medical emergencies, having to perform highly complex tasks involving reading and interpreting test results, diagnosing, prescribing and advising, all draw heavily on cognitive resources and eventually promote the activation of the impulsive brain system. Other factors include time pressure, hunger and experience, where increased experience and therefore behavioural repetition of clinical actions (which facilitates habit formation), lowers the functioning of the reflective system and increases use of the impulsive system.

One fascinating study found that prisoners are more likely to be granted parole early in the day or after the judges have taken their lunch break – variables that should have no bearing on legal decisions.[3] The researchers studied 1112 judicial rulings made by eight experienced judges in Israel over a 10-month period. Each day, a judge considered 14–35 cases in succession, and their deliberation for each case lasted about six minutes. The researchers found that the likelihood of a favourable ruling peaked at the beginning of the workday after the judges had breakfast, or after a food break, compared with later in the sequence of cases. At the start of the day, the judges gave favourable rulings to about 65 per cent of cases, but this number gradually dropped to nearly zero with each decision session before lunch. It then jumped back up to about 65 per cent after the judges took their lunch break. As the judges made repeated rulings, they showed an increased tendency to rule in favour of the status quo, despite the severity of the particular prisoner's crime, prison time, gender and ethnicity. So if you're ever unfortunate enough find yourself standing in front of a judge, you're anywhere between two and six times more likely to be released if you're one of the first three cases versus the last three cases considered.

The judges are more lenient after a meal break because the food helps replenish their mental resources. We'll dig deeper into how to replenish our own mental resources later in this chapter.

## THE REFLECTIVE–IMPULSIVE MODEL

The reflective–impulsive model (RIM) is a social and behavioural theory suggesting that our reflective and impulsive brain systems function in parallel. It proposes that the impulsive system is always active, whereas the reflective system may be disengaged as a default, then become engaged as required. This means that our baseline state is impulsive/habitual, and we only engage in intentional thought when we need to. I visually think of this theory as a piano player who at particular moments of a song uses both hands to play, while at other times uses just one hand. In the same way we, at times, use both our reflective and impulsive brain systems, while at other times we use only one or the other. We engage our reflective system when we're performing a new or complex task or learning a new skill, and our impulsive system when we're acting out a familiar behaviour. The interaction between the two brain systems can be what we call synergistic (where the systems work in tandem) or antagonistic (where the systems are in opposition).[4]

As an example of a synergistic interaction, take an experienced nurse working at a blood donation bank. The nurse has drawn blood from patients thousands of times throughout their career. They may draw blood from the patients' arms without engaging their reflective system because they don't need to think about drawing blood – it's a familiar and automatic action. But there may be patients whose veins are less visible. To carry out the behaviour in this instance, the nurse needs to engage their reflective system in order to assist their impulsive system. The nurse won't be able to draw blood completely automatically, as they need to focus on finding the less visible vein, but they can also rely on their impulsive system to carry out the rest of the actions required to do the job.

An antagonistic interaction on the other hand, happens when the reflective and impulsive brain systems are working towards incompatible agendas. For example, take a person who sets their alarm to get up for an early morning run. When the alarm goes off, they may be tempted to snooze it or turn it off and indulge in a longer sleep. At the same time, their reflective system is prompting them to get up and go for their planned run. This antagonistic activation may be accompanied by feelings of conflict and temptation. They want to go for a run but they also want to sleep in. To win the reflective–impulsive brain battle, the person could try to stop entertaining the idea of snoozing and sit more in their reflective system by getting out of bed. They could focus on all the benefits they will gain from running or how good they'll feel afterwards. It's a mental practice we can all learn to master.

The RIM explains that our reflective system is like a sensor light that turns on only when we enter a room and walk past the sensor. Only when we need conscious and deliberate thought do we engage our reflective brain system. Habitual behaviour is therefore generally considered the default mode of response: we rely on our habits unless the situation requires us to overrule them through explicit deliberation and self-control.[5]

*

In my early thirties, I took up powerlifting for about four years. It actually took me that whole time to realise that my body is not made for powerlifting. Power sports like powerlifting, strongman (strength athletics) and sumo wrestling are best suited to bodies with shorter limbs, larger sizes and the ability to pack on muscle easily. I have long limbs and a slim frame, and I'm quite tall. My coach nicknamed me LL Cool-G – Long-Lever Cool-Gina.

Powerlifting consists of three attempts at achieving maximal weight on three different lifts: squat, bench press and deadlift. It's all about lifting heavy weights and doing it with the right technique. Even though I would never be a powerlifting champion, I loved the training. I found the resilience I gained from lifting heavy weights spilled over into other areas of my life, and I developed a new level of mental strength overall.

When I first started powerlifting, I couldn't tell you the difference between a dumbbell and a barbell; by the end of my training, I had competed in a small local competition and deadlifted more than double my body weight. On comp day, I realised that I was the only competitor in my weight range, so I was competing against myself; the other competitors were 20–50 kilograms (45–65 pounds) heavier than me – I told you my body wasn't built for this sport.

Deadlifting is arguably one of the most complex lifts you can do in the gym. It's an all-encompassing compound movement that targets a series of major muscle groups. To perform a deadlift with correct form, you have to think of your foot positioning, your barbell grip, the bend in your knees, the angle of your chest and back, your chin positioning, bracing your back, abs and glutes, not to mention focusing on a whole sequence of breathing. All of this and you haven't even lifted the bar off the ground yet. It took me about two years to perfect my deadlift form. When I first started, I was able to focus on only two or three things, like the positioning of my feet, my bar grip and my breath, while the rest of my body would be out of form. Before I lifted the bar off the ground, my coach would prompt me to adjust all the necessary components: 'Knees bent, butt down, brace lats, suck it in, tight grip, chin down, chest up, big breath, hold and lift.' With time, and countless hours of practice, I was able to deadlift with good form, without my coach's prompts.

The technique that once took a high level of cognitive focus started becoming habitual, and my body naturally automated my deadlift form. My lifting became more efficient, and I could flow into the movement with little cognitive attentiveness. But here's a plot twist: no matter how many times I repeat a deadlift, it will never become a fully automated action. That's because it's a complex behaviour, so although it can include habitual properties, it will always require a bit of conscious thought compared with more simple behaviours. Walking, for example, can be mostly automatic because it's a simple behaviour.

I wanted to share my deadlifting story to illustrate that it's not always easy to compartmentalise a behaviour into either intentional or habitual − sometimes it can be both, and some behaviours will lean more towards one brain system than the other.

# SUMMARY

» There are two forces that govern our behaviour: intention (reflective) and habit (impulsive).

» Our reflective brain system is slow, effortful, intentional, conscious, analytical, contemplative, logical, decision-making, reasoning, self-regulating and rational. It is responsible for our deliberate behaviour.

» Our impulsive brain system is fast, effortless, habitual, impulsive, subconscious, intuitive, reactive, spontaneous and reflexive. It is responsible for our automatic habits.

» The stronger our intention the weaker the habit strength, and the weaker our intention the stronger the habit strength.

## Chapter 4

# Habit triggers

I WOULD DEFINITELY DESCRIBE MYSELF as having a sweet tooth. From the moment I finish a meal, my friends start counting down from eight seconds because they reckon it only takes me that long to reach for dessert after a meal – and they're not wrong. The only other time I'd indulge in dessert, apart from gelato at the beach or when I'm travelling, used to be at the petrol station. I'd stop in to fuel my car and I'd grab a chocolate bar while I was at the counter. I'd then proceed to eat it in the car as I drove to my next destination. This all happened in a very mindless fashion. It didn't matter what time of day it was or if I was even craving chocolate. Going to the petrol station meant buying and eating a chocolate bar.

It wasn't until I was cleaning out my car one day that I realised I had a chocolate bar problem. Wrappers filled and decorated the side pocket of the driver's door and I had only myself to point to as the culprit. I clearly love chocolate, but I wanted to choose to eat chocolate when I felt like it; I didn't want chocolate to choose me. The way I was eating it – the mindless, subconscious, reflexive way – was representative of the fact that I was not in control.

I was a few weeks into my PhD, researching all things to do with habits. I was sitting at my desk looking at the habit loop – cue, routine, reward – and the penny dropped. My chocolate habit was cued by going to the petrol station. It was in that moment that I realised the power and influence of habit triggers, not so much because my chocolate habit was something I struggled to break, but more because of how mindless and automatic it was. I wasn't even aware of my behaviour; one minute I was filling up my car and the next I was eating a chocolate bar. I didn't choose this habit mindfully, it was automatically triggered. After all, a habit is the process in which our behaviour is influenced by a prompt to act based on well-learned associations between triggers and behaviours.

## WHAT ARE HABIT TRIGGERS?

Triggers are the external or internal cues that prompt a habit. They can be as simple as hearing an alarm clock in the morning or as complex as feeling a sense of anxiety in a particular situation.

A habit trigger is defined as an event that kicks off the automatic urge to perform a habit. A trigger is known to activate, set off, bring about, cause, generate, produce, prompt, provoke, spark, start, elicit, set in motion or cue a habit. I use the words 'trigger' and 'cue' interchangeably in this book – they mean the same thing.

As we saw earlier, smokers, particularly those attempting to quit, often report that environmental stimuli trigger lapses or interfere with their thought processes and daily activities. These people don't necessarily light up because they want a cigarette, but because they're habitually accustomed to smoke in response to a specific environmental trigger – such as with their morning coffee, during their lunch break or while socialising or drinking alcohol.

Triggers are one of the main factors that set habits apart from behaviours. Every habit starts with a trigger, whereas behaviours

---

## Without triggers, we don't have habits.

---

are not triggered but intentionally enacted. Triggers are arguably the most important part of creating and breaking habits, because without triggers, we don't have habits. Understanding our triggers, therefore, is essential to creating positive and lasting habits. By identifying and modifying the triggers that lead to unwanted habits, we can reprogram our brain to stop performing those unwanted habits or to form new, wanted habits instead. In this chapter, we will explore the different types of habit triggers, how they work, and how to use this knowledge to our advantage.

## FIVE KEY HABIT TRIGGERS

Experiments have shown that almost all habit cues fit into one of five categories:

1. time
2. location
3. preceding event or action
4. emotional state
5. social situation.

These five triggers include both external and internal cues. External triggers – such as time, location, preceding event and social situation – are visible. Internal triggers, on the other hand – such as emotions, thoughts or physical sensations like feeling tired or hungry – come from within ourselves.

## 1. Time

Our circadian rhythm (our body clock) and the society we live in make time a powerful trigger. We generally wake up, drink coffee, exercise, go to work, eat our meals and go to sleep at similar times of the day.

In Australia, and especially in Queensland where I live, shops and cafés open early and close early. Cafés open at around 6 am and close at 2–3 pm. In other parts of the world, however, cafés might not open till 10–11 am and don't close till midnight. This contributes to the way we socialise in different places around the world. In Queensland we might go out for an early morning breakfast or coffee, whereas if we were in Europe, we might catch up with friends over lunch instead.

Time is a useful habit trigger because it's objective, predictable and guaranteed to happen every day. Common time habits include waking up at the same time every morning, or having a set time for lunch.

I'm a morning person. I like to get up and start my day early. One of my time triggers is 5.30 am, when I get up and do some exercise. I also tend to eat my meals at similar times of the day: breakfast at around 8 am, lunch at midday and dinner at about 6 pm. My snacks are sprinkled throughout the day.

If you want to use time to trigger a habit, start by using an alarm, a calendar event or an app notification as a reminder.

## 2. Location

Location is one of the most influential habit triggers because environment drives behaviour. The locations we frequently encounter – home, office, gym, car – are already associated with countless habits, both wanted and otherwise.

Sitting on the couch might trigger you to scroll mindlessly through social media on your phone; going to the movies might trigger you to buy popcorn; getting in your car or sitting on an aeroplane might trigger you to fasten your seatbelt. Your environment is a strong driver of your behaviour.

To use location as a trigger when developing a new habit, you can start by putting an obvious reminder in the specific place where you want your new habit to be triggered. For example, you could stick a post-it note on your computer monitor to remind yourself to take five deep breaths when you get into the office, or put your medication next to the kettle where you make your morning cup of tea.

Maybe you want to eat more fruit. You could have fruit cut up and ready in the fridge, directly at eye level, so it's the first thing you see when you open the fridge door. The trick is to make it convenient and easy to access.

If you want to break a habit using location, you can apply the same strategy but in reverse – you want to create environmental barriers to that unwanted habit. For example, if you're finding yourself mindlessly non-hungry snacking on certain foods, place those foods in an inconvenient location, such as on a hard-to-reach shelf in the laundry or garage. You're still welcome to grab those snacks anytime you wish, but you might find that not having them within arm's reach and having to go to a different room, grab a stepladder and get the snacks from the top shelf creates space for mindfulness and reduces your non-hungry snacking. Sometimes those barriers are just too inconvenient to make the effort of getting your snacks worth it.

Say you often find yourself scrolling through social media when you're sitting on the couch at home. Try sitting on the other side of the couch or, even better, on the other side of the room. You could try leaving a journal, book or hobby item (such as a sketchbook) on your coffee table near your couch to encourage you to pick it up instead of your phone.

Or maybe you're trying to break the habit of ordering takeaway because it's costing you too much money. But every time you go into the kitchen you see the takeaway menus on your fridge. You could try replacing the menus with printouts of recipes that are easy, quick and you know you'll enjoy.

Our environment drives our behaviour. If there's a jar of candy sitting on your desk, you're likely to reach over and snack on it throughout the day. We need to create an environment that's conducive to our goals and that will support the habits we want to create.

---

## Our environment drives our behaviour.

---

### 3. Preceding event or action

Habits often operate in a web, where one habit feeds off another. Once one habit is activated, the rest of the web of habits becomes activated, one by one. For example, turning on your computer at work might trigger you to check your emails.

Many of our existing habits are automatic responses to preceding events or actions, and the compilation of these is what makes up our routines. When the initial triggered action is completed, it sets off the rest of the routine, similar to a domino effect. For example, waking up triggers taking a shower, which triggers getting dressed, which triggers walking to the kitchen, which triggers eating breakfast, which triggers brushing your teeth, which triggers leaving for work, and so on.

The best way to use preceding actions to trigger new habits is to group the new habit you want to create with something you're already doing regularly. For example, if you want to start flossing, then you can use brushing your teeth as the trigger. The ritual of brushing your teeth becomes the trigger, and flossing becomes the new habit.

It's important to try to create a natural flow when you're working with preceding event triggers. Attach your new habit to something in your routine that would naturally occur with your new habit. It makes sense to attach flossing with brushing your teeth. It wouldn't make as much sense to attach flossing with something like showering because there's no association between dental care and showering.

## 4. Emotional state

We will do whatever we can to avoid experiencing uncomfortable emotions, but sometimes we avoid or distract ourselves from those negative emotions by developing unwanted habits. For example, we may get the urge to snack when we're feeling bored even though we're not genuinely hungry; or we may scroll through social media when we're feeling lonely, which only gives us a false sense of community and doesn't create true connection; or we may drink alcohol when we're feeling stressed, which doesn't actually solve anything.

Emotions can be subtle triggers because we're not always consciously aware of how we're feeling. I can easily convince myself that my boredom is hunger when it's really not. I can also tell myself that playing video games is going to help reduce my anxiety, but it unfortunately doesn't work like that. Those quick fixes provide a very short-lived reward but they don't really help us feel better. In most cases, we actually end up feeling worse.

The first step to using emotional triggers to our advantage is to understand and identify our emotions so that we can change or eliminate the emotional triggers for our unwanted habits. The activity at the end of this chapter will help you identify your triggers for both your wanted and unwanted habits.

You can start today by replacing your unwanted habits with healthier habits in response to emotional triggers. Give yourself what you're really looking for – reducing stress, feeling connected or improving your mood. A new trigger, for example, could be: 'When I'm feeling bored, I'll listen to a new podcast.'

Other positive habits that can address undesirable feelings include:

- exercising – releases endorphins and improves mood
- deep breathing and mindfulness meditation – reduce stress and increase calmness
- expressing gratitude – has been linked to increased positive emotions, increased resilience and creating stronger relationships
- journalling – can increase mindfulness and self-awareness
- listening to music – improves mood
- spending time with loved ones – strengthens connection and community.

## 5. Social situation

The people you spend regular time with and your perception of social norms have an inevitable influence on your habits. If your work colleagues have a habit of putting on a spread of food during your board meetings, you have an increased chance of snacking during meetings, even when you're not hungry. Or if your partner goes out to walk the dog each morning, you have an increased chance of developing a habit of walking in the morning. That's why it's very helpful to spend time with people who share similar lifestyle values and goals to your own.

Social accountability has also been shown to significantly increase habitual performance of a desired task.[1] For example, you're much more likely to go to a yoga class if you sign up with a friend rather than going on your own.

The people that you surround yourself with form part of your environment. If you want to reduce the amount of alcohol you drink or late nights out, consider reducing the time you spend with people who contribute to those unwanted habits or don't support your goals.

---

## The people you surround yourself with form part of your environment.

---

## COMMON TRIGGERS FOR EVERYDAY HABITS

- Switching off your morning alarm
- Taking a shower
- Brushing your teeth
- Starting the coffee machine
- Pouring a cup of tea
- Feeding your pet
- Putting on your shoes
- Getting in the car
- Starting the car
- Arriving at work
- Putting down your work bag
- Sitting down at your desk
- Switching your computer on
- Walking into a meeting
- Feeling the urge to snack
- Switching your computer off
- Sitting down on the bus, train or tram
- Turning off the television at night
- Plugging in your phone to charge
- Lying down in bed

# SUPERCHARGING YOUR TRIGGERS

Research shows that the most effective triggers are those that are one or more of the following:

1. specific
2. salient (obvious)
3. consistent
4. automatic
5. inevitable.

Effective triggers strongly and consistently remind us to perform our desired habit, so it's valuable to be aware of these trigger characteristics when we're creating new habits. Using effective triggers not only makes those habits easier to initiate, but ensures they develop quicker.

## 1. Specific

Specific triggers are clear and precise and leave no room for misinterpretation. For example, a more specific trigger than 'after dinner' would be, 'after I finish eating dinner'. 'After dinner' could be any time between finishing eating and going to bed, so using the more specific trigger 'after I finish eating dinner' reduces that time to directly after eating. This obviously helps create a more specific plan and a tighter trigger time.

## 2. Salient

A salient trigger is one that is noticeable, pronounced or obvious, such as placing your walking shoes by the front door. Every time you see your walking shoes, you are reminded of your goal to exercise and are prompted to go for a walk. The visual cue of the walking shoes acts as a reminder to perform the habit of walking regularly.

Another example could be setting a reminder on your phone for a specific time each day to take your supplements or medication. The alarm sound and notification serve as a salient habit trigger to prompt you to take your supplements or medication at that particular time.

In one study, researchers observed people who recently moved to a new house, splitting them into two groups. They gave the intervention group free bus tickets and personalised travel schedule information. The control group were not given any tickets or travel information. The researchers concluded that the intervention group were significantly more likely to use public transport than the control group. Having salient information at their fingertips made changing their transportation habits significantly more likely.[2]

## 3. Consistent

A consistent trigger is something that happens every day (or at least most days of the week) with reliable frequency. For example, a trigger that might occur every day is 'after getting dressed in the morning', whereas a trigger that might only occur on weekdays is 'after getting ready for work'.

Consistent triggers include anything we do regularly: eating breakfast, drinking a morning coffee, brushing our teeth, etc.

## 4. Automatic

An automatic trigger is one that occurs on its own without any ongoing effort. It's something we can set and forget. An example might be 'when my alarm goes off at 7 am'. You can set your alarm to go off every day without any manual input. The same is true of recurring calendar reminders.

A friend of mine does shift work, so his schedule is out of sync with the more usual Monday to Friday working week. To remember to take the bins out, he has a weekly recurring reminder on his phone to tell him when it's bin day.

### 5. Inevitable

An effective trigger is one that is inevitable, which means you'll definitely encounter the trigger during your waking hours as a result of your environment or routine. Examples could be 'leaving my office for the day' or 'getting out of bed' or 'when I feel hungry'. Feeling hungry, for example, is a natural and inevitable signal your body gives you when it's time to eat. In this case, feeling hunger serves as an inevitable habit trigger for seeking out food.

## SUMMARY

» Triggers are crucial to forming new habits, as habits are always triggered.
» There are five key triggers: time, location, preceding event or action, emotional state and social situation.
» Effective triggers are specific, salient, consistent, automatic and/or inevitable.

**ACTIVITY 1**

## What triggers your habits?

Take out your journal or notebook. Can you identify a habit that you perform in response to each of the triggers below? (You may have habits with overlapping triggers from more than one of these categories – that's perfectly okay.)

- Time
- Location
- Preceding event/action
- Emotional state
- Social situation

## ACTIVITY 2

# Cue monitoring

In your journal, draw up a table like the one opposite, which starts at 5 am and goes through to 11 pm. Make sure you leave yourself lots of writing room. Your task is to identify the typical cues in your life – this is called cue monitoring.

Once you have filled out the table, you will be able to use that information to create new habits through cue–response association (we'll talk more about this in Chapter 5). All you need to do now is write down your typical weekly routine. I've filled in Monday in the table as an indication of the sorts of things you could include. The next step is to add the triggers involved – this may be the time or place, the activity that you just completed (preceding action), your emotional state or who you are with.

Some examples of cues include: the time you wake up, brushing your teeth, eating breakfast, the time you leave for work, sitting down at your desk, where you have lunch, who you usually spend evenings with, and so on.

If possible, it's best to fill in the table the moment each cue occurs rather than trying to do it at the end of the day or week, because it can be difficult to remember the necessary details.

### Your lifestyle patterns

Once you've filled in the table, see if you can identify any patterns from your cue monitoring. Write them down in your journal so you can start to build awareness of your common cues and lifestyle routines.

# Habit triggers

| Time | Monday | Tuesday | Wednesday | Thursday | Friday | Saturday | Sunday |
|---|---|---|---|---|---|---|---|
| 5–7 am | 5.30 am Wake up 6.00 am Walk dog | | | | | | |
| 7–9 am | 7 am Eat breakfast 8 am Leave for work | | | | | | |
| 9–11 am | 8.30 am Get to work 9 am Drink coffee and eat snack | | | | | | |
| 11 am – 1 pm | 12 pm Eat lunch | | | | | | |
| 1–3 pm | 2 pm Daily meeting 3.30 pm Eat snack | | | | | | |
| 3–5 pm | 4.30 pm Leave work | | | | | | |
| 5–7 pm | 5 pm Get home 6.30 pm Eat dinner | | | | | | |
| 7–9 pm | 7 pm Pack lunch for tomorrow and watch TV | | | | | | |
| 9–11 pm | 9 pm Start bedtime routine | | | | | | |

# Chapter 5

# How to create new habits

HABITS ARE THE BUILDING BLOCKS of our lives. They shape the way we think, act and respond to the world around us. Whether they're the morning routine that kickstarts our day or the unconscious decisions we make throughout our waking hours, habits have a profound impact on our lives. What we do habitually makes up much of what we do entirely. In fact, it's estimated that up to 70 per cent of our waking behaviour is made up of habitual behaviour.[1] We are creatures of habit, and most of the time our action dial is turned towards autopilot. Research shows that habits are the only proven method for achieving long-term success with behavioural goals. So having healthy habits that are aligned with our values and goals can shape our life in the way we desire.

> What we do habitually makes up
> much of what we do entirely.

But I won't sugarcoat it – while habits can be incredibly powerful, they can also be difficult to change. Whether it's breaking an old habit or forming a new one, the process of habit change can be challenging, but the rewards can be immense. In this chapter, we will delve into the art of creating new, healthy habits, and explore the key principles and strategies for forming new habits that stick.

## WHY CREATE HEALTHY HABITS?

Developing healthy habits not only provides us with freedom by reducing the effort and energy required to maintain them, but also frees up extra time and mental space for pursuing other priorities. Similar to brushing your teeth even when you're tired, these habits become automatic and effortless, which leaves more of your energy available for more meaningful pursuits.

If you weren't already convinced that creating healthy habits could significantly benefit your life, here are some of the ways it does just that:

- **improved physical health and greater potential longevity:** Healthy habits, such as regular exercise, healthy eating and adequate sleep, can lead to improved physical health, reducing the risk of chronic diseases and promoting longevity.
- **enhanced mental wellbeing:** Habits such as meditation, mindfulness and stress management can help improve mental health and reduce the risk of anxiety, depression and other mental health conditions.
- **increased energy and productivity:** Habits such as regular exercise and getting enough sleep can lead to increased energy and improved focus, which can optimise performance and productivity.

- **improved relationships:** Habits such as active communication, empathy and kindness can improve relationships, leading to greater satisfaction and happiness in our personal and professional lives.
- **better self-esteem and confidence:** Having positive mindset and self-talk habits can improve self-image, increase self-esteem and boost confidence.
- **greater sense of autonomy:** Healthy habits can provide a sense of control and autonomy, empowering us to take charge of our lives and achieve our goals.

## THE HABIT-FORMATION FRAMEWORK

The advice for habit formation is ultimately simple: consistently repeat an action in the same context. But although the method of change is simple, it's not always easy. Change requires deliberate action, and action often requires us to silence short-term temptations in order to achieve long-term goals. This is how we change the narrative and create a different life.

The habit-formation framework describes the three stages to creating a new habit – not to be confused with the five steps for creating a new habit, which we'll go through later in this chapter. The habit-formation framework is more of a bird's-eye view of the habit-formation process.

The three stages of the habit-formation framework are initiation, training and maintenance. Initiate a new behaviour, train yourself in that behaviour through repetition, and maintain the new behaviour through consistency. Essentially, this is how we achieve goals: we decide on a goal we want to achieve, we take action towards that goal, then we achieve and maintain that goal – in theory anyway.

## 1. Initiation

In this initial stage of habit formation, you decide to form a new habit and take the first step towards making it a part of your daily routine. This involves setting a clear habit goal, identifying a trigger or cue, and starting to perform the habit consistently.

During this stage, you're setting out the plan, the intention for action. For example: 'When I get home from work, I'm going to walk the dog for 30 minutes.'

There's no doubt you've set a goal before and experienced the challenge of taking the first step. Going out for your first walk or to your first Pilates class, eating your first mindful meal, making your first positive self-talk statement. The thing is, we're comfortable in our routines, even if those routines aren't serving us. So the first step towards doing something different from our norm often feels like a hill or even a mountain to overcome. And overcoming that mountain requires self-regulation skills we in the habit biz call intention formation, planning and deliberate action initiation – which are all just fancy words for 'effort'.

---

## We're comfortable in our routines, even if those routines aren't serving us.

---

I told you I wouldn't sugarcoat it. There would be no point in giving you some steps to follow and leaving you in the dark about what it's really like to make changes in your behaviour. So I'm here with the raw, unfiltered truth, taken from the scientific literature and from seeing hundreds of people set out to change their habits.

You see, at the heart of every single moment we are presented with a choice. We can make a decision to do, say or pursue what's really important to us, or we can let fear and complacency make a decision to keep us shackled in the same old routines. Considering you're here reading this book, I'd say you're ready to make some positive changes in your life – go you!

## 2. Training

In the training phase, you start to actually implement the new habit and work towards making it part of your routine. This is where you consistently repeat the behaviour in your chosen context (thus creating context-dependent repetition).

This training phase requires willpower and motivation because you're doing something different from your usual routine. A great way to increase motivation in this phase is reflecting on the positive outcomes that are likely to occur if you create this new habit.

If I said to you that if you practised 10 minutes of meditation before bed every night you would sleep better, improve your focus and attention, reduce overeating, enhance your mood and improve your immune function,[2] it would seem that meditating is a great investment of your time and worth doing.

Now it's your turn. Take a moment to think of a habit you want to create. It can be anything, big or small. Once you've thought of a habit, I want you to write down in your journal or notebook all the benefits that practising that habit will have in your life. For example, if your new habit is increasing your level of physical activity, your list of benefits could include improving your sleep quality, feeling stronger, helping to manage your weight, boosting your energy levels, and improving your mental wellbeing. Make sure the benefits on your list are things you value. As you reflect on this list, your level of motivation to take action towards your new habit will significantly increase. Another excellent way to increase motivation is to track your habits, which we will cover later in this chapter. (And Chapter 12 is dedicated to motivation.)

In order to be successful in creating your new habit, you have to ensure it's something that's meaningful to you and your life. You won't succeed if you're doing it because of external factors such as someone else wanting you to. Motivation can be either intrinsic or extrinsic. Intrinsic motivation is driven by our own interest or enjoyment of the action, and by personal reward such as living our values or a sense of personal satisfaction. Extrinsic motivation, on the other hand, is driven by a desire to achieve external rewards such as money, recognition, pleasing others or avoiding punishment. Make sure your motivation for creating your new habit is intrinsic.

Studies consistently show that intrinsic motivation is more likely to lead to strong intentions and sustained changes in behaviour compared with extrinsic motivation, which seems only to change behaviour in the short term.[3] Extrinsically motivated behaviours represent a means to an end and we're therefore less likely to engage in them. For example, if I were to offer you $10 for every step you took in a day, you would be extrinsically motivated to walk as many steps as you could, but as soon as I took away that offer, your motivation to walk more than usual would likely vanish.

We're much more likely to stick with pursuing a goal if it's founded on personal investment and a sense of fulfilment rather than external rewards. Intrinsic motivation fosters a growth mindset, where we start to view challenges as opportunities for learning and growth rather than solely focusing on the outcome. This can lead to a greater sense of purpose and a deeper connection to the habit being changed.

Add to your earlier notes on your chosen new habit and its rewards by responding to this journal prompt: *Why creating this new habit is important to me.*

## 3. Maintenance

In the maintenance stage of the habit-formation framework a habit finally starts to form and to feel like second nature. By this stage you've developed mental associations between the cue and the habit (the cue–response association), and you've successfully transferred the habit from your reflective to your impulsive brain. In this maintenance stage, your chosen habit persists over time with minimal conscious thought or effort when you encounter the triggering cue. You've reached a level of automaticity.

The habit is now an automatic part of your daily routine, and you can continue to enjoy the sustainable and long-lasting benefits it brings to your life. Here's to long-term outcomes.

## THE FIVE STEPS FOR CREATING NEW HABITS

The best way to get through the three stages of the habit-formation framework and make your habits stick is using these five steps for creating new habits:

1. Decide on a goal you'd like to achieve.
2. Choose a simple action you can perform on a daily basis that will move you towards your goal.
3. Plan when and where you will perform your chosen action – to create a cue–response association using the habit loop.
4. Each time you encounter the cue from step 3, take action by performing your chosen habit.
5. Track your progress using a habit tracker.

Let's have a detailed look at each of these steps.

### 1. Set a goal

Setting achievable goals can be an art, which is why Chapter 14 is entirely dedicated to just that. When you're deciding on a goal you want to achieve, make sure it's realistic and intrinsically motivated (i.e. you're doing it for yourself).

## 2. Choose a simple action

You may need to do several things to achieve your goal. For example, if my goal were to get a better night's sleep, my actions to achieve that goal might include going to bed and waking up at similar times of the day, avoiding screens an hour before bed, and limiting my caffeine and alcohol intake, among other things. The actions you choose should be simple and achievable. You may wish to focus on doing one action at a time.

---

The actions you choose should
be simple and achievable.

---

## 3. Plan your cue–response association

This step is about planning when and where you will perform your chosen action(s) in order to create a cue–response association as per the habit loop. You want to be consistent: choose a time or place you encounter every day. This cue will become the first part of a two-part sequence: 'When I [encounter cue X], I will [perform action Y (which will later become a habit)].'

Your 'When I' becomes an anchor because it's a stable routine in your life. You will use anchors like this to trigger your new desired habits. For example, if I want to avoid screens an hour before bed, I would decide on my bedtime, say 9 pm, and work backwards to turn off all screens at 8 pm. To help me get into this habit, I could set an alarm to go off at 8 pm or set my screens to turn off automatically at that time.

Review the example triggers and your cue monitor from Chapter 4 for inspiration in finding triggers for your new habits. Once you've identified potential triggers, you can pair your desired habits with them to create a cue–response association. Psychologists call this an implementation intention. Write this down using the formulation: 'When I [cue], I will [habit].'

For example:

- When I brush my teeth, I will floss them too.
- When I hear my alarm at 7 am, I will go for a 30-minute walk.
- When I start the coffee machine, I will feed my dog.
- When I sit down at my desk, I will take five deep breaths.
- When I put my head on my pillow, I will think of one thing I'm grateful for.

## 4. Take action

It's one thing to plan a great cue–response association and intend on forming your new habit, but it's another thing altogether to actually take action towards that plan. This step is simply about performing the chosen habit.

The human mind is conditioned to look for explanations, and it creates reasons for why the things we want are not possible – such as a lack of time or energy. This happens because our brain assumes that accomplishing what we want will require dealing with unfamiliar situations. Since unfamiliar environments require the brain to do a lot of work, it prefers us to stay in familiar environments and routines instead. Being mindful of this human shortcoming is very empowering.

You can start disrupting your brain's efforts to keep you in the familiar by creating some distance between yourself and your thoughts. When you notice your mind starting to give reasons for why something's impossible, try thinking: 'Aha! You're coming up with excuses again. You want to stay in the familiar. Thanks, brain, but I don't need that. I'm okay with doing something different.'

---

## Sometimes it's best to not think too much and just do.

---

I can't tell you how many times I planned to go to the gym then came up with a hundred reasons why staying in bed was a better idea. It's too hot, it's too cold, I'm hungry, I have a big day, I'm tired, I worked out yesterday, and so on. Sometimes it's best to not think too much and just do. Now I wake up and just get on with it. The less I listen to my thoughts, the more likely I am to follow through with my workout – and I've never regretted a workout.

### 5. Track your progress using a habit tracker

Research shows that self-monitoring allows our minds to transition from a state of 'mindlessness' to a state of 'mindfulness'.[4] A habit tracker is essential for monitoring our progress, but research shows that using a habit tracker also significantly increases the number of times we perform a new habit and therefore increases automaticity so that we can create our habit faster.

Self-monitoring helps us to remember to perform the new habit and gives us a sense of reward. You know how we give children a gold star when they've done something good? The funny thing is we don't seem to grow out of that reward response as adults. Giving ourselves a tick for achieving a habit makes us feel good and motivates us to perform that habit again.

Using a habit tracker is not simply a mechanical tracking process. It has numerous benefits, such as increasing motivation, bringing to mind goal-relevant information and triggering self-reflective responses – which ensures the desired behaviour occurs more often.

Some research even shows that creating a new habit is only possible if you're self-monitoring. In one study, as soon as the participants stopped self-monitoring, they stopped performing the habit. A meta-analysis (a highly reliable systematic synthesis of the findings of multiple scientific studies on the same topic) of the results of 19 intervention studies with a total of 2800 participants showed that the interventions using self-monitoring were significantly more likely to achieve the desired outcome.[5] Self-monitoring and taking action go hand in hand, so this is an essential step towards successfully creating a new habit.

Habit trackers come in all shapes and sizes. There are paper-based or app-based trackers (see the activity at the end of this chapter for links to both). The most important thing is that they're handy to use and they create a sense of mindfulness regarding the habits in question.

When you give yourself a tick, I want you to take a moment to be proud of yourself. Just a small mindful moment to acknowledge that you achieved your chosen habit for the day. This reinforces the reward centre in your brain and helps you feel motivated to do it again. It really makes a big difference. It doesn't have to be an elaborate or audible 'Well done', it can just be an internal acknowledgement that you achieved what you set out to do, because that's worth celebrating.

## Bonus step: Evaluate, reassess and redesign

You want to know that your new habit loop is working and you're regularly performing your chosen habit in response to its trigger. After several days or several weeks (the timing will be different for each person), you want to evaluate your progress and, if required, reassess your cue–response association and redesign your plan.

To do this, simply review your habit tracker and determine whether your chosen cue is effectively triggering the desired habit and if you're consistently performing that habit. If you're hitting a good streak and performing your new habit regularly, then awesome, you don't need to change anything.

If you're finding that you're not increasing the frequency of your new habit, that indicates that you need to rework your habit loop. You may need to change your trigger, or you may need to assess whether your chosen habit is realistic and achievable.

It's important to note that with time it will get easier to perform your new habit, and within about 10 weeks you should find that you're doing your new habit without even having to think about it; it will feel like second nature.

Use the activity coming up to follow the five steps and create your new habit.

## SUMMARY

» The habit-formation framework describes the three stages for creating a new habit: initiate a new behaviour, train yourself in that behaviour through repetition, and maintain the behaviour through consistency.

» The five steps to creating a new habit are:

1. Set a goal.
2. Choose a simple action.
3. Create a cue–response association.
4. Take action: when you encounter the habit trigger, perform the chosen action.
5. Track your progress using a habit tracker.

# Five steps for creating new habits

To transform your goals into habits, choose a simple action that you want to become a habit. Choose something you can do on a daily basis, which will move you towards your goal. Then pair your chosen habit with an already existing cue to successfully create a cue–response association. Let's go through the process step by step. Use each stage as a journal prompt to plan out how you will achieve your new habit.

## 1. Set a goal

Decide on a goal you would like to achieve. If you would like some inspiration, you could look at the list of healthy habit examples on my website: drginacleo.com/post/healthy-habit-examples.

## 2. Choose a simple action

Pick something you can do on a daily basis that will move you towards your goal. This action will eventually become your new habit.

## 3. Create a cue–response association

Plan when and where you will perform your chosen action. Make sure it will allow you to be consistent. Choose a time or place you encounter every day without too much trouble, then create an implementation intention: 'When I [encounter X], I will [do Y].'

## 4. Take action

Each time you encounter the cue, perform your chosen habit.

## 5. Use a habit tracker

Each time you perform your new habit, mark it off using a habit tracker. Visit drginacleo.com/book to download a paper-based habit tracker, or see the list of habit tracker apps there.

## Bonus step: Evaluate, reassess and redesign

After several days or weeks, reassess how successful your cue–response associations have been and redesign your plan as necessary, either by starting the five steps from scratch or finessing one or two of them. Measure your cue–response success by simply reviewing your habit tracker and determining whether your chosen cue is effectively triggering your desired habit and if you're performing that habit consistently. Make sure you note down your new plan in your journal as before, in a way that makes it easy to consult and implement.

## Chapter 6

# How to break
# old habits

WE'VE ALL SAID, 'I CAN'T help it, it's a habit.' Habits are powerful drivers of our behaviour, but they can be difficult to change, especially when they've become ingrained over a long period of time. But with determination, discipline and, most importantly, the right strategies, it's possible to break even the most stubborn of habits and create new, positive patterns of behaviour. In this chapter, we will explore the science behind why we do the things we don't want to do, and the most effective strategies for breaking those unwanted habits.

I do a lot of corporate speaking about habits as part of my work. I give presentations to staff members of large companies and organisations about how to form new habits and break their old, unwanted habits. One of the activities I love doing is what I've termed the 'habit confessional', and it's exactly what it sounds like. I ask the audience to think of an unwanted habit in their life, something that isn't serving them or their goals, and confess that unwanted habit to the person sitting next to them. It's an amazing activity because it shows having unwanted habits is a very real human experience we all share. Even the most successful, smart, wealthy, fit people have unwanted habits. And their habits are no different from yours or mine. They confess to things like drinking too much coffee, scrolling on their phone for hours before bed, or eating when they're feeling bored or anxious. We're all human and we all have habits we'd like to kick – yes, even me! The fact that you're imperfect is not a sign that you've failed, it's simply a sign that you're human and, more importantly, that you still have more potential within you.

How do you know if you have unwanted habits? Ask yourself where are my habits leading me? Are they moving me towards or away from my goals? What will my life look like if I maintain my current habits for the next five years? Ten years?

---

## The fact that you're imperfect is not a sign that you've failed, it's simply a sign that you're human.

---

Your direction is much more important than your speed. If you're heading in the right direction you'll eventually reach your desired outcomes, but no matter how fast you go, if you're going in the wrong direction you're still getting nowhere.

The automaticity of habits means that breaking your existing habits requires different and altogether more effortful strategies than making new ones. By the end of this chapter, though, you'll have the tools and knowledge you need to break those unwanted habits.

## WHY WE HAVE UNWANTED HABITS

Do you ever find yourself stuck in the same old cycle? Frustrating, isn't it? I completely relate to that feeling. How can a smart, strong, independent person be defeated by a block of chocolate or the snooze button? You want to go to bed earlier, but you scroll through social media a bit too long again. You want to save more money, but those sales are just too alluring.

## Comfort in the familiar

One reason we get stuck doing things we don't want to do is that, as we saw earlier, our brain assumes that achieving what we want will involve dealing with unfamiliar situations. Since unfamiliar environments require our brain to do a lot of work, it prefers us to stay in our familiar situations and routines instead. Our brain, therefore, creates reasons why the things we want are going to be too hard: 'I don't have enough time' or 'I'm too tired'. We are creatures of habit after all, and transitions disrupt the comforting rhythm of the routines we've established.

Our brain associates familiarity with safety, even if familiarity isn't what we want or need. But not doing something different and being stuck in unhelpful patterns is a form of self-sabotage. It's a fear-based projection mechanism where the known negative outcome feels safer than the potential danger of the unknown. Among a whole range of other reasons, we self-sabotage because we underestimate our capabilities or because we're afraid of failure or commitment.

The good news is, you can rewire your brain. When you notice your mind starting to give you reasons for why something's impossible, try thinking, 'Thanks, brain. This will require a bit of effort, but the same old thinking will give me the same old results.' Then just get up, create some distance between your thoughts and actions, and do the thing you want to do. Your brain and body will thank you for it. (It's also important to practise self-care, though. If you're genuinely tired or ill, then rest and try again another day.)

## Rewards

There's another simple explanation for why we have unwanted habits. We know that the habit loop includes a cue, a routine and a reward. So that means that every habit we have – wanted or unwanted – gives us some kind of reward, even if that habit is undesirable for us in other ways.

Say, for example, you started eating dessert every night as a way to enjoy something sweet after dinner, and you did that several nights in a row. The more you continued to eat dessert after dinner, the more automatic it became, and it eventually became a craving and a habit. This habit may not help you achieve your health goals, but it does offer you the reward of satisfying your sweet tooth.

Or maybe you decided to skip your morning walk because it was cold and dark and you got to sleep in a little longer. You intentionally chose to not go for your walks. But when the season changed and it became sunny again, you found yourself out of your morning walking habit and in a new not-walking habit. Not going for your walk isn't going to help you be more active, but it does allow you to sleep in a little bit longer, which is also rewarding.

Another classic example is having a glass of wine in the evenings. While on the one hand it might help you relax after a big day, on the other, it negatively impacts your quality of sleep, which makes you more fatigued the next day.

If you reflected on your unwanted habits, you would find that there's a reward at the other end of each of them. But sometimes the consequences of the unwanted habit outweigh the reward, so it's important to break those habits in order to live a happy and healthy life.

One of my favourite authors, Brianna Wiest, describes this inner conflict in her book *The Mountain Is You*.[1] For our purposes, the 'mountain' of the title is our unwanted routines and behaviours.

Wiest says that we can think of our problems like mountains, pushed up by the inexorable forces of geology – or daily life. Our personal mountains could be more tangible, like interpersonal or work problems, financial hardship, addiction or disordered eating, or they could be emotions we find overwhelming. These mountains arise when our needs clash, and our reflective and reflexive minds are at odds. To scale our personal mountain and overcome the issues that are limiting us we must find a resolution between these two parts of ourselves, our awareness and our impulses.

Some of the obstacles we encounter will be beyond our control, simply part of life. But long-lasting problems arise after a lifetime of dealing with what life has thrown at us. We have coped, but to do so we have made accommodations and taken on pain that has built up slowly into a mountain that stands between us and a happier future. That process, too, will remain with us, but in absorbing its lessons we have become the master of our destiny and of ourselves.

If you're finding yourself repeating the same unwanted patterns, take comfort in knowing that it's never too late to break a habit. Habits are malleable throughout our life, so if you want to break an unwanted habit, you absolutely can. It doesn't matter how old you are or how long you've been performing that habit, a leopard *can* change its spots. I've worked with clients in their seventies who've broken habits they've had for more than 50 years. If they can do it, so can you.

Remaining attached to our unwanted habits is an act of self-sabotage. To see real change in our lives we must be willing to let those habits go. The first step in breaking a habit is deciding to do so and accepting that it's going to be challenging at times. Breaking habits is not easy, but with enough self-awareness, perseverance and consistency, it's absolutely achievable. What a relief!

# HOW TO BREAK UNWANTED HABITS

There are two proven methods for breaking habits. I call them *reprogramming* and *restructuring*. Reprogramming is all about replacing the unwanted habit with a new, desired habit – that is, reprogramming a new habit in response to the existing cue. Restructuring involves restructuring your environment to avoid the habit trigger altogether. Let's have a look at each of these methods in more detail.

## Reprogramming

Have you ever been told or told yourself 'Just stop doing that' or 'Don't do this'? Just don't eat when you're not hungry, just don't finish everything on your plate if you're already full, just stop watching so much television, just stop being negative, just stop procrastinating. It doesn't work. I've certainly said these things to myself many times before, but it's never worked. I'd still finish all the food on my plate even if I wasn't hungry. To explain this, let's think back to the habit loop. We know that our habits are triggered by a cue and result in a reward. Because all habits offer some sort of reward, it can be difficult to simply eliminate them, which is why advice like 'Just stop doing it' rarely works.

Instead, you need to replace an old habit with a new habit that provides a similar reward. We cannot simply unlearn associations, we have to learn new associations in their place.

For example, if you eat whenever you feel bored, 'Just stop eating' isn't going to help you break that habit because it won't meet your desire not to be bored. Instead, you need to deal with being bored in a different way. When you feel bored, you could call a friend, go for a five-minute walk outside, or perhaps even start learning to play a musical instrument. Your new healthier habit needs to be triggered by boredom and reward you by meeting your need for stimulation.

Breaking old habits using reprogramming works by keeping the same cue and the same reward of the habit loop and simply changing the routine. A client I've worked with, I'll call her Vanessa, was in the habit of drinking a glass of wine every night when she got home from work. She believed it helped her unwind (that was her reward). But Vanessa's doctor told her she needed to have at least two alcohol-free days a week. She was happy to follow the doctor's advice, but she'd often be halfway through a glass of wine before realising what she was doing. She would mindlessly pull out a wine glass from the cupboard, open a bottle of wine and pour the wine into the glass. She realised this was a strong and automatic habit for her. Vanessa's habit cue was getting home from work, her routine was drinking a glass of wine and her reward was unwinding.

She couldn't not go home, so she couldn't avoid the cue. To break her wine-drinking habit, she therefore needed to replace the glass of wine with a different habit that would still help her unwind. We used the same cue (getting home from work) and the same reward (unwinding), but we experimented with a few different ways to help her unwind, such as a cup of herbal tea, a hot shower, doing some deep breathing, stretching, meditating and reading. She enjoyed having a cup of herbal tea and that eventually became her new habit. To help her avoid slip-ups, we moved her tea mugs to where the wine glasses used to be and moved the wine bottles into an inconvenient, hard-to-reach spot in the house. Now, when she habitually reached for a wine glass, she was met with tea mugs, which reminded her that her new habit was to have a herbal tea instead of wine. I touched base with Vanessa as I was writing this chapter three years later. She still has her cup of herbal tea after work, and she's completely kicked her old wine-drinking habit.

Reprogramming works in the brain by changing our neural connections. In Chapter 1, I wrote about Hebbian learning, which describes the principle that if one neuron fires and then another neuron fires, the first neuron will connect to the second neuron, making them more likely to fire as a pair. So if you were bitten by a dog as a kid, you might have developed a fear of dogs. Because your 'dog' neuron fired, then your 'pain' neuron fired, dog became connected to pain.

The reverse of this theory and relevant to breaking old habits is anti-Hebbian learning. In anti-Hebbian learning if you already have a connection between two neurons and you fire the first neuron without firing the second neuron, the connection weakens. This 'unlearning' rule is why if you have a fear of dogs and you're exposed to friendly dogs over and over again, you might unlearn your fear of dogs. The 'dog' neuron gets fired without the 'pain' neuron getting fired, and so the connection weakens until eventually the 'dog' and 'pain' neurons aren't likely to fire together again. This is how we break habit loops, this is how we unlearn old patterns of behaviour, this is how we reprogram our brain to act in a different way when we're faced with a habit trigger.

Using the reprogramming method to break old habits takes experimentation and a bit of trial and error. The reward that one action will give you might not be the same reward another action gives you. Luckily for Vanessa, having a herbal tea helped her unwind so she no longer had the urge to have a glass of wine. For someone else, tea might not cut it. They might need to go out for an evening stroll or take a warm shower. We need to adopt an attitude of curiosity and be experimental with the process.

The simplest way to start practising habit reprogramming is to distance your response from the trigger. Say, for example, that when you climb into bed you have a habit of scrolling on your phone and it's a habit you'd like to break. Instead of picking up your phone straight after getting into bed, pause for five minutes, 10 minutes, even just two minutes, to leave enough time between the trigger (getting into bed) and the habit (scrolling on your phone). Over time, the neural connection will weaken and the habit will no longer be automatic. Between the trigger and the habit there is a space, and in that space is our power to choose what we do next. In our choice lies our growth and our freedom.

## Restructuring

Research shows that people break habits most dramatically when they move to a new house, change jobs or go on holiday.[2] Because their environment has been radically restructured, they are no longer triggered by the old familiar cues. We can create this effect simply by changing our triggering environment. Remember, our environment drives our behaviour.

---

## If we remove the trigger, the habit is no longer going to take place.

---

Restructuring is all about changing your environment to eliminate the triggering cue – the first ingredient in the habit loop – altogether. If we remove the trigger, the habit is no longer going to take place. No trigger = no habit.

If having dinner laid out on the dining table in front of you triggers the habit of going back for seconds when you're no longer hungry, then you could remove that trigger by dishing your dinner straight onto your plate and leaving the rest of the food in the kitchen. Or if standing on your balcony and drinking a cup of coffee triggers a morning habit of smoking a cigarette, you could change the triggering environment by not going out onto the balcony to drink your coffee in the morning but instead sitting in the lounge room. Social scientists call this an 'upstream intervention', because it's intervening before the habit is performed.

Studies show that our intentions will tend to predict our future behaviour when we perform a behaviour in varying contexts.

But when we perform behaviours in stable contexts, past behaviour becomes the strongest predictor of future behaviour.[3] For example, if you exercise at different times of the day, then your intentions will drive your future exercise behaviours. But if you exercise at a similar time each day, then that cue–response association will drive your future exercise behaviours. The stronger the cue–response association, the more likely you are to unintentionally continue with that habit.

I worked with another client – I'll call him Sam – who had a habit of going through the drive-through of a fast-food chain on his way home from work. He would order a combo meal and eat it on his drive. Eventually, Sam's wife asked him to have dinner with the family instead, and Sam wanted that for himself too. The next day, he started driving home from work and without a second thought pulled into the drive-through of the fast-food chain and ordered the same combo meal. He was feeling disappointed with himself but felt motivated to get it right the following day. The next day came around and he tried again, this time telling himself he wouldn't stop anywhere on his way home, but as soon as he saw the fast-food chain, he said it was like a giant magnet that pulled his car into the drive-through (of course, there were no magnets; Sam just had a very strong habit). Although he didn't order the same combo meal, he still ate too much to enjoy dinner with his family that night. This is when Sam approached me to help. I identified straight away that his cue was seeing the fast-food chain, his routine was driving through and his reward was effortlessly satisfying his hunger.

I pulled the map out and worked out that if Sam took a different route home, he would avoid the fast-food chain and only add an additional minute to his drive. So after our chat, he drove the new route home and for the first time in more than a year enjoyed a wholesome dinner with his family. He waited several days to see if his fast-food habit was really broken, or if this was just the honeymoon phase of doing something new. He then called me to let me know that he'd genuinely broken his old habit, that not seeing the fast-food chain meant he drove straight home. He said he'd forgotten what it was like to even crave the fast food, that he genuinely didn't even think about it. I could hear Sam's wife in the background yelling, 'Thank you, Dr Cleo.' More than a case of out of sight out of mind, if you don't initiate the habit loop with the cue, then there's no habit to be acted on. You wouldn't try to put on your seatbelt when you sat at your dining table because that's not the trigger for putting on your seatbelt, sitting in the car is.

I spoke with Sam and his wife recently. He's lost weight, his blood sugar levels and blood cholesterol have improved significantly, and his kids are very happy to have Dad back at the dinner table.

Our environment is a strong driver for our behaviour, so restructuring our environment can change our habits. College students' daily habits of reading, exercising and watching television were studied by researchers to see what happened when they moved from one university to another.[4] They found that the students' habits remained the same in the new college as long as their habit triggers, such as location and social setting, were similar. For example, if their new dorm-mates exercised then the students continued to exercise. But when the environmental triggers for their habits changed, so did their habits. If their new dorm-mates didn't read regularly like their old dorm-mates did, the students cut down their reading time.

New environments remove automatic cue–response associations and spur us to make new or different decisions. For example, in the same study of college students, a change of college made the students more likely to ask themselves things like, 'Should I really be watching television?' or 'Am I actually enjoying this exercise?' When they were in their new environment, they started to think about their habits rather than merely repeating them. We become more mindful and less on autopilot when our environment changes. This gives us an opportunity to act from our values, goals and intentions rather than being guided by automatic cue–response associations that may not be serving us.

## A four-step process for breaking unwanted habits

There's a valuable activity at the end of this chapter to help guide you through a four-step process for breaking unwanted habits. In summary, those steps are:

1. Identify an unwanted habit in your life.
2. Investigate its cue(s).
3. Reflect on its reward(s).
4. Determine whether reprogramming a new habit or restructuring your environment would be more applicable.

## Frozen habits

During a transition or change in circumstance, environmental triggers are disrupted. When we go on holiday, for example, our habits can be temporarily halted, or frozen. The key word here is 'temporarily', because when we are re-exposed to the triggering environment (when we get home from holiday), the old habits can become unfrozen. We might think we've broken that habit, but we just haven't been exposed to the cue that triggers it for a period of time.

For example, Amira has a habit of going to Pilates after work with her colleagues. When Amira took two weeks off on annual leave, she didn't attend any Pilates classes. She thought her healthy habit of regular exercise had surely fallen away. But when she returned to work, Amira started going to Pilates with her colleagues again.

## PRACTISING ABSTINENCE

I personally don't like the idea of complete abstinence from something, because the last thing we want to do is create a sense that we can't exert self-control. I remember, when I was in my twenties, trying to reduce how much chocolate I ate. One of my strategies was not to have chocolate in the house, but when I would go to friends' houses, or work meetings where chocolate was on offer, I turned into a chocolate-eating monster and initiated an unhealthy all-or-nothing mentality. Nevertheless, for very stubborn or addictive habits, some research suggests that going 30 days without the substance or behaviour could result in important changes in the brain that help with breaking the habit.[5]

Dr Anna Lembke, a professor of psychiatry and specialist on the opioid epidemic, suggests in her book *Dopamine Nation* that 30 days is about the average time it takes for the brain to reset reward pathways and for dopamine transmission to regenerate itself.[6] In other words, it takes on average 30 days to feel good and happy again without the substance or behaviour we feel so strongly drawn to. One study took a group of men diagnosed with depression who were addicted to alcohol. The men were placed in a hospital where they received no treatment for depression and had no access to alcohol. After four weeks, 86 per cent of the men no longer met the criteria for depression. By depriving themselves of alcohol, which gave them a high sense of reward and therefore a hit of dopamine, their brain's reward system was able to find a healthy balance again.[7]

During those 30 days, two key benefits take place. Firstly, we are able to widen our lens and pay attention to and enjoy other things in our life – we can expand the repertoire of things we enjoy doing. Secondly, we can look back and see the true cause and effect between performing our unwanted habit and its impact on our life and the people around us.

Of course, saying 'Just stop for 30 days' is much easier than actually doing it. Depending on the habit you're trying to break, days one to 10 are going to be the hardest. In fact, those first 10 days can sometimes really suck. You might feel agitated, angry, anxious or impulsive. But once you get through those first 10 days, you'll start to feel so much better. There's a better life on the other side of the mountain, so keep going, you can do this. I've met people who've broken the strongest habits and addictions. If they can do it, you absolutely can.

If, after the 30 days, you decide you want to go back to your unwanted habit but in moderation, you can use a self-binding strategy to achieve this, such as only doing it on Mondays and Fridays, or only for 10 minutes a day, or whatever limit you set for yourself. Most of the time, your view of the unwanted habit will change and you won't go back to doing it like you used to. (But do bear in mind that this of course won't work for dangerous addictions, such as drugs and alcohol, where lifelong abstinence is the only way.)

---

> I've met people who've broken the strongest habits and addictions. If they can do it, you absolutely can.

---

In *Dopamine Nation*, Dr Lembke describes a patient she worked with who had a video game problem. He was depressed and anxious and eventually dropped out of college. He was convinced that video games were the only thing that alleviated his depression, but in fact they were driving it. When he abstained from video games for 30 days, he felt better than he had in years. He eventually went back to playing video games, but he decided to do it differently. He wanted to play less and to have a healthier attachment to gaming. He managed to accomplish that by only letting himself play certain games and avoiding the ones he found too addictive, and he only let himself play with friends and not strangers. By implementing these self-binding strategies, he was able to bracket off his video game playing in a way that helped him limit his use.[8]

Is something holding you back from living your best life? Might it help to abstain from it for the next 30 days?

## SUMMARY

» It's never too late to break a habit. Habits are malleable throughout your entire life, so if you want to change a habit, you can.

» Every habit in your life – both wanted and unwanted – provides you with a reward.

» You can break habits by either:
   1. reprogramming a new habit response to your existing cue (replacing the unwanted habit with a desired habit)
   2. restructuring the existing cues (avoiding the triggering environment).

» Creating space between a trigger and a habit weakens the neural connections over time and thus breaks the automaticity of the habit.

» Habit strength and strong intentions moderate the effectiveness of breaking habits.

» The four steps to breaking unwanted habits are:
   1. Identify an unwanted habit in your life.
   2. Investigate its cue(s).
   3. Reflect on its reward(s).
   4. Determine whether reprogramming a new habit or restructuring the environment would be more applicable.

» Abstaining from a behaviour or substance for 30 days can be helpful in breaking stubborn habits or addictions.

**ACTIVITY**

# Breaking old habits

As with forming new habits, you can change the cue–routine–reward cycle to break unwanted habits, either by reprogramming or restructuring.

To change your habits, you need to know how they work. Habit mapping is a great tool for understanding why you do the things you do, so you can effectively break your unwanted habits.

To map your habits, use the templates below or opposite. Draw up the diagram in your journal and fill in your responses.

### A four-step process for breaking unwanted habits

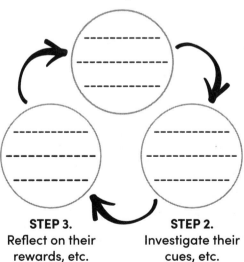

**STEP 1.**
Identify unwanted habits, etc.

**STEP 3.**
Reflect on their rewards, etc.

**STEP 2.**
Investigate their cues, etc.

## Steps 1–3: Habit mapping

**STEP 1.**
Identify
unwanted habits
Identify up to three
unwanted habits in
your life.
*e.g. Eating when I'm
not hungry*

**STEP 2.**
Investigate
their cues
Write down the cues
that are triggering
the unwanted habit.
*e.g. When I'm feeling
restless or bored*

**STEP 3.**
Reflect on
their rewards
List the rewards you
receive from performing
the unwanted habit.
*e.g. Eating gives me
something to do*

## Step 4: Select a breaking method

For each habit you wish to break, determine whether reprogramming a new habit or restructuring your environment would be more appropriate. A method that works for one habit may not be as effective for other habits. The method you use should depend on whether you can avoid the trigger or not. You probably can't, for example, avoid going to or from work or getting into and out of bed.

If reprogramming is more appropriate, write down the new habit you'll complete in place of the old unwanted habit (bearing in mind that the reward should not change). For example:

> Cue: 'When I get home from work.'
> ~~Old habit: 'I will have a glass of wine.'~~
> New habit: 'I will have a cup of herbal tea.'
> Reward: 'Unwind from the day.'

If restructuring is more appropriate, write down how you intend to avoid or modify the trigger. For example:

Cue: ~~'When I drive home from work and pass a fast-food chain.'~~

Habit: 'I order a combo meal with a medium fries and cola.'

Restructured cue: 'Drive a different way home from work.'

Reward: 'Enjoy dinner with the family.'

Make some notes on how you'll break each of your three unwanted habits. You may feel a bit unsure as you first try to do this, and that's perfectly okay. It's one of those skills you need to practise to fully grasp.

## Chapter 7

# The neuroscience of habits

WHAT HAPPENS IN OUR BRAIN when we're creating new habits and breaking old ones? Can an old dog really learn new tricks, and can a leopard change its spots?

I'm a firm believer that if you understand how something works, you can learn to change it. That's why I want to explain the wonders of the human brain and detail how you can use your brain power to create the life you desire. Let's start with the difference between the mind and the brain.

## MIND VERSUS BRAIN

Our mind and our brain are not the same thing, although they both have tremendous power over our body and our actions. Our brain is a physical organ, part of the visible, tangible world of our body. It is composed of neurons and cells, and it uses electrical and chemical signals to communicate within itself and with the rest of our body. Our brain is the physical structure that enables our mind to exist and function.

Our mind is a more abstract concept that refers to the subjective experiences and mental processes that emerge from the activity of our brain. Our mind is part of the invisible, transcendent world of thought, feeling, attitude, belief, emotion, perception, memory and imagination. Our mind is shaped by various factors, such as genetics, environment and experience, and day after day it is building and reprogramming our brain.

Essentially, the mind and the brain are a unified system. As the brain changes the mind changes, and as the mind changes the brain changes.

## THE HUMAN BRAIN

The brain is our most complex organ, and its primary objective is to keep us alive. It does this through our neural pathways – chains of nerve cells that transmit messages to our body. These cells help us to breathe, eat, walk, feel, think and communicate – the basic essentials of survival. While our brain, at 1.5 kilograms (3¼ pounds), makes up approximately 2 per cent of our entire bodyweight, it uses a massive 20–25 per cent of our energy every day.[1]

The brain's basic building blocks are cells known as neurons, and we each have an estimated 100 billion neurons in our brain. Each of those brain cells has 1000–10,000 connections to other cells – it's a serious spaghetti bowl up there. If you were to lay out the brain's neural connections in a straight line, they would be around 5 million kilometres (3 million miles) long. That's nearly 125 round-the-world trips. Similar to electricity moving through a city's power grid, information is passed along these neural connections through a series of electrochemical messages. The more times these messages journey down the same beaten track, the more solid and formed those tracks become. In the context of unwanted habits, they are the tracks to our self-sabotaging impulses – our unwanted habits.

Just as computers are hard-wired with electrical connections, the brain is hard-wired with neural connections. These connections link together its various lobes and also link what we take in through our five senses – sight, smell, sound, taste and touch – with our physical actions and how we move.

That's what makes our brain the control centre of our entire body. It's like the power station that connects our every thought, movement and feeling. As humans, we can plan ahead, solve problems, experience emotions and store memories.

## NEUROPLASTICITY

Scientists used to believe that our brain didn't change after childhood, that it was hard-wired or 'fixed' by the time we became adults. But recent advances tell us that this is simply not true. We have discovered that the brain can and does change throughout our lives – it is adaptable, plastic in the sense of malleable. Neuroscientists thus call this feature neuroplasticity. Our brain has the ability to be shaped or formed by new activity – even into old age.

Think of your brain as a dynamic town plan with billions of roads and pathways and highways. Some of these roads are well travelled – these are your habits, your established ways of thinking, feeling and doing. Every time you think in a certain way, feel a specific emotion or practise a particular task, you strengthen that road. It becomes easier and more efficient for your brain to travel that pathway.

Say you think about something differently or choose a different emotion or learn a new task – you're essentially carving out a new road. If you continue travelling that road, your brain begins to use this pathway more, and this new way of thinking, feeling or doing becomes second nature; it resembles a well-used highway. Simultaneously, the old pathway gets used less and less and weakens, becoming more like a back alley.

This process of rewiring our brain by forming new connections and weakening old ones is the wonder of neuroplasticity in action. Neuroplasticity is defined as the ability of the brain to form and reorganise neural connections, especially in response to learning or experience. In other words, it's our brain's ability to change continuously throughout our life, both structurally and functionally.[2]

Neuroplasticity describes a sequence of processes that take place as our emotions, behaviours, experiences and thoughts physically change the way our brain functions. Everything we think, feel and do is transmitted via neural circuits in our brain. These same thoughts, feelings, actions and experiences can change and sculpt the very circuits they travel along.

The good news is, you have the ability to learn and change by rewiring your brain. In fact, if you've ever changed a habit or thought about something differently, you've experienced neuroplasticity first-hand.

When I learned that I had the power to reshape my brain, I felt incredibly empowered. I realised that no matter what habits I had in my life, I had the power to change them and that it would get easier and easier.

## Can the adult brain learn and change?

During infancy and our childhood and teenage years, our neuroplasticity was switched to *on*. In the adult brain, however, the plasticity switch sits towards neutral. The older brain is still plastic and remains plastic to the end of our life. We can learn, change and master new skills as adults, but it requires a bit more persistence. We're all capable of learning to speak a new language at any age, but we're not going to pick it up as easily as if we learned to speak it as a child.

With this knowledge, we can see that our brain will support the behaviours we repeatedly perform and discourage the behaviours we

> When we procrastinate on taking action,
> we're not just delaying doing the task, we're
> actually reinforcing its neural pathways
> so that we procrastinate even more.

perform rarely. This means that our daily actions matter. When we procrastinate on taking action, we're not just delaying doing the task, we're actually reinforcing its neural pathways so that we procrastinate even more.

This concept helped me realise that every time I repeated an unwanted habit I was reinforcing it in my life. It helped me get rid of my excuses. I no longer said 'Just this once' or 'I'll start next week'.

## OUR BRAIN ON HABITS

Various biological and physiological mechanisms come into play in our brain when we're forming new habits or breaking old ones, including neurogenesis, synaptic strengthening and synaptic pruning. You don't need to remember them by name, but knowing how they work is both fascinating and helpful when you're reshaping your life.

- **neurogenesis:** This is the process by which our brain creates new neurons. It takes place when we're learning a new skill or going through a new experience. Our brain can also generate new neural connections through these new experiences. For example, when we're creating a new habit, our brain learns the cue–response association and links those two things (the cue and the response) together. Our brain also creates new neural connections with old neurons. For example, when we're breaking an unwanted habit and we reprogram a new habit in place of the old one, our brain learns to connect the new habit to the old habit trigger. We therefore learn to perform our new habit rather than our old one whenever we encounter the existing trigger.

- **synaptic strengthening:** The actual strength of neural connections is adaptable and can be changed. That means we can create stronger connections between neurons, which leads to long-term change and adaptation (habit formation). These are what we generally refer to as our strong habits, the habits that are really ingrained in our life. We achieve synaptic strengthening through repetition. When we repeatedly perform the same action in response to the same trigger, our brain strengthens the neural connections between the trigger and the action. Simply put, the more you repeat a habit loop, the stronger the habit will get.

- **synaptic pruning:** I love this one. The process of synaptic pruning is like a gardener trimming and pruning a tree to remove the dead or unnecessary branches, allowing the healthy branches to grow and flourish. In the same way, our brain eliminates old, weak or unused neural connections to optimise cognitive function and improve efficiency. The less we perform a habit, the weaker its neural connections become, until eventually our brain learns that it doesn't need those neural connections any more (because they're not being used) and gets rid of them. This is what happens in our brain when we're breaking old habits. So a leopard *can* change its spots after all.

Neurons that fire together wire together, and neurons that are out of sync fail to link.[3] We have the power and ability to completely rewire our brain through strengthening or pruning our neural connections, which in turn changes our automatic actions or our habits. This is the power of neuroplasticity.

---

## We have the power and ability to completely rewire our brain.

---

Rewiring your brain for success comes down to commitment, consistency and context-dependent repetition.

## IMPORTANT, REWARDING, CRUCIAL FOR SURVIVAL

It's easy for me to live an active lifestyle because the benefits I gain from movement are important to me and they align with my values. Among many other positives, being active helps me concentrate during the day and sleep better, puts me in a better mood and energises me. I'd describe exercise as my therapy.

We can supercharge our adult brain's innate capacity for neuroplasticity when we believe that a change is important, rewarding or crucial for survival. How do we do that? At the risk of sounding like a motivational speaker, I'm going to ask you to find your 'why'. Why does making this change or achieving this goal matter to you? How will it benefit your life? Who do you want to become?

Answering these questions and really reflecting on your answers will help you find the necessary motivation to take action towards your goals and make those important brain changes. Having clarity around your goal and the benefits of achieving that goal creates confidence, drive and excitement.

The language you use to talk to yourself matters. Are you trying to learn to play the piano or are you a musician? Are you trying to get fit or are you an active person? Your identity and the way you see yourself can shape your actions and influence the choices you make. For example, if you see yourself as a kind and compassionate person, you are more likely to volunteer at a local charity or help someone in need. Or if you believe that smoking is harmful to your health, you are less likely to take up smoking. And if you do, you may experience cognitive dissonance, an uncomfortable mental conflict that occurs when our behaviour is inconsistent with our beliefs, values or attitudes.[4] A classic example is when someone tells a lie and feels uncomfortable about it because they fundamentally view themselves as an honest person. A mental conflict takes place due to the contradiction between knowing they did something wrong and thinking they are an honest person.

So instead of focusing on distant goals, make your goal pursuits your identity. You can start reshaping your sense of identity right now by completing this sentence, 'I am [healthy/calm/confident/disciplined/successful/etc.].' Creating a coherent narrative is critical to our ability to find meaning, resolve our cognitive dissonance, and build a social identity around our lived experiences.

Cognitive dissonance reduces our drive to reach a reward. For example, we know that things like eating highly processed food or smoking aren't good for us. But the reason fewer people smoke now than ever before in history isn't because of their knowledge that smoking is a bad habit; it's not because of the campaigns that show the negative health effects of smoking; it's not because we know that smoking is linked to cancer and other chronic diseases. The most effective messaging in the battle against smoking was showing young adults videos of rich men sitting around a table laughing at how much money they were making from the health problems people were experiencing due to smoking.[5] They made being a non-smoker anti-establishment and activated the same sense of rebellion that would previously have made them turn to smoking.

We are all vulnerable to marketing. Researchers have shown people with food addiction how the food industry manipulates us by designing food to be addictive. They showed them the months of research and the millions of dollars that go into product development, the ingredients they use and the chemically exaggerated flavours that create a taste sensation so appealing that we keep wanting more. The food industry has cleverly exploited sugar, fat and salt in a way that sends our biology haywire. They know how to make their food hit the spot and drive our reward system so that we want more and more of it and essentially eat more of their food than their competitors'. Once this veil was lifted and participants learned about the big business that makes food addictive, a mental conflict took place between their behaviour and their values. Consequently, there was a huge reduction in their food addiction and their consumption of highly processed food.[6]

I saw this effect taking place in my life when I learned how social media developers create these platforms with the objective of keeping us scrolling for as long as possible, because the longer we're scrolling, the more money they're making. It started with the introduction of infinite scrolling, which allows us to keep scrolling through content endlessly without any break or end point. Then there were push notifications to alert us when there's new content or updates: 'Sally posted a product on marketplace.' Do I really need to know that? I really don't but sometimes I feel like I need to see what Sally's selling. These notifications create a sense of urgency and a fear of missing out, compelling us to check our accounts frequently. Then there's the allure of personalised content, where cleverly designed algorithms show us the posts we're most likely to engage with based on our previous behaviour and interests. They do this because it creates a sense of relevance and familiarity that keeps us coming back for more.

But social media took it too far by playing with our sense of self-worth through social validation. Research shows that the feedback we get in the form of likes, comments and shares lights up the reward system in our brain and, after time, we can feel depressed, lonely and empty without it.[7] I could go on about the gamification in the form of points and badges that incentivises us to stay logged in, the techniques for creating social norms such as indicating that our close friends are online when in fact they're not, and many, many others. We almost have to wonder how much free choice we really have when we're up against computer engineers, researchers and social psychologists who understand our brain and how to create an addictive user experience better than we do. I don't know about you, but I lost interest in aimlessly scrolling on social media when I discovered these manipulation tactics. I still post on my socials, but you will rarely find me scrolling or spending time on social platforms in my idle time. Maybe it's the rebel in me, but I like being anti-establishment. I want to be in control of my time and my brain's reward system.

Dig deep, find your why, make it meaningful to you, and believe that you already are the person you want to be.

# SUMMARY

» Our brains are continuously changing throughout our lives – that's the wonder of neuroplasticity. Our neural connections change every day and we have the power to rewire our brain and change our life.

» An old dog *can* learn new tricks – through neurogenesis; and a leopard *can* change its spots – through synaptic pruning.

» Neurons that fire together wire together, and neurons that are out of sync fail to link.

» Habits are an excellent representation of the power of neuroplasticity.

  • We create new neurons and synaptic connections through a new skill or experience, and we strengthen neural connections through repetition, which leads to long-term habit change.

  • We shed old, weak synaptic connections when we don't perform a specific habit for some time.

» The adult brain's innate capacity for neuroplasticity can be supercharged when we believe the change is important, rewarding or crucial for survival.

# Chapter 8

# Micro habits

WORKING IN THE FIELD OF behaviour change, I'm often speaking with people who want to make changes in their life. We've all set New Year's resolutions and goals to become better versions of ourselves. I think when done right, goals can be an invaluable tool for helping us do better and be better. But all too often what I see with people who want to overhaul their lives is a list of goals that resembles Santa's Christmas list rather than realistic aspirations. We want to lose weight, get fit, pay off our debts, start a gratitude practice, travel more, meditate every day, drink more water, be better parents, better partners, better friends. It's a lot!

Our brains are only capable of making up to three changes at once, so by limiting the number of goals you set for yourself to three or less, you will significantly improve your chance of achieving those goals, without overwhelming your brain. To take it a step further, if you focus on just one change at a time, you're much more likely to achieve it than if you try to focus on multiple changes.

## SIMPLICITY CHANGES BEHAVIOUR

Research shows that the easier the change in behaviour we want to make, the more consistent we will be in performing it, and therefore the better and more sustained the outcomes we will achieve.[1] Large or complex changes are not only more difficult to achieve but more difficult to sustain. Simplicity changes behaviour. Creating small, consistent changes adds up to lifestyle changes more effectively than trying to create big changes. This is because simple changes require less willpower and motivation than large or complex changes.

In Chapter 9, we'll learn that self-control is a finite resource that gets exhausted – a concept known as ego depletion. We cannot therefore consistently or reliably depend on our self-control, especially when we're not feeling particularly motivated, or when life throws a hurdle at us. Our motivation is like a wave – it ebbs and flows from day to day and from moment to moment.

The graph opposite shows our level of motivation on the vertical axis and time along the horizontal axis. Over time, our motivation levels naturally fluctuate from high to low and back again. Line A represents behaviours that are challenging to perform and therefore require higher motivation, and line B represents behaviours that are easy and require less motivation. You can see that when our motivation is low, we're unlikely to consistently perform challenging behaviours such as going out for a run or reading a whole chapter of a book. But when our motivation is low, we can still regularly perform easier behaviours such as going for a leisurely walk around the block or reading one page of a book.

---

To achieve and sustain our desired habits,
it's important to keep the need for
motivation and willpower as low as possible.

---

**Motivation for hard versus easy behaviours**

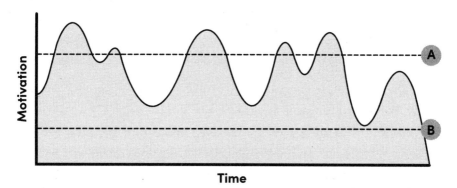

A = Hard, inconsistent behaviours
B = Easy, consistent behaviours

We know that consistency is the key to creating new habits, so to achieve and sustain our desired habits, it's important to keep the need for motivation and willpower as low as possible. We do this by breaking down those desired habits into bite-sized pieces. I call those pieces micro habits.

## MICRO HABITS

A micro habit is a bite-sized form of your desired habit. By bite-sized I mean a smaller, simpler version of your desired habit. You could think of a micro habit as an action that requires little effort, something so small it's easy to say yes to doing.

For example, if your goal is healthy eating, it's much easier to eat a piece of fruit every day than completely overhaul your entire diet. Or if your goal is to do more exercise, it's much easier to take a 15-minute walk every day than to run a marathon.

If you take on too big a goal all at once, you might be able to push on with it for the first few days or even a couple of weeks, but eventually your motivation will wear thin. Whether it's because you're dealing with screaming kids, work stress or feeling tired, the result is you end up back doing what you've always done. This is why it's much more productive to initiate bite-sized habits that you can perform consistently. Eventually your brain will rewire itself and recognise that habit as second nature.

Baby steps may seem like an unlikely route to achieving your goals. We naturally want to achieve our goals as quickly as possible. But research has shown over and over again that big changes are difficult to achieve and we will actually have much more success if we make small changes and do them consistently.[2] Walking for 15 minutes a day may not seem like much exercise, but 15 minutes of walking added up over a month or six months would likely be more activity than trying to run a marathon and only training a few times before giving up.

## Compound the benefits

It's easy to overestimate the importance of big one-off actions and underestimate the value of small frequent actions. There's a common misconception that big changes require big, grand actions. We think that to lose weight we need to be on a very restrictive diet, or to get fit we need to exercise vigorously every day, or if we want to save money we must forgo all our surplus luxuries (goodbye going to the movies or enjoying a meal at a restaurant). But the reality is, we can very rarely sustain those big actions. It's impossible to stay on a restrictive diet for long periods, and never going out to the movies or to enjoy a meal at a restaurant in the name of saving money is unreasonable. It's the small, achievable actions done consistently that make big achievements happen. Just as money in a bank account multiplies through compound interest, the benefits of micro habits compound as we repeat them. If you clean out just one shelf in the cupboard and you repeat that action with a new shelf several times over the course of the next few weeks, you will eventually have

---

## Change the small things and big things happen.

---

a cleaned-out cupboard. But if you wait to feel motivated enough to clean out the entire cupboard at once, it's likely to stay cluttered. Change the small things and big things happen.

Your trajectory is also much more important than your speed. Every step you take in the right direction moves you towards your goals, no matter how small that step. It's much more productive to move slowly in the right direction than fast in the wrong direction. Small progress is still progress, and micro habits are what will help you achieve that.

### Ignite motivation

Micro habits also set you up for some early easy wins. If you give yourself a realistic goal, like reducing your screen time by five minutes, and you achieve that goal, your brain triggers a reward pathway that helps you to experience pleasure and satisfaction. This reward pathway ignites motivation and plays a crucial role in prompting you to want to perform that behaviour again. So by achieving a goal, even a teeny-tiny goal, you reinforce the behaviour and neural pathway that led to the reward.

### Boost self-efficacy

Do you believe in your ability to achieve your goals? I hope so. The strongest predictor of motivation and success is the belief in our own ability to achieve the goals we set for ourselves. This belief is known as self-efficacy. High levels of self-efficacy predict ultimate success.[3]

Self-efficacy is not self-image, self-worth or any other similar construct. While self-esteem focuses more on 'being' or feeling that you are perfectly acceptable as you are, self-efficacy focuses more on 'doing'. It's having a can-do attitude and taking action when met with a challenge, and it's knowing that you're up to that challenge.

Albert Bandura, a professor of psychology who introduced the concept of self-efficacy, said, 'People's beliefs about their abilities have a profound effect on those abilities.'[4] And Henry Ford said, 'Whether you think you can, or you can't – you're right.'[5]

Imagine someone who is learning a new language. If they have high self-efficacy, they may believe that they have the skills and determination to become fluent, even if the process is challenging. This belief in their ability can motivate them to practise consistently, seek out resources and support, and persist through setbacks. Ultimately, their high self-efficacy can lead to them successfully learning the language, reinforcing their belief in their own abilities, and building confidence for future challenges. I spent six months in South America travelling off the beaten track, exploring small remote towns. The locals didn't speak much English in the places I travelled, so to get around or to order a meal I had to learn a bit of Spanish. I would watch subtitled cartoons because they used basic vocabulary that I was confident enough to learn. I believed I could learn some Spanish and I did. I wasn't able to have a political conversation with someone, but I could communicate enough to make connections and travel with ease.

Let's imagine that you feel incapable of achieving a goal because you don't have enough experience. Having thoughts and feelings about not having enough experience creates feelings of anxiety and stress, which can activate the sympathetic nervous system and put you in a state of flight, fight or freeze. In this state, your creativity and productivity are disabled, your brain is no longer focused on the benefits of achieving the goal, and you start procrastinating on the steps you could be taking in the present. This results in you seeing that you're not doing the things that deep down you want to do, which reinforces your original thought of being incapable of achieving your goal. Lack of self-efficacy is a vicious cycle.

Start by thinking of the kind of person you need to become to make your goals possible for yourself. Do you need to be more open-minded, courageous, balanced, disciplined, resilient? Think about the times you've demonstrated those characteristics in the past and start replacing your thoughts of self-doubt with beliefs that you can be – and in fact are – the person you need to be to achieve your goals.

Every time you face doubt and push right past it, you prove to yourself that you are capable. Every time you feel fear and do it anyway, you display an inner strength. Every time you quash your excuses and do it anyway, you honour the greatness inside you that wants to be heard. That's how confidence and self-efficacy grow: one small, courageous move at a time.

---

## Every time you face doubt and push right past it, you prove to yourself that you are capable.

---

Examples of self-efficacy include a student who is not particularly gifted in a certain subject but believes in their own ability to learn it well. Or an expectant mother who is nervous about caring for a new baby but believes that she has what it takes to succeed, no matter how difficult it will be.

Small changes increase self-efficacy because we're more likely to achieve small changes than big changes. By setting ourselves an achievable micro habit, we get positive reinforcement when we attain it, which further increases self-efficacy. It's a beautiful cycle: achieving micro habit = positive reinforcement = increase in self-efficacy = achieving micro habit. Micro habits boost self-efficacy and self-efficacy promotes behaviour change – and thus builds habits. Other factors that increase self-efficacy include affirming self-talk ('I can do this'; see Chapter 15), previous success at changing other behaviours or habits, and encouragement from others.[6]

It's for these reasons that I believe micro habits, along with triggers, are the most important concept in the implementation of sustainable change.

## HOW MICRO IS A MICRO HABIT?

I learned a lot from working with a client named Billy, who was carrying a significant amount of extra weight. He had a personal goal to walk around his local park, which was a 5-kilometre (3-mile) loop, but when I met him he hadn't done any exercise in years. I could see that the idea of walking was challenging for him, mainly because he lacked confidence in his ability to be active. So for the first week I asked Billy just to put his walking shoes on. After taking a few days to find his shoes, Billy would put his walking shoes on each day and walk around the house. We then worked on him walking out to his letterbox and back. Then he became curious as to what was down the road, so he walked to the end of his street and back. As the days passed, Billy started walking around the block, until eventually he was able to successfully walk the 5-kilometre loop around his local park. He was of course, thrilled. Billy lost weight, built his confidence and went on to run a 10-kilometre (6-mile) race. What started with putting his sneakers on ended in an achievement he describes as 'unimaginable'.

What I learned from working with Billy was that the intensity, duration and frequency of a micro habit will be dependent on each person's circumstances and capacity for change. Let's take two people who want to be more active. While for one of them their first micro habit might be just to put on their walking shoes, for the other it might be to go for a 20-minute walk each day. The key is to make the micro habit small enough for you to perform it consistently.

Examples of micro exercise habits to get you moving could include:

- doing 10 push-ups against the kitchen counter while waiting for the kettle to boil
- staying in a wall-sit position while waiting for the toaster
- balancing on one leg for the time it takes to brush your teeth
- doing squats in the ad breaks when watching television.

You may have heard the 'Do 1 per cent better every day' message. The idea is that if you can get 1 per cent better each day for one year, you'll end up 38 times better by the time you're done ($1.01^{365} = 37.78$). In all honesty, I'm not a fan of this idea at all because I don't think it's practical, applicable or relevant in most cases. How can you tangibly divide a behaviour by 100 to know what 1 per cent looks or feels like? And maybe you have the capacity to do more than 1 per cent; if you stick to 1 per cent and your progress is too slow, you will likely lose motivation and give up on your goal altogether.

The other point to make here is that sometimes *maintaining* a new habit is the goal, and you don't have to improve on that every day. For example, if I want to meditate for 10 minutes a day, then 10 minutes is what I'm aiming for. I don't need to do 1 per cent better than 10 minutes each day. So instead of trying to do 1 per cent better every day, just do something small enough that you can't say no to doing it. I might not make time for a 10-minute meditation

---

I like to say,
'Seek rituals, not results.'

---

every day, but I can always do two minutes. I like to say, 'Seek rituals, not results.' The idea is to just show up, do what you can when you can, and gradually build on that routine.

As a micro habit starts to feel natural and automatic, you can increase its intensity, duration or frequency until you achieve the full desired habit. For example, if your ultimate goal is to walk 10,000 steps per day, start with just 2000 steps. Once walking 2000 steps a day feels natural and habitual, build up to 4000 steps a day, then 6000 steps a day and so on, until you reach your goal of 10,000 steps a day.

My dear friend Kate, who is a graduate of my habit practitioner course, calls herself a micro habit convert. Kate went from 'aim for the stars', 'all or nothing' and 'do or die' to incorporating micro habits into her own life as well as those of the clients she coaches. 'About a decade ago,' she says, 'I was a lot heavier than I am now. I tried lots of different behaviour-change techniques, but none of them worked. So I started to make really small changes to my life and lifestyle. At first it was just a 10-minute walk, then I gradually extended that. I just made lots of little tweaks.' Kate is now happy with her weight and exercises regularly. When I asked her what the most effective strategy was when she was incorporating micro habits into her life, she said, 'What I've found is really important is choosing micro habits that are based on things that make me feel good and fit in with my life, because otherwise I'm not going to really want to keep doing them.'

You become what you want to be by consistently being what you want to become each day. You can change your life, transform your daily routines, make new choices, build new habits, shake things up and start over in any moment. The key is not falling for the 'go hard or go home' mentality, which does not work in the long term. The key is opting for small, simple actions that are not only easier to achieve but are also significantly easier to maintain in the long term.

> You become what you want to be
> by consistently being what you want
> to become each day.

Start with doing one push-up, drinking one glass of water, paying a small amount towards one debt, reading one page, making one sale, deleting one old contact, walking one lap. Start with an action you can easily do. As Vincent Van Gogh put it, 'Great things are done by a series of small changes brought together.'[7]

## Finding the sweet spot between fear and boredom

Imagine for a moment that you and I are playing tennis together. We are at the same skill level and it's point for point. We've played tennis together before and some games you win and some games I win. It's a close match, but you know that with a little more oomph you could beat me.

Where is your motivation level right now if you had to place it on a scale of 1 to 10, where 1 is not at all motivated and 10 is very motivated? Most people say something around 9–10. You might be feeling very motivated because you know you can win this game.

Now imagine I've jumped off the court and you're faced with one of the greatest tennis players of all time, known for her mighty serve, powerful playing style and mental toughness on the court: the incomparable Serena Williams. It's just you and Serena and she's about to serve you the ball.

Now where is your motivation level on a scale of 1 to 10? If it was me, I would feel defeated and completely overwhelmed. I'd probably want to throw my racquet as far as I could and run off the court before Serena has even had the opportunity to touch the ball. My motivation would be a weak 1 out of 10.

This time, imagine Serena Williams hops off the court and she's replaced with a five-year-old child. The racquet in the child's hand spans the length of their body and it's the first time they've set foot on a tennis court.

Where is your motivation level now? Most of us will not be feeling overly motivated to give this game our all. We will likely have low levels of motivation because we know we could easily win this game without putting in too much effort. Our motivation might be around a 2 or 3. In fact, we might have an opposite high motivation to let the child win, although the savage ones among us might be thinking, 'I'm going to crush that kid.'

When our goals are too big, we lose motivation because we feel overwhelmed and defeated. And in the same way, when our goals are too small, we also lose motivation because we're not being challenged and achieving the goal is not overly exciting.

The edge of comfort is the sweet spot. It's the space between fear and boredom, where we're not too uncomfortable, but we're also being challenged. At mild to moderate levels of activation, the brain is in its optimal state to learn. At very low levels or very high levels of activation or arousal, learning is inhibited. Research shows over and over again that the highest amount of effort occurs when the task is moderately difficult, and the lowest amount of effort occurs when the task is either very easy or very hard.[8]

**The relationship between task difficulty and effort exerted**

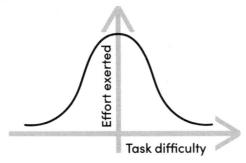

Fear is a symptom of overarousal. This occurs when our goals are too big or too challenging, or far exceed our skill level or capacity. You will know this is happening to you if you're struggling to start your goal or if the idea of doing it seems overwhelming. If this is the case, rework your micro habit so that it's manageable and achievable. At the opposite end of the spectrum, boredom is a symptom of under-arousal. This is when your micro habit isn't challenging you enough. This might manifest in you thinking the goal is super easy and you can achieve it anytime, and yet you still don't take action towards doing so. If this happens, move the goalposts and set yourself a slightly bigger, more challenging goal.

## Just show up: instigation versus execution habits

When I get up in the morning, I usually walk over to the kitchen and make myself a cup of tea. Interestingly, the actual tea I drink is different every day. Some days it's English breakfast, other days it's chai, this morning it was white rose and vanilla. Every now and then I have a hot chocolate. I instigate the same habit, which is having a hot drink in the morning, but my execution is always different. Instigation is like the *on* button – it's habitually deciding to do something; execution, on the other hand, is the *play* button that moves the habit along – it's habitually doing that thing.

A habitually instigated behaviour is one you are cued to do automatically – for example, brushing your teeth in the morning. Habit execution describes habits that facilitate progression through a sequence of actions – for example, how you dry yourself after a shower or how you make a cup of coffee.

I have a habit of going to the gym most mornings, but I don't have a habit of working out. I know this because I habitually get to the gym but the workouts I do are always different; I have to actively think about what I feel like doing on any particular morning. I have an instigation habit of making a cup of tea and going to the gym, but I don't have an execution habit for those behaviours. I habitually decide to make a cup of tea and go to the gym – those decisions are automatic and subconscious. But the actual execution of the habit is something I have to think about – what tea do I feel like, what workout will I do today?

Why this matters is because a growing number of scientific studies suggests that an instigation habit, not an execution habit, predicts how frequently a behaviour is performed. People who are automatically triggered to 'go for a walk' (i.e. they have an instigation habit) will go walking more consistently and frequently. Their habit is deciding to walk. If you only have an execution habit of walking, it's not likely that it will help you walk more frequently, because you have to still decide whether to take a walk or not. The habit is the walk itself, which only happens after making a conscious (non-automatic) decision to do something that involves walking. Take Levi, for example. He likes to take his puppy for a walk around the park. He doesn't walk every day; he just likes to go when he feels like it or remembers to. When Levi does go on his walk, he always takes the same route – down the path and across the road to the park – and then he walks the track around the park. Levi never considers taking a different route or going to a different park. Going for a walk is not Levi's habit (he does not habitually decide to go for a walk; there is no habit instigation); his habit is walking around the park when he is walking for another purpose (he habitually walks the same route; this is habit execution).

---

You just need to get into the
habit of starting. Become the person
who shows up every day.

---

You actually don't need to fully automate your behaviour to promote maintenance, because forming an instigation habit (i.e. habitually deciding to do something) could be sufficient to maintain that behaviour. Don't focus on trying to create a perfect plan before you've done the thing that's fundamental to that plan, which is just showing up. You just need to get into the habit of starting. Become the person who shows up every day. What happens after that is not the focus. Focus on just showing up; just start.

The activities at the end of this chapter will help you create micro habits successfully. So grab your notebook or journal and complete those now to start achieving your micro habits today.

## SUMMARY

» Our brains have the capacity to make up to three changes at once.
» Creating small, consistent changes adds up to lifestyle changes more effectively than trying to create big changes.
» The easier the behaviour you want to change, the more consistent you will be in performing it, and therefore the better and more sustained the outcomes will be.
» A micro habit is a bite-sized form of your desired habit and an action that requires little effort.
» The intensity, duration and frequency of a micro habit will depend on each individual's circumstances and capacity for change.
» The strongest predictor of motivation and success is self-efficacy.

» We lose motivation when our goals are too big or too small. The edge of comfort is the sweet spot. It's the space between fear and boredom, where we're not too uncomfortable but we're still being challenged.

» A habitually instigated behaviour is one you are cued to do automatically (deciding to do it is habitual). Habit execution describes habits that facilitate progression through a sequence of actions (doing it is the habit). Focusing on habit instigation – just starting the habit – results in greater consistency and frequency of the desired behaviour.

---

**ACTIVITY 1**

## Micro habits in practice

Review the desired habits you wrote down in the activity in Chapter 5 and break those habits down into micro habits. Think of the minimum sustainable action of that habit. Make your micro habits so small that you can't say no to doing them. For example, if the habit you want to establish is writing a page every day, your micro habit could be writing a paragraph every day. This means that you develop a habit of writing that you can improve upon over time by gradually increasing to a whole page.

Write your micro habits in your journal so you can't forget them and so it will be easier for you to track your progress.

As your chosen micro habits start to become more natural and automatic, you can either add other micro habits to your routine, or instead increase the intensity, duration or frequency of the initial micro habits.

## ACTIVITY 2

# Keep it real

I like to call the prompts for reflection below the 'Keep it real' questions. Answering these will help you determine if you want to implement the micro habits you chose in the previous activity.

**1. Are you willing to commit to implementing this micro habit every day for the next month? How about three months, or six, or 12?**

If you're not willing to commit to implementing this micro habit every day, then it's likely not achievable or it's likely that achieving the goal isn't important enough to you. Your answer to this question needs to be a clear yes. If not, you need to rethink your micro habit.

**2. If you do perform this micro habit every day, what change will result?**

For example, if you meditate for 10 minutes a day, you will be more mindful and calm, you may even improve your sleep.

Small actions add up to big results. Really take the time to reflect on the results your micro habits will have, because they serve as a powerful motivator and remind you why you're doing this in the first place.

**3. Does the pain of not doing it outweigh the pain of doing it?**

Every change requires some sort of sacrifice. Change isn't easy, so you need to really want to make the change. Is it worth it? Why?

**4. How will you hold yourself accountable?**

Accountability fosters an environment where your habit can be sustained. You can be accountable to a friend, spouse, coach or your habit tracker.

After reflecting on the 'Keep it real' questions, make any necessary adjustments to your desired habits. Make sure you note them down in your notebook or journal.

# Chapter 9

# Where is our self-control?

Do you grab the fresh donuts in the breakroom or reach for the piece of fruit? For most people it can be a challenging call. We face countless decisions like this each day and it takes self-control to say no. At times, it can almost feel like a physical struggle to keep yourself from indulging in an afternoon sweet treat or splurging on another barista coffee. I've thought to myself countless times, 'I wish I had more self-control' – but that was before I learned more about self-control and willpower – and their limitations.

Self-control is defined as the capacity of an individual to alter, modify, change or override their impulses, desires and habitual responses. It's used interchangeably with willpower because it's the same executive function – the ability to delay gratification and resist short-term temptation in order to achieve long-term goals, and the capacity to exert control over thoughts, feelings, impulses or well-conditioned or habitual responses. Self-control is a crucial skill to have, and despite what you might think about your own self-control, we all have it.

Often people think of their willpower when they want to change a behaviour that requires significant mental or physical effort, such as giving up smoking, resisting dessert even though they have a sweet tooth, exercising regularly, saving money when they're used to spending it, and so on.

In this chapter, we'll take a look at how self-control works, why we feel like we don't have enough of it, how to improve our level of self-control and, most importantly, how not to be dependent upon our self-control so that we can achieve our goals long-term.

## SELF-CONTROL

When we're exerting self-control, we can, for example, say no to the extra pizza slice we don't need; we can regularly meditate, floss our teeth, have positive self-talk, study or go to work on a sunny day when we'd rather be at the beach; we can get up early to exercise and go to bed on time, even when it's not natural for us to do those things. The ability to attain deliberate control over our impulses and abstain from gratifying our immediate wants and desires is an essential life skill that enables us to engage in goal-directed behaviour and eventually achieve our desired outcomes.

But despite the human capacity to regulate the self, many behavioural and social problems can stem from persistent slips in self-control. While genetic, socioeconomic and systemic issues play a huge part, problems such as excess weight, drug misuse, violent crime, poorly managed finances (including personal debt and gambling), sexually transmitted diseases, and some chronic diseases (such as some cases of cancer and heart disease) have their roots, directly or indirectly, in self-regulation lapses. This can be explained, at least in part, by the fact that self-control is an exhaustible resource we can't depend on in the long term.

Think of self-control as like a muscle. Just as a muscle requires energy in order to apply force, behaviours that demand self-control require energy; in both cases we can't be too hungry or tired.

In the same way that muscles become fatigued with sustained exertion, which results in a reduction in their ability to exert further force, self-control draws from a limited 'reservoir' that depletes with demand, resulting in a reduced capacity for further self-regulation.

Imagine picking up a dumbbell to do bicep curls. After a few curls, your arm is going to get fatigued and you'll need to put the dumbbell down and rest your arm before doing another set of curls. Self-control works in the same way: the more you use it, the more exhausted it gets. After a long, hard, emotional day, the last thing you'll want to come home to is a chicken salad. You'll crave chocolate cake, cheese and that extra glass of wine.

Or say you're on a weight-loss program that involves a strict diet and exercise regimen, both of which require a lot of self-control. You start off with heaps of energy, but as your self-control muscles get weaker with sustained use, you get exhausted and fall off the wagon. You might pick yourself up and try again, and again, and again, but your self-control muscles don't have the energy required to continue on this strict diet because you're physically, emotionally and/or mentally depleted. Eventually, you get exhausted and feel as though you just can't continue any more and you give up on the program altogether – this is the yo-yo dieting trap.

Self-control is also a universal resource – it doesn't discriminate between work demands, life demands and emotional demands. Whether you have a tough day, the kids are screaming, you're stuck in traffic, you have an altercation with someone, or you're tired or hungry, you're using up your limited reservoir of self-control. Simply, the more demand you put on your self-control, the less you have of it for other tasks.

You could think of self-control as like a bank account. Each day you start with a certain amount in your account. As you go about your day, life's demands debit funds from your account. The more you debit, the less funds you have to spend on other things. On a day where you debit a lot of your funds, your account will reach zero earlier than on a day where you haven't debited a lot of funds. On the days where you still have surplus funds, you have enough self-control left to splurge on more demanding tasks. But on the days where life has debited much of your self-control funds, you're less likely to have the capacity to do other challenging things, such as regulating your emotions, sticking to your diet, doing a hard workout, and so on.

We're living in a time when we seem to be working longer hours and sleeping less than ever before. We consume more news and media, and we're expected to be available via email at any time of the day. So it's no wonder we feel exhausted and depleted.

## EGO DEPLETION

The state of diminishing self-control was first conceptualised as ego depletion by Sigmund Freud in 1923. Here, 'ego' is used in the psychological sense as the part of the self that mediates between the world and your desires and impulses; it's the part of you that engages executive functions such as self-control and decision-making. And 'depletion' has its usual meaning of a reduction in the quantity of something. Ego depletion, therefore, describes the phenomenon of the exhaustion of our self-control.

Freud was fond of the analogy of the horse and rider, where the horse represents life and the rider represents self-control. He said that the rider is generally in charge of steering but is sometimes unable to prevent the horse from going where it wants to go.[1] Ego depletion was later tested in the 1990s by social psychologists. In 2010 researchers conducted a meta-analysis of 83 studies and found that ego depletion had a significant effect on self-control and task performance.[2]

One team of researchers ran a fascinating series of studies where they kept 67 participants in a room that smelled of freshly baked chocolate-chip cookies.[3] On a table, two bowls of food were displayed: one containing the freshly baked cookies and the other red-and-white radishes. The participants thought they were in a food-tasting study. Half the group were asked to eat two to three cookies and the other half were asked to eat two to three radishes; they weren't allowed to eat anything other than the food assigned to them. The researchers stepped out of the room, which naturally increased temptation among the radish eaters to reach for a sneaky cookie. Some of them looked longingly at the cookie display, and in a few cases even picked up the cookies to sniff them. But they were strong and resisted temptation. Meanwhile, the cookie-eating group, were loving these delicious cookies and didn't have the same kind of temptation to indulge in the radishes.

The research team then gave the participants a second, supposedly unrelated exercise, which appeared to be a logic puzzle, where they had to trace out a complicated geometric shape without lifting their pencil from the paper. Unbeknown to them, this puzzle was unsolvable – it was literally impossible to do. The researchers simply wanted to see how long each group would persist in a difficult task. The effects of ego depletion were immediate and undeniable. The cookie eaters persisted to solve the impossible puzzle for 19 minutes – double the time of the radish eaters, who only attempted the puzzle for an average of eight minutes. The radish eaters used up so much self-control in resisting the cookies and forcing themselves to eat raw radishes that they could no longer find the will to fully engage in another taxing task; they were already too exhausted.

In the world of psychology, the key finding of this study was a breakthrough: self-control is a general strength that's used across different tasks, and it gets depleted. This proved that self-regulation is not a skill to be mastered or a rote function that can be performed with little consequence. It really is like using a muscle – after we've exercised it, it loses its strength, gets fatigued and becomes ineffectual, at least in the short term. This research would go on to serve as the foundation for at least 1280 other studies involving everything from consumer to criminal behaviour. It would, for instance, help show that people are energised by positive messages, and explain why we're more likely to engage in retail therapy after a relationship breakup or to eat too much after a long day.

Another study had two groups of people in different rooms. The first room had rows of tables filled with sugary snacks, the second had a few sugary snacks but nowhere near as many as the first room. The participants in both rooms were asked to refrain from eating the snacks for a short period of time before the researchers put them out of their misery and allowed them to eat as much as they wanted from their respective tables. While the participants in both groups spent time resisting the desirable snacks, the group in the first room with lots of sugary snacks ended up caving and eating significantly more than the group in the second room, who weren't exposed to as much temptation and therefore hadn't needed to use as much of their self-control.[4]

When I think back on my teenage dieting days, I find myself deeply relating to this phenomenon. The more I restricted what I was 'allowed' to eat, the more I binged on the very same foods I was trying to avoid. This went on into my early to mid-twenties and it made me feel like a sham dietitian. Here I was giving people advice on how to eat a balanced diet and limit discretionary foods, when I was bingeing on chips and chocolate on my drive home from the clinic. I desperately wanted to have more control over my eating, but the harder I tried, the further I would fall. And I wasn't just tumbling over a little hurdle every now and then – no, it felt like I was falling headfirst into a bottomless one-way black hole. I was frustrated with myself; I lost my self-confidence and, in many ways, my self-love. Instead of seeing that restriction was causing this cycle of self-sabotage, I blamed myself for not having enough self-control. I would fall off the wagon and wait till the next Monday came around to start the next fad diet, which was really just restricting a different set of foods. Dieting, at its core, is restrictive eating, so no wonder 95 per cent of people who lose weight on diets end up putting all the weight back on.

## The forbidden fruit effect

In psychology, the forbidden fruit effect refers to the experience we have when we make something off limits and it becomes more desirable. This term is often used in the context of consumer behaviour, where we are more likely to want something if it's restricted or taboo, creating a sense of excitement and thrill around the forbidden item.

Several psychological factors influence the forbidden fruit effect, including scarcity, curiosity, rebellion, attraction to taboo and, of course, ego depletion. In many cases, the forbidden fruit effect can be seen as a manifestation of ego depletion, where we use up our self-control in one area and end up giving in to temptation and indulging in whatever it was we were trying to restrict. We don't tend to overindulge on broccoli and kale when we're ego depleted; we tend to reach for chocolate, chips, cheese, wine and other tempting treats. The idea isn't to say yes to all temptation so that we don't deplete our self-control, but rather to manage our levels of self-control so that we're using it for the things that really matter and that align with our values and goals.

## DEPLETING OUR SELF-CONTROL

Our self-control can become depleted in many other ways than resisting cookies. These include exerting initiative, prolonged focused attention, stress, fatigue, burnout, sleeplessness, calorie restriction, low blood sugar levels, experiencing negative emotions such as anxiety or depression, and making an excessive number of decisions.

All of these factors present a pattern, which is that they all require a degree of effort to overcome.

It's no wonder that overnight shift workers report twice as many attention failures and 36 per cent more errors.[5] A study by SleepFoundation.org found that tired employees take more time to react in critical situations. In professional settings, impaired reaction times may mean missing an important phone call or not responding quickly in a conversation. For other professionals, such as doctors, first responders and truck drivers, slow reaction times can be the difference between life and death. Lack of sleep can also leave people feeling more irritable, angry and vulnerable to stress. In stressful or negative situations, the emotional reactions of tired people become amplified, leading to overeating and further irritability. These over-reactions are a manifestation of their wearied self-control.

Working in the field of behaviour change, I commonly hear it said that the reason people don't change is that they're lazy. But I think what appears to be laziness is often exhaustion. When we're making a change in our life, we're obliged to do something different, something new, something unfamiliar. If we do what we've always done, we'll keep getting the same outcomes, so change requires us to replace our familiar, comfortable behaviour with something different, and doing that requires self-control. We're no longer acting from our efficient and subconscious neural pathways but instead forging a new neural connection in our brain. We're teaching our body to move in a different way in response to our old habit triggers. We're using our reflective brain rather than our impulsive brain, and that requires effort.

Take your morning routine as an example. You have a system for getting out of bed, showering, brushing your teeth, getting dressed, and you've been doing it for so long that it's become effortless and subconscious. Now imagine having to completely reinvent that morning routine from start to finish. You'd be able to get through it, but it would require a great deal of self-control. You would have to actively think of every action in your previously automatic routine, and that's exhausting. What looks like laziness is so often exhaustion. Change simply wears us out. Ego depletion has been associated with less engagement in physical activity and following a healthy diet, and poorer success with reducing alcohol intake and quitting smoking.[6]

---

## You are not a lazy failure, you are ego depleted.

---

In one study, 128 college students were randomly assigned to either an ego-depletion group or a control group. The control group were given one page of text from a biology textbook and asked to cross out every *e* on the page. The depletion group were given two pages from the biology textbook. The first page contained the same instructions that the control group received. The second page, however, contained much more complex instructions: 'Cross out every instance of the letter *e* except for when the *e* is adjacent to another vowel or is one letter removed from another vowel.' Just the thought of that task has my brain in a scramble! The control group finished their task in about five minutes, while the depletion group took about 15 minutes. The researchers then showed both groups of students a range of healthy and unhealthy foods. The students in the depletion group responded faster to the unhealthy food than to the healthy food. But the students in the control group, who weren't ego depleted, showed no difference in their responses to either food option. This study showed that even if we're motivated to eat healthy food, when our self-control resources are depleted, our mind and body become more geared towards reaching for unhealthier foods because we don't have as much willpower to pick the healthy option.[7] You are not a lazy failure, you are ego depleted.

We experience demands on our self-control resources every single day. These range from simple, tedious demands to more taxing demands – anything from persisting with extended boring tasks such as filing or data entry to dealing with difficult customers; coping with setbacks, which is exacerbated when we're under time pressure such as a deadline; and resisting temptations to overeat, mindlessly scroll on our phones, smoke cigarettes or drink too much alcohol. Any situation that requires us to persist against the path of least resistance will deplete our self-control.

Sometimes, making decisions requires careful consideration and evaluation of all our given options – for instance, looking at the options when taking out a loan. Other times, making a judgement call requires us to refrain from purchasing something that we really want (but admittedly don't need), such as a new surround sound system. Both situations require mental effort, which can be exhausting. After spending time considering your options or refraining from spending, you may end up spontaneously breaking your budget and splurging big. We only have so much self-control before it inevitably runs out.

Chronic ego depletion refers to a long-term state of ego depletion, often observed in people who spend long periods of time exerting effort. For example, long-term dieters, or people with chronic pain conditions or severe test anxiety. One experimental study measured participants' inherent states of ego depletion by having them complete a questionnaire.[8] The researchers then asked the participants to select a goal to adhere to for three weeks, ranging from weight loss to spending less time online. They found that those with higher chronic ego depletion needed to exert a greater level of effort to achieve their goals than those who had lower chronic ego depletion. The researchers concluded that chronic ego depletion increases the likelihood that we will fail in regulating our behaviour, suggesting that it's difficult for people in an ego-depleted state to adhere to goals.

Instead of trying to make positive changes in our life through an impossibly difficult state of ego depletion, we should be shifting our efforts towards replenishing our self-control first, so that we have the energy, motivation and focus we need to achieve our desired outcomes. Otherwise, we're essentially an exercise in futility.

## REPLENISHING OUR SELF-CONTROL

Successfully regulating the self contributes to many positive outcomes, such as success at school, at university and in the workplace; healthy personal relationships; greater physical and mental health; a greater capacity to cope with life's problems; and reduced susceptibility to social harms such as drug misuse and criminality.

Although our self-control is an exhaustible resource, the good news is that we can do a range of things to replenish its stores. While depleted self-control is useless to us, replenished self-control can be our superpower. This is an essential yet commonly overlooked strategy for change.

We know that self-control is depleted through effort, so the opposite of effort will replenish our self-control. This includes things like rest, sleep, meditation, taking periodic breaks throughout the day, feeling positive emotions such as happiness and joy, viewing scenes of nature, and increasing our blood sugar levels.[9] Any action we take that reduces stress will heal our mental fatigue, and increase our capacity to exert further self-control.

---

While depleted self-control is useless
to us, replenished self-control
can be our superpower.

---

Practically speaking, this is what each of the factors that replenish self-control can look like:

- **rest:** Slow down, read a book, take a moment to breathe deeply, sit in nature.
- **sleep:** Create a sleep routine to ensure you're getting seven to nine hours of sleep a night.
- **meditate:** Try a meditation app such as Headspace or Calm to help you make time for calming your mind every day.
- **pause:** Take a 10-minute break each hour. This gives your brain a rest and helps to restore mental fatigue. Don't get caught up scrolling on your phone; give your brain a genuine rest – take a walk outside or listen to your favourite music.
- **feel positive emotions:** Spend time with loved ones, watch a funny video, cuddle your pet, whatever it takes to reinvigorate your mind.
- **view scenes of nature:** Research has shown that viewing images or scenes of nature can help reduce stress, improve mood, and increase attention and focus, which in turn can help increase self-control.[10] Additionally, spending time in natural environments has been shown to have a positive impact on self-control, likely due to the combination of physical exercise and exposure to the calming effects of nature. Get outside, sit in a park or on the beach, or walk around the neighbourhood if you live or work in a place where there are trees or picturesque bodies of water.
- **increase blood sugar levels:** The human brain accounts for approximately 20 per cent of the body's total energy consumption, and its main source of fuel is glucose. Glucose comes from carbohydrates, so our brain needs carbs to function and to replenish our self-control levels. If you're feeling mentally fatigued, snack on some fruit, which contains

natural sugars; whole grains such as brown rice, wholegrain bread and oats; or starchy vegetables such as potatoes, parsnips, beetroot and corn.

- **change perspective:** When facing potential stressors, the way we view what we're experiencing – our perspective – can exacerbate or minimise our stress. Do you focus on the bad day, or do you see it as a mildly low point in an overall great life or even a learning experience? You can relieve a significant amount of stress and create a more positive life without making any changes to your circumstances. Research shows that people who have a more positive and optimistic outlook on stress tend to experience lower levels of stress and are better able to maintain self-control in the face of stressful situations.[11] On the other hand, people who view stress as a threat or experience negative emotions in response to it struggle more with self-control. If you change your perspective, you change your experience. Adopting a growth mindset, where you see stress as an opportunity for growth and development, can help improve your self-control in the face of stress. Distancing yourself from negative outcomes is also a very helpful strategy. Ask yourself if this stressor will impact your life in five or 10 years from now. Most of the time, the answer is no and we can feel a sense of relief in knowing that whatever is causing us stress is temporary and will eventually pass.

During your workday, all of these except maybe sleep, are achievable. You could easily rest, meditate or press pause on your day for 10 minutes. I recommend setting an alarm so you're not distracted for too long, but if you need more rest time then take it, because you will be much more productive working from a place of rest than a place of stress and depletion.

I'm often asked, 'If self-control is like a muscle, can you strengthen it?' The answer is yes, kind of. We can train ourselves to need less self-regulation for the same task by regularly doing that task. When we regularly train at a task that requires self-control, we reduce the ego depletion effect, just as training a muscle increases its endurance and strength. We can also strengthen our self-control with stress management, and with our attitudes and beliefs, which have been shown to play a role in shaping willpower.[12]

## THE BODY CONTROLS THE MIND

In Chapter 10, we will take a look at how stress impacts our ability to create new habits and break old ones. Spoiler alert: the more negative stress we're feeling, the less self-control we have. Stress creates ego depletion, and ego depletion makes change very challenging. So being able to manage negative stress and reframe it in our mind is a critical practice in the pursuit of changing our habits and improving our lives. Our mindset matters because it shapes our physiology – how our body functions. How stress impacts you will depend on the narrative you place around it.

Most of us think that stress is bad and we try to avoid it at any cost, but what if it could work for your benefit? What if you could take all that energy racing around your brain and your body and transform it into something helpful?

Stress management is a very individual thing – what works for one person may not be as effective for the next. But what we all have in common is that we hold stress and tension in our body and that our body controls the mind. You might not be aware that you're feeling stressed until you notice your hands are clenched or your stomach feels uneasy, or your neck and shoulders are tight. I tend to hold stress in my jaw; I find myself clenching my teeth when I'm stressed and often I'm not even aware that I'm carrying that tension until I feel my jaw muscles tense up.

## Checking in with your body

Becoming aware of how stressed you are is the first step towards releasing it. To do this effectively, check in with your body and your breath. How is your body feeling? Are you carrying tension? Are your muscles clenched or relaxed? Is your heart racing? Are you taking in shallow breaths? Research shows that by focusing on our body and bringing our thoughts back to the present moment, we can significantly reduce stress, anxiety, self-referential thoughts and thinking negatively about ourselves.[13]

Try doing a mindful (i.e. conscious) check-in with your body now. You can literally work stress out of your body and feel a sense of relief by shifting your focus from the stressful thoughts (which are active in the part of your brain called the amygdala), towards the more experiential (in the part of your brain called the somatosensory cortex, where information from our senses is processed).

I practised this many times during exposure therapy. My psychologist would get me to think of a trauma trigger – the smell of coffee, for example. I would be on the edge of a panic attack, but she guided me to let go of the thought and focus on the sensations in my body. I felt a tightness in my stomach, my heart was racing, my eyes were wide open, and my palms were sweaty. As I continued to focus on the sensations going on in my body, I noticed that those physical symptoms faded away. The first time I did it, it took about 15 minutes to de-escalate from my anxious state; the second time it took 10 minutes, then five minutes, until eventually I could work the stress out of my body and feel relief in a matter of seconds. I use this strategy time and time again and it never fails me.

Mindful check-ins aren't only for managing trauma triggers and phobias. Research looking at people with strong food cravings showed that if they did a mindful check-in, they significantly reduced those cravings – which, as we all know, is very difficult to achieve. I'm a strong believer that everyone would benefit from checking in with their body and bringing themselves back into the present moment.

## Deep breathing

Deep breathing is one of the most immediate ways to calm our stress and anxiety, because deep breaths directly activate the natural de-stressing part of our nervous system, our parasympathetic nervous system. Slow breathing tells our body that we no longer need the resources to run or fight. There are numerous breathwork techniques, but you don't need to complicate things – simply let your breath flow as deep down towards your belly as is comfortable without forcing it. For five minutes try breathing in gently through your nose and gently out through your mouth. Some people find it helpful to count as they breathe.

Neuroscientists recommend the box breathing technique, which is slowly inhaling for four seconds, holding at the top of the chest for four seconds, exhaling deeply for four seconds, then holding at the bottom of the chest for four seconds. Simply put, that's breathing in and holding, then breathing out and holding. You can do this technique almost anywhere, which is why it's a great habit to incorporate into your daily routine. You can do it standing, sitting or lying down. Using breathwork to reduce negative stress is a common practice among monks and modern meditators alike.

## Movement

Movement is also a powerful way to inject an immediate and positive lift to your mood state. Movement benefits us in two primary ways. Firstly, it helps us shift our focus from our mind to what we're feeling in our body. This again works by shifting our focus from the amygdala to the somatosensory cortex – in other words, from processing fear and threat to experiencing physical sensations such as touch, body position, pressure and temperature. Secondly, every time we move our body, we're releasing a whole cocktail of beneficial neurochemicals in our brain. These mood- and reward-boosting neurochemicals include dopamine, serotonin, noradrenaline (aka norepinephrine) and endorphins, all of which work to both increase positive mood states and decrease negative ones. Movement is like giving your brain a hug. Studies show that it only takes 10 minutes of walking to get those mood-boosting effects.[14] If you're in an office, you could take a short walk around the block, or walk up the stairs. If you're at home, you could play your two favourite songs and dance around in your living room. Get creative with how you want to move. I've had clients hula-hoop for 10 minutes, while others have taken the opportunity to walk the dog or vacuum the house. Whichever way you choose to move your body, just 10 minutes will help to reduce stress and make your anxiety feel less all-consuming.

Some people also find that a change of scene is a helpful strategy for reducing stress. We know that our environment drives our behaviour, but it can also drive our thoughts. A change of scene can therefore have a big effect on helping us change our thoughts. Find a place of comfort, whether that be in nature, with your pet, looking through pictures that bring you joy, or listening to music that soothes your soul. Having an accessible safe zone you can turn to for just a few minutes can do wonders for reducing stress and shifting your headspace.

## SELF-CONTROL AND HABITS

Because our levels of motivation and self-control change from day to day and moment to moment, our goal should be to rely less on our self-control. To do that, we need to lean on our habits, because habits don't need self-control once they're formed. Habits operate from our impulsive brain, which uses very little mental energy. That's why we tend to fall back on our habits when we're ego depleted or our motivational energy is directed elsewhere.

We need to use self-control when we're starting to form a new habit, but once that habit becomes automatic, that habitual behaviour will happen even when we're tired. Relying on our habits rather than on our self-control is how we achieve long-term outcomes and reach our goals.

## SUMMARY

» Self-control works like a muscle: the more you use it, the more exhausted it gets.

» Self-control is a universal resource.

» Depletion of self-control is called ego depletion.

» Things that deplete self-control include exerting initiative, prolonged focused attention, stress, fatigue, burnout, sleeplessness, calorie restriction, low blood sugar levels, experiencing negative emotions such as anxiety or depression, and making an excessive number of decisions.

» Things that replenish self-control include rest, sleep, meditation, taking a pause, feeling positive emotions, viewing scenes of nature, increasing blood sugar levels and changing perspective.

» Habits do not require self-control to be performed.

» Relying on our habits rather than on our self-control is how we achieve long-term outcomes and reach our goals.

**ACTIVITY**

# Refuelling your self-control

Taking the table below as your template, use your notebook or journal to write down ways you can implement or improve on each of the listed replenishing strategies.

| Self-control replenishment strategy | My commitment |
| --- | --- |
| To improve my rest, I will ... | |
| To improve my sleep, I will ... | |
| I will make space to meditate at these times ... | |
| I will take periodic breaks at these times ... | |
| To feel positive emotions, I will ... | |
| To view scenes of nature, I will ... | |
| To increase my blood sugar levels, I will eat ... | |

## Chapter 10

# How long it really takes to change a habit

ONE OF THE MOST COMMON things people ask me is how long it takes to change a habit. One of my favourite responses is to debunk the myths about this timeline. The idea that it takes 21 days to create or break a habit is sprinkled like confetti all over the internet, and in many motivational talks, inspirational quotes and self-help advice. But despite its popularity, there has never been any scientific evidence to back the claim that it takes 21 days to change a habit – it's quite simply a long-lived myth. Its origins are not entirely clear, but the idea was first popularised in the 1960s by a plastic surgeon named Dr Maxwell Maltz, who claimed that it took his patients about 21 days to adjust to changes in their appearance following facial surgery. In his book *Psycho-Cybernetics*, Maltz also wrote that among other changes, it takes us about 21 days to get used to a new home.[1]

People assumed that if it takes 21 days for the mind to change its perception of these things, then it must take 21 days for neuroplasticity to occur and, therefore, 21 days to change habits. No research was ever conducted to back up this claim, however, and the idea has since been debunked by numerous studies.

## HOW LONG DOES IT REALLY TAKE TO FORM A HABIT?

While most of us find making a change relatively easy, maintaining that change is evidently a lot tougher. Some people might be lucky enough to make a change and stick to it, but most of us will have to keep trying. The good news is, the science suggests we'll get there in the end.

Our current estimate of how long it takes to change a habit is 66 days. The study that's often referred to as the basis for this figure was conducted by researchers at University College London.[2] The researchers recruited 96 participants and asked them to choose a behaviour they could do every day that they wanted to turn into a habit. It had to be something they didn't already do, so participants chose things like eating a piece of fruit or drinking a glass of water with lunch or doing 50 sit-ups in the morning. They were asked to perform their chosen behaviour every day for 84 days and track their progress with a habit tracker.

The time it took for the participants to turn their behaviours into automatic habits varied depending on the individual and their chosen behaviour. Some participants formed a habit in as little as 18 days, while for others it took more like 254 days (more than eight months). The average time it took participants to reach automaticity of their chosen habit was 66 days. So we can conclude that it takes on average 66 days to form a new habit.

If I keep 66 days, or roughly 10 weeks in mind, then I'm more likely to stick with practising the habit and tracking my progress for at least that long. After 10 weeks, I would hope that the habit has reached automaticity and become embedded in my life. If not, then I know it's at least well on its way.

# FACTORS THAT AFFECT HABIT-FORMATION TIME

The length of time it takes to change a habit can vary widely depending on numerous factors, including how habitual you are as a person, how consistent you are in performing the habit, the complexity of the habit, your level of motivation, your environment, the value of the reward, and how stressed you are. Having an understanding of these factors can help you change your habits quicker and with a higher strike rate. So let's get into the crucial things to know.

## How habitual you are as a person

Some of us are naturally more habitual than others. Some of us prefer structure and routine, while others prefer spontaneity and flexibility.

Ironically, even though I'm a habit researcher, I'm not naturally a very habitual person. When a friend asked me recently what I usually do on a Sunday, I struggled to give her an answer because I don't have a usual Sunday routine – every Sunday looks different. Sometimes I go to the farmers' market, other times I go to the beach, or go on a hike, or catch up with friends. Sometimes I spend the morning with family and the afternoon baking. I don't have a 'usual' schedule. I actually feel suffocated when I'm bound to a rigorous routine. I value spontaneity, flexibility and never having two days the same. It's probably why I've never had a full-time job – I've worked full-time hours, but never in the same place. I couldn't tell you what I'm having for breakfast tomorrow; I could only tell you that it won't be the same as what I had today (home-made muesli, if you're wondering). Or maybe it will be – I will only know right before I prepare it. I will routinely go to the gym, but it won't be on the same days each week, and I like doing different exercises when I'm there. I prefer to go to different holiday destinations and try different restaurants – even if I'm not going to enjoy them as much as the ones I've already been to.

I thrive on doing things differently and being in unique settings. I like having a plan, but the plan will be different each day. Writing this book, some days have looked like waking up and writing for a few hours first thing in the morning, while on other days I've started in the afternoon, and other days it's been split up throughout the day between other tasks. Some days I write for one hour and other days I'll spend the whole day at my desk typing away. I even mow the lawn and vacuum out of sequence – much to my husband Mitch's horror.

Mitch thrives on structure and routine. When he mows the lawn, he creates perfect straight lines in the grass, unlike my crop-circle impersonations. Since the day Mitch and I met, he's been eating the same meals for lunch and dinner. He has an ice bath first thing in the morning and likes to have a sauna in the afternoons before walking our dog, Macy. These events all take place at the same time of day, every day. He is predictable, systematised and habitual. If I make a salad without adding carrot, Mitch thinks we must be out of carrots, because when he makes salad, carrot is always an ingredient.

Personalities that are more habitual by nature will potentially form habits quicker than more flexible personalities. This is not to say that it's harder for a more flexible person to form a habit, but they may just require more repetitions of the habit until they achieve a true level of automaticity. This is only anecdotal evidence of course, but in our house, Mitch forms habits quicker than I do and I break habits quicker than he does. The important point is that we can both very successfully form new habits and break old ones. I hope that one day soon we will have empirical research on measured personality types and their disposition to acquire habits telling us what kind of temperaments are likely to acquire habits or successfully break habits the fastest. This would be a breakthrough in behavioural science because we could tailor habit-change plans to each individual's personality type. Ahh, that's the dream!

There is some evidence that people with natural self-control are more likely to develop and maintain healthy habits compared with those naturally low in self-control. People who have a high conscientiousness score – characterised by a tendency to be organised, responsible, productive and dependable – are more likely to form and maintain habits over time. But self-control and conscientiousness are personality traits that we can develop; they are not immutable personality types or temperaments.

Until we have more research, you can simply reflect on whether you would call yourself a habitual person or not. Do you like order, predictability and structure? Do you have a usual Sunday routine? Do you tend to eat the same breakfast each day? Do you walk the same circuit? Do you have good impulse control? Do you like to avoid making mistakes or are you willing to take risks? How comfortable are you with ambiguity? Do you readily welcome change?

## Consistency

I like to say that the secret sauce to changing our habits is consistency. Reaching automaticity can be thought of like filling a jar with water – when the water level reaches the top of the jar, we have achieved automaticity. Every time you repeat a behaviour in a consistent context, you are putting a drop of water in your jar. The more you repeat the behaviour, the more drops of water you put in your jar, until it eventually fills to the top and your habit reaches automaticity.

The way habits develop is not a linear process. Although automaticity increases steadily each day we repeat a behaviour, early repetitions seem to result in a higher spike in automaticity than those later in the habit-formation process. The 444th repetition of a behaviour does not have the same reinforcement impact on a habit as the fourth repetition.[3] So it's critical to focus especially on consistency in the early phases of creating a new habit, because that's when a lot of the magic happens. If behaviours are not performed consistently enough, they will simply stay as behaviours and never achieve the status of being a habit. For our brain to really solidify a habit as our new normal, we need to perform that habit consistently each time we encounter its trigger. Once we reach the peak of automaticity for a habit, we hit a plateau at which the behaviour can't become more automatic, even with further repetitions. So keep on keeping on, until the behaviour feels automatic and habitual.

Amateurs practise until they get it right; professionals practise until they can't get it wrong.

## Missed opportunities

This leads me to what happens if you miss a day. Say you're consistently performing your new habit and life throws you a curve ball (as it does) and you miss a day of performing your habit. When researchers tested participants' habit strength after they missed a day of performing their new habit, they found that for habits that were still being developed, the habit-strength score (see page 32) was reduced a minimal amount after one missed day, but it jumped back up again once they got back into that habit.[4] The following day, the habit-strength score was not significantly different from before the missed day, and one missed day had no long-term impacts on automaticity. In other words, all is not lost. Although repetition of a behaviour is essential to creating a habit, a few missed opportunities won't derail the process.

Having said that, missing a whole week or longer of performing a habit has noteworthy consequences, reducing the likelihood of performing the habit in the future and hindering habit acquisition. It's inevitable when you're forming a new habit that you will have off days or days where you'll forget to do it. It's perfectly fine to miss a day or two, but just make sure you get back on the horse as quickly as you can and focus on consistency.

## The complexity of the behaviour

The complexity of a particular behaviour impacts the development and strength of automaticity. Automaticity is reached quicker for easier, simple actions (e.g. drinking a glass of water), than for difficult, more complex actions (e.g. doing 50 sit-ups). We can assume that there's usually water around, so it's accessible and within reach, and drinking it is also quick and fairly easy, but doing sit-ups might be impacted by our location, or what we're wearing. I can't imagine doing 50 sit-ups on an aeroplane, for example, or at a restaurant. Our brain doesn't have to think as much about drinking a glass of water as it does about doing 50 sit-ups.

We're much more likely to be consistent with a simpler behaviour than a more complex one. A study that put this theory to the test found that participants were compliant with drinking a glass of water 93 per cent of the time compared with only 80 per cent for eating a piece of fruit or 86 per cent for doing some form of physical activity such as exercising for 15 minutes or doing 50 sit-ups.[5] Participants in the exercise group took one and a half times longer to reach automaticity than the water drinkers and fruit eaters. This further supports the idea of creating micro habits rather than aiming for big, complex goals. It's consistency, not intensity that will help you achieve your goals.

---

### We're much more likely to be consistent with a simpler behaviour.

---

## The value of the reward

I remember setting a New Year's resolution once to start a gratitude journal. I'd read an article that suggested gratitude was linked to improvements in general wellbeing, so I thought I'd give it a go.

I found that I really struggled to find the motivation to sit down and write out three things I was grateful for each day. I would procrastinate by doing other, meaningless things or put it off to the next day. It's not because I wasn't grateful. I was. I just didn't fully appreciate the reward or the outcome that I would achieve from this gratitude practice. A few months later I came across a research paper that detailed all the benefits that come with practising gratitude – things like reducing symptoms of depression, anxiety and stress; a greater sense of contentment and fulfilment; improved sleep; decreased blood pressure; reduced inflammation; and so on. It had me at reduced inflammation and improved sleep, because I highly value those outcomes. It was as if this research article came with its very own motivation fairy who smacked me straight in the face, because ever since I read it, my lack of motivation for practising gratitude has vanished, and creating the habit of a daily gratitude journal has been effortless.

The greater the perceived value of the reward, the quicker and stronger the habit develops. Habits get stronger when the behaviour is reinforced by a positive reward, such as feeling stronger, sleeping better, noticing your body change, or having a more positive and healthier mindset. How much you value the reward associated with a particular behaviour will determine how likely you are to repeat that behaviour. It's therefore important to really check in with yourself and reflect on how your new habits are benefiting your life.

## Reward prediction error

Rewards produce learning. Pavlov's dog hears a bell, sees food and salivates. When this effect is elicited often enough, the dog salivates merely on hearing the sound of the bell. There are mathematical formulae going all the way back to the 1970s that map out this kind of reinforcement learning.

Our brains determine and store reward value. Reward prediction error is a dopamine signal involved in learning from rewards and punishments. It occurs when there's a difference between the reward we expected and the reward we actually receive. This signal plays a key role in predicting most if not all forms of learning, including habit formation, as it helps to reinforce actions that lead to positive outcomes.[6]

When we perform a behaviour and receive a reward that's better than we expected, there is a positive prediction error, which reinforces the behaviour and makes us more likely to repeat it in the future. On the other hand, if the reward is less than we expected, there is a negative prediction error, which can make us less likely to repeat that behaviour in the future.

Say, for example, you want to eat more healthily and lose weight, so you decide to have a salad for lunch instead of your usual ham and cheese croissant. You love your ham and cheese croissant, and the bakery you go to does them really well, so naturally, you're hesitant about ordering the salad. But with your health in mind, you get the salad anyway. Turns out, the salad is surprisingly delicious and satisfying. In this case, the actual reward exceeded your expectations, resulting in a positive prediction error. This can reinforce the behaviour, making you more likely to choose salad for lunch in the future.

On the other hand, say you decide to eat the salad for lunch and you expect to feel good about your healthy choice, but instead you find that the salad just didn't hit the spot and you're still a bit hungry and dissatisfied. In this situation, the expected reward was the feeling of satisfaction from making a healthy choice, but the actual reward was less than expected, resulting in a negative prediction error. This makes you less likely to choose a salad for lunch again in the future.

A great US study demonstrated this when researchers asked participants to bring into the lab their favourite highly processed food or drink – things like twinkies, potato chips and sugary drinks. The participants described feeling out of control around their chosen items. They thought they wanted that food because it would taste and feel good, and no doubt because the food marketing told them they would be happy and successful after eating or drinking it. The researchers then asked the participants to eat their food slowly or drink their drink slowly, really paying attention to the flavours and the satisfaction they got from it.[7] Interestingly, nearly 100 per cent of the time, the participants reported that they were disappointed with their experience, which of course led to them feeling significantly less desire to eat that food again.

The same strategy has been used to help smokers quit their smoking habit.[8] As the smokers were drawing in a breath of nicotine smoke, researchers asked them to mindfully describe what smoking tasted like. Some compared it to licking a burning newspaper, others to swallowing ash, and others to inhaling burnt tyres. They also reported that smoking made them feel dizzy and made them cough. When the researchers followed up the participants to see if they were still smoking months later, they found that the majority had quit their smoking habit, attributing their cessation mainly to not liking the taste of cigarettes. It's often the anticipation of getting something that drives our behaviour; reducing its reward value will lessen our brain's drive to seek out that thing we're craving.

One of my very first jobs as a teenager was working in an ice-cream shop. I love ice cream and I would eat my own weight in ice cream at the end of every shift – I really was not an asset to the company. I regularly tasted all the flavours, but my favourite was a mocha ice cream with roasted almonds and a rich chocolate ribbon. I was obsessed with this flavour. One of my happiest memories from working there was when a customer ordered a large ice-cream cake with my favourite mocha flavour but never collected it and I got to take it home. When my mum picked me up after I'd finished my shift,

I sat in the passenger seat of her car and devoured this cake with a small plastic spoon. Two decades later, the ice-cream shop still sells the same flavoured ice cream. I visited the shop with some friends the other day and ordered a scoop, but it tasted different. The chocolate ribbon was less chocolatey and there were fewer roasted almonds mixed through the less creamy ice cream. The recipe had changed and the reward of nostalgia and deliciousness that I expected from the ice cream was less than I anticipated; I experienced a negative prediction error. As a result, I'm less likely to choose that flavour again in the future, or I'll lower my expectations of that particular flavour.

I tried my friend's ice-cream choice, a caramel praline flavour. I was not expecting it to taste so good – how can anything exceed the deliciousness of chocolate? – but it was seriously yummy and extra creamy. The reward of a creamy ice cream exceeded my expectations resulting in a positive prediction error. This may make it more likely that I will try new flavours in the future. The reward I experienced was even greater because it was unexpected. I didn't think I'd like any ice-cream flavour more than my usual favourite, but I did.

Dopamine neurons fire when we encounter unexpectedly good things. If I suddenly tap you on the shoulder and hand you a sweet, your dopamine neurons will light up for the sweet. If I keep tapping you on the shoulder and keep giving you a sweet, your dopamine neurons will stop firing for the sweet, because while sweets are great, it's no longer unexpected that one is coming. Instead, your dopamine starts firing in anticipation of the tap itself, because you can now reliably predict that a shoulder tap means a sweet is coming (a good thing). But you don't know when the tap is coming next, so the tap on the shoulder becomes the unexpectedly good thing.

If I were to tap you on the shoulder and then not give you a sweet, your dopamine neurons would drop below baseline, below the level of dopamine you had before I started tapping your shoulder.

This process of learning through prediction error is a key mechanism by which our brain adapts our behaviour to changing environments.

You may not be able to trick your brain into thinking that something will be less rewarding than it really is, so just being aware of your reward prediction error and not overestimating the likely reward that you will get from performing a particular behaviour can help reinforce good habits.

## Stress

You know when you get an urgent email from your boss, and you start to get sweaty palms and an empty sensation in your stomach? If your brain cells could talk, they would say, 'Welcome back, stress and anxiety.' Stress has a huge influence on our capacity to make or break habits. As a broad generalisation, the more stressed we are, the harder we find it to create new habits and to break old ones. We also tend to fall back on our old habits when we're feeling stressed.

Stress is a natural physiological and psychological response that helps us deal with difficult situations or perceived threats or challenges. It's present any time we feel overwhelmed or when life's demands seem too great for our capacity or resources. There's good and bad stress, and there's acute (sudden and short-lived) or chronic (long-term) stress.

---

The more stressed we are, the harder we find it to create new habits and to break old ones. We also tend to fall back on our old habits when we're feeling stressed.

---

People who can successfully manage stress and uncertainty have higher resilience. When stress is hindering our life, though, it becomes problematic. Much of life is about meeting challenges, and managing stress is part of that. So it really comes down not so much to what's causing us stress, but how we respond to it.

Stress uses a tremendous amount of energy, so if we're in a stressed state all day, we're going to feel exhausted, which depletes our self-control. Consequently, we enter a state of ego depletion, making behaviour change exceptionally difficult. Anything that increases our stress decreases our ability to focus. Our thoughts are the most common source of stress; we keep stress alive in our head through our thoughts and ruminations. This type of stress is so exhausting. Studies show that people with chronic stress – the type of stress that doesn't have a simple or quick solution – don't produce as many mitochondria (tiny bodies in our cells that produce energy).[9] Mitochondria are often referred to as 'powerhouses', as they help turn the energy we take from food into energy that our body can use. Mitochondria production is strongly correlated with our thoughts and feelings. The more stressed we feel on a particular day, the less energy we have. To mitigate this, we should adopt a daily practice of focusing on the things that went well that day. Go to bed with a grateful heart and a positive focus. I do this with Mitch, and nothing drives him more crazy than me asking him what went well in his day just before he nods off. But he's a good sport and we always have a beautiful time sharing what we're grateful for (well, at least I enjoy it, and Mitch is happy to oblige).

Another important exercise we should all practise more often is radical acceptance. And I don't mean accepting stress in our life, but rather, radically accepting when a situation is out of our control. That might be a traffic jam, the weather, a delayed flight or how other people act. Professor Elissa Epel, author of *The Stress Prescription*, gives a great analogy to illustrate the importance of radical accept-ance.[10] She says that stressing about things we can't change is like pulling a rope that's attached to a brick wall. We're doing this because we're stressed and because we want to see change. But the wall isn't going anywhere. All we're really doing is chafing our hands. She recommends letting go of the rope and giving ourselves freedom to manage the situations we can control.

Take a moment to write down the stressful situations in your life. Then put a circle around the ones you can't change. Just recognising that can be incredibly powerful, because we can put the baggage down and give ourselves some relief, some freedom from the big space that stress is taking up in our mind and in our body. We get to loosen our grip and give ourselves greater capacity to manage the things in our life that we *can* control. Radical acceptance is a practice, not a one-off exercise. We need to make it a habit, a way of life, an identity. Otherwise, all that unhelpful stress will keep taking up too much precious mental real estate, which is important and necessary for creating change. We can't fight a riptide; we need to let go and flow with the direction of the tide.

## Reframing stress

I want to emphasise that not all stress is bad for us. Some stress helps us feel alive, gives us a sense of drive and purpose, and increases our cognitive capacity. A complete lack of stress makes it difficult to feel a desire to engage in activities or make changes. Think of a lioness chasing a zebra, for example. They are both feeling stressed, but they're experiencing that stress completely differently in their mind and body. The lioness is feeling excited because she might be getting dinner soon; she's motivated, alert and feels a healthy dose of challenge. The zebra, on the other hand, is experiencing a great deal of threat and panic; his life is a risk and he's frightened at the possibility of what might happen if the lioness catches up with him.

We get to shape whether we're the lioness or the zebra. Rather than dreading stress and getting stressed by stress, we can reframe our thoughts to see stress as empowering and motivating and a sign that our bodies are doing exactly what they should be doing. We feel that anxious pang in our stomachs when we're doing great and exhilarating things, like riding a roller-coaster, competing in a game or going on a first date. This short-term stress inspires and motivates us, focuses our energy, and enhances our performance. It's the kind of stress that makes us feel excited and allows us to live outside our comfort zone. Studies show that when people perceive stress positively, they perform better, solve problems more effectively, feel more positive emotions, and recover more quickly from stressful situations. One study from Harvard University that illustrated this particular effect was titled, 'Turning the knots in your stomach into bows';[11] it's all about perspective.

So how we perceive stress and how we manage it will greatly influence how quickly it takes us to create new or break old habits. In the previous chapter, you will find a few stress management tips to help you unwind and jump start neuroplasticity.

The influence of stress explains why there's such a big range – 18–254 days – for how long it takes to reach automaticity and create a habit. If you and I performed exactly the same habit for exactly the same length of time, we would not necessarily have reached the same level of automaticity. You might be more habitual than I am, or you might be more consistent in performing the habit, or I might perceive the reward as greater than you do. It's a very loose scale, but now you know the factors that influence how long it takes to change a habit, you might not feel so discouraged if it takes a while.

## Speeding up the habit-forming process

We can speed up the process of reaching automaticity because habits are strengthened by consistency, low complexity, environmental conduciveness (using obvious, inevitable and specific triggers like the ones we talked about in Chapter 4), and positive *affect* (our tendency to experience positive emotions and interact with others and with life's challenges in a positive way). Are you a glass half full or half empty kind of person?

In the same way, trying to form a habit is very difficult and will take much longer if you're not consistent, you're trying to form a very complex habit, your environment is not conducive, you tend to have a negative mindset, or you are chronically stressed and therefore ego depleted.

## HOW LONG DOES IT TAKE TO BREAK A HABIT?

I wish I had a straightforward answer, because if we could count down to a guaranteed day when those unwanted habits will no longer be part of our lives, it would be so much easier to commit to breaking them. But unfortunately, there is currently no empirical evidence as to how long it takes to break a habit. It's a very difficult question to answer because we all have different habit strengths, so comparing one person's habit to another is like comparing apples and oranges – it can't be done fairly or objectively.

I mentioned in Chapter 6 that it takes on average 30 days for the brain to make important changes that help in the process of breaking old habits. So we have that as a baseline for change, but there are several factors that contribute to the time it takes to break a habit, such as the actual habit we're trying to break and our level of commitment and motivation. Breaking a habit can also be influenced by various factors, such as the strength of the habit, our environment and social support, and the level of stress and other external pressures present in our life. For example, breaking a habit that's deeply ingrained and associated with strong rewards may be more challenging than breaking a habit that's newly acquired.

Ultimately, breaking a habit requires consistency; commitment; and a willingness to be curious and kind with yourself, try new strategies, and make changes to your environment and daily routine.

Perseverance underpins most success stories of change. One study of smokers shows that it can take anywhere from six to 30 attempts to finally quit.[12] While that many attempts may seem disheartening, it's important to stay realistic about the need to keep on keeping on.

## Factors that affect habit-breaking time

Some key factors that influence how long it takes to break a habit include:

- **how strong the habit is:** The stronger the habit, the more you do it, and the greater the reward you get from it, the longer it will take you to break it.
- **how aware you are of your habit trigger:** You know how you're sometimes halfway through doing something *then* you realise you're doing it? The more aware you are of your triggers, the less likely you are to perform that unwanted habit and the quicker you will break it.
- **how appropriate your alternative habit is:** If you're trying to reprogram a new habit using the same cue and reward but your new habit isn't actually giving you much of a reward, it will be harder to break the original habit. Say, for example, you're trying to break a habit of scrolling too much on social media, and your reward is a perceived sense of connection. If you choose to read a book instead, you're not actually achieving connection by reading a book, so you're still going to be craving scrolling on social media. Your alternative habit needs to match your needs and desires.
- **how much you want to break it:** The stronger your goal and your intention to break your unwanted habit, the quicker it will be gone from your life. Create strong implementation intentions (as you did in Chapter 5) – it's about developing

those cue–response associations, the 'If … then' or 'When I … I will' plans – and use a habit tracker.

- **how much you're dreading the change:** Believing change is possible can be undermined by 'anticipatory anxiety'.[13] This occurs when we expect and fear withdrawal symptoms when changing a habit, such as smoking. The anticipated discomfort is usually greater than the actual experience, but it can paralyse any attempt to test reality. Rather than focusing on what you're losing by giving up smoking or alcohol, or any other addictive substance or behaviour, think of what you will gain – improved health, better sleep, longevity, more money, and so on.

## Curiosity and kindness

One of the key things to making a habit stick is the reward you get from performing it. You keep acting out your unwanted habits because they give you a reward. Eating in response to feeling anxious makes you feel a little better – your brain learns that and prompts you to eat every time you feel anxious. But to break that cycle and override the reward response, you need to bring awareness in. When we become aware of the rewards we get from our unwanted habits, we learn that most of the time they're not actually serving us. Take emotional eating, for example. If you eat when you're feeling anxious, the act of chewing and certain compounds in the food do make you feel slightly better in the moment, but it doesn't take long for that anxiety to return. If you really take time to notice the flow-on effect, you'll find that you most likely feel even more anxious than before, and that may be compounded by feelings of guilt, shame and mental fatigue.

Psychiatrist and neuroscientist Dr Jud Brewer tested this with his patients by asking them to be curious and pay attention to the real rewards from overeating each time they felt the urge.[14] After they did this 10–15 times, the reward value of overeating dropped below zero, which means it was no longer rewarding for them. It doesn't take a lot of time, only 10–15 repetitions, to change the reward systems in our brain. Our brains are very adaptable and are constantly learning and unlearning through this reward system – all we need to do is pay attention. We have been distracted by willpower as the dominant paradigm, but we just need to reshape our brain through our reward mechanism by bringing in curiosity and awareness. Once we learn that something isn't rewarding, we become disenchanted with it and we can change that behaviour without trying to force ourselves or using too much willpower.

To apply this strategy, start by noticing the physical sensations in your body. What does anxiety actually feel like? Are you truly hungry right now or do you want to suppress an uncomfortable emotion or sensation? This curiosity will help you recalibrate your awareness of your body and then your mind. Then, once you become comfortable with noticing your physical sensations, next time you're performing an unwanted habit, simply ask yourself, 'What am I getting out of this?', 'How is this serving me?' You can do this with any type of unwanted habit, from worrying too much to biting your fingernails or being self-critical.

You can then ask yourself, 'What do I really need in this moment?' Is it rest, connection, tackling something you've been procrastinating on? Come home to yourself and be curious and kind to yourself. When creating new habits or breaking old ones, it's important to remember that setbacks are normal and to focus on progress rather than perfection.

I worked with a client I'll call Bella, who had a habit of worrying too much. She described this unhelpful habit as taking over her mind. She worried about whether she packed the kids enough lunch for their school day, she worried about her and her husband's job security, she worried about a potential natural disaster occurring, she worried about eating too much when out with friends, she worried about not saying the right things in a social setting, she worried about saving for retirement even though she and her husband were on a great financial trajectory, she even worried about the potential of it raining on their family holiday in two months' time. Thinking about any or all of these things is not necessarily a bad habit – worry is a normal part of life – but when we don't manage it properly, it becomes overwhelming and interferes with daily functioning, as it did for Bella.

I asked Bella to start by noticing what worry felt like in her body. She described muscle tension, especially in her neck and shoulders, a racing heart, shallow breathing and a knot in her stomach. This was the first time that Bella leaned into what her body was experiencing when she worried. She had thought that worrying would reduce her anxiety, but was starting to realise that worrying was actually creating many of the same symptoms as her anxiety created and making her anxiety worse. At this point, Bella's brain started reprogramming the reward value of worrying. The reward prediction error was tipping from positive to negative, making the idea of worrying less appealing for her brain.

I then asked her, 'How does worrying serve you?' She said it gave her a false sense of security because it made her feel like she was making plans for her potential concerns. I dug deeper and asked Bella, 'How often does the outcome change because of your worrying?' If she worried about not packing the kids enough lunch or the potential of it raining on their holiday or a natural disaster occurring, would the outcome change? Would the kids miraculously have more food for lunch or the rain clouds part or the natural disaster decide to go elsewhere because Bella was worrying about it? No, of course not. Worrying only gave her a false sense of security because it gave her the illusion that she was doing something to address her anxiety. But in reality, she was just ruminating on her concerns and falling into a cycle of focusing her attention on the negative possibilities rather than the positive ones. When she weighed up the pros and cons of worrying, the balance clearly tipped towards it being an unproductive and even a harmful habit. This awareness was again helping Bella's brain recalibrate the reward value of worrying towards negative.

Finally I asked her, 'What do you really need when your mind starts to worry?' Through mapping her worry habit, Bella recognised that she often worried in response to her anxiety. Her trigger was feeling anxious, her habit was worrying, and her reward was a false sense of security. Bella also recognised that what she really needed was to reduce her anxiety, and she could do that through deep breathing and taking a short break. After a few weeks, Bella's mind became a place of calm and peace. She would still worry every now and then, but it wasn't taking over her mind as before or creating the extra anxiety she used to experience. It was an awesome outcome and a demonstration of the power of curiosity and awareness.

## ARE HABITS DIFFERENT FOR MEN AND WOMEN?

Over the past few decades, researchers have mostly agreed that gender doesn't play a major role in the experience of habits – it's the same for both men and women. But more recent research is teaching us more about the brain and how different genders may be triggered and motivated by different things.

For example, one study from Yale University's School of Medicine involved people with an addiction to cocaine or who regularly drank alcohol.[15] They conducted brain scans of the participants as they showed them photos of scenes that, in previous interviews, had increased their stress levels.

For the women in the study, exposure to stress-related cues triggered addiction impulses. For example, seeing a photo of a child in potential danger caused the women to crave cocaine or a glass of wine. Men, on the other hand, were much less affected by stress.

The men's addictions were triggered when they were exposed to drug-related cues, such as photos of someone at a bar, or of a needle or line of cocaine. The women were much less impacted by those drug-related cues.

This teaches us that to reduce ego depletion and help us stay on track with our habits, women should focus on reducing their stress levels and men should focus on creating a healthy environment where they will be less likely to be triggered to perform unwanted habits.

Another interesting study looked at exercise habits of 1719 men and women to determine who was more likely to start working out.[16] When men felt like they had an exercise-friendly neighbourhood and that they had the personal capability, they started exercising, whereas the women started exercising if they had sufficient family support. When you think of this from a traditional or even biological perspective, the men's responsibility has historically been to keep the community healthy, while the women's responsibility has been to care for and nurture the family. So it's no wonder that men and women need certain conditions to successfully stop unwanted habits or start new, healthy ones.

Anecdotally, we can also assume that perhaps men are more triggered by external or environmental cues whereas women are more internally or emotionally and socially driven. But the science of gender and habits is still in its infancy, and we hope to have more answers in the future.

## IS IT EASIER TO FORM GOOD HABITS THAN TO BREAK BAD ONES?

As I said earlier, I don't like describing habits as good or bad, but of course some habits serve us while others are detrimental to our lives. In theory, it's not easier to make or break good habit associations than it is to make or break bad habit associations. Having said that, most of us can agree that bad habits are often inherently more pleasurable or rewarding than good habits. Pressing snooze on your morning alarm, snacking when you're not hungry, or mindlessly scrolling on your phone are arguably more pleasurable than eating healthy meals, sweating it out at the gym every day, or drinking enough water. There's certainly a reason why many bad habits stick easier than good ones. In day-to-day life then, it can be more difficult to weaken a bad habit than to strengthen a good one, but this of course depends on how strong the bad habit is and how much you want to form the good habit.

## SUMMARY

» It takes on average 66 days to form a habit, ranging from 18 to 254 days.

» The time it takes to change a habit depends on how habitual you are as a person, how often you repeat the behaviour, the complexity of the task, the value of the reward, and the amount of negative stress in your life.

» There is currently no empirical evidence as to how long it takes to break a habit.

» Breaking a habit requires consistency, commitment, a willingness to be curious and kind with yourself, trying new strategies, and making changes to your environment and daily routine.

## ACTIVITY

# Getting curious

In Chapter 6 you mapped out three unwanted habits by identifying their triggers, routines and rewards. For this activity, you can use the same habits you previously identified or map out different ones by writing down the cues, routines and rewards for three of your unwanted habits (see the example on pages 103–104). You might want to draw them in a circle using the format below.

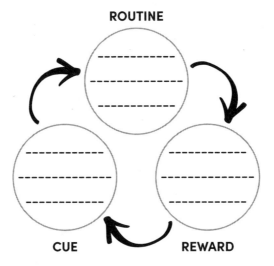

Now, for each of the unwanted habits you mapped earlier, ask yourself the following three questions and reflect on your answers.

1. What sensations are happening in my body when I'm performing this habit?
2. What do I get from performing this habit?
3. What is it that I really need?

# Chapter 11

# The recipe for change

A MULTITUDE OF FACTORS INFLUENCES our behaviour and the decisions we make. Why we do the things we do is guided by the culture we grew up in or have been exposed to, our awareness and perception of the world, our social influence, our self-efficacy, our attitudes and values, our level of motivation and, of course, our habits.

World-renowned professor of health psychology Susan Michie developed, with her team, a framework to help us understand the factors that influence our behaviour. They classified these into three key categories: capability, opportunity and motivation (shortened to COM-B, where B is behaviour).[1]

The COM-B framework describes how every behaviour change requires us to have capability, opportunity and motivation. This means that if change is not happening, then we are likely missing one of these factors.

- **Capability** describes our physical and psychological capability to engage in the desired behaviour. It includes having the necessary thought processes, comprehension, reasoning, knowledge and skills. Capability is being able to do what you want to do.

- **Opportunity** includes all the factors that lie outside of us that make the behaviour possible or prompt it. Opportunity can be our physical or social environment (social opportunity includes the cultural climate that dictates the way we think about things). Opportunity is having the resources, time and social acceptance to do what we want to do.

- **Motivation** is defined as the brain processes that energise and direct behaviour. It's our reason for acting in a certain way. Motivation can be automatic (habitual) or reflective (planned, intentional). It can also activate or inhibit our behaviour. We can be motivated to do something, such as exercising; or motivated not to do something, such as smoking. We'll take a deep dive into all things motivation in Chapter 12.

### The COM-B framework

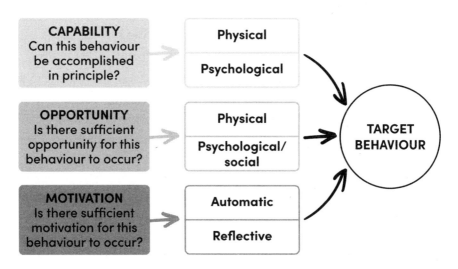

## THE COM-B TANGO

Our behaviour is a result of the interaction between capability, opportunity and motivation. For example, we can be motivated to do something because we have the capability and opportunity to do it. Sometimes we take action then the motivation follows, so the act of doing can influence motivation. There's a dance, a tango, that takes place between capability, opportunity and motivation.

Think of a habit you've wanted to create, such as having a daily meditation practice. If you don't have the capability to do something, you're not likely to do it. You first need to know how to meditate before you can start meditating.

---

There's a dance, a tango, that takes place between capability, opportunity and motivation.

---

To mitigate this, let's assume you download a guided meditation app to increase your capability to meditate. So now you know how to meditate. But say the app is down, or the kids are having a tantrum in the next room, or it's time to leave for work. Without the opportunity to meditate, you simply can't do it. You could have high levels of capability and motivation, but still not meditate if you're not presented with an opportunity to do so.

In the same way, you could have high levels of capability and opportunity to meditate but still not do it unless you have the motivation to do so. If you're not convinced that meditating is beneficial for your mental and physical health, then you're likely not going to have enough motivation to actually take time out of your busy schedule for a moment of Zen.

You can see how behaviour happens when there's an interaction between capability, opportunity and motivation, and that we need all three in order to enact or change a behaviour. Using the COM-B framework to identify why we might not be taking action towards a particular goal can be really useful, as it allows us to understand which component or combination of components could affect the desired transformation. For example, with one desired behaviour change the only barrier might be capability, while for another it may be enough to provide or restrict opportunities, and for yet another to boost our motivation. Or we may need to change all three components.

## PERFORMING YOUR OWN 'BEHAVIOURAL DIAGNOSIS'

To make behaviour change – either start a new behaviour or stop an old one – the first step is performing a 'behavioural diagnosis'. This involves asking yourself two simple questions:

- *Why* are these behaviours as they are?
- *What needs to change* for the desired/unwanted behaviours to occur/cease?

The next step is examining your capability, opportunity and motivation for those behaviours.

For example, if your goal is to drink more water, you would ask yourself: 'Why don't I drink enough water even though I want to?' Your COM-B analysis might then be:

- Do I have the *capability* to drink water? Yes, of course I have the physical ability and knowledge to drink water.
- Do I have sufficient physical and social *opportunity* to drink water? Yes, I have plenty of water around and it's a socially acceptable behaviour.
- Am I *motivated* to drink water? Hmmm, no, perhaps not.

You've now identified that you have the capability and opportunity to drink water, but you may need to work on your motivation if you're to increase how much water you drink.

The next question is, what needs to change? The answer is extremely simple: you need to increase your motivation for drinking more water.

How can we increase motivation? We'll get to that later in this chapter, as well as in Chapter 12, which is all about mastering motivation. Just know that you have the ability to change each of the COM-B components and achieve sustained habit change.

## MAKING CHANGE HAPPEN

This chapter's activity guides you through completing a behavioural diagnosis for behaviours that you want to start performing or those you want to stop performing.

Once you identify an insufficiency in capability, opportunity or motivation to perform (or not perform) a particular behaviour, you can work towards increasing that component of the COM-B system and achieving the desired change.

### Maximising capability

To maximise physical and psychological capability:

- Develop specific goals and plans to change. Implementation intentions ('If … then' plans; pages 80–1) are an excellent strategy.
- Upskill by getting the necessary education or training to be able to perform the behaviour. This could include doing workshops, using online resources, watching training videos or engaging in one-on-one coaching.
- Self-monitor using a habit tracker (pages 82, 86).

- Simplify the behaviour so that it's more manageable using micro habits (see Chapter 8).
- Create a supportive social environment and have someone to be accountable to. This could include family, friends or a peer support group.

## Maximising opportunity

To maximise physical and social opportunity:

- Create a supportive physical environment that will provide opportunities to perform the behaviour. For example, if you want to eat more healthily, place healthy food options at the front of the pantry and the occasional treats in a hard-to-reach area. Or if you want to read more, place your book in a spot where you're likely to see it, such as on the couch, coffee table or kitchen bench.
- Avoid the habit cues that are triggering the unwanted habit (restructure your environment; page 95).
- Have a social support network or connect with people with similar goals. This can help to create a supportive environment and increase social opportunities.
- Shake things up and change your routines and environments.
- Have on hand the resources you need to perform the desired behaviour. For example, if you want to develop a habit of flossing your teeth, make sure you have floss in the bathroom ready to use.

## Maximising motivation

To increase motivation for a desired behaviour or reduce motivation for continuing an undesired behaviour:

- Create positive reinforcement by rewarding your changes. Reward has a very powerful influence on behaviour. Rewards can include anything that you enjoy doing, such as taking a bath, watching a movie or buying a new outfit.
- Develop appropriate beliefs and ideals, such as a deep understanding of how this change can benefit your life. I'm motivated to practise a good sleep routine every day because I appreciate how important sleep is for my health and wellbeing. It's also important to know that other people approve of the change you're making.
- Make the change relevant to you personally. Finding personal meaning or enjoyment in the behaviour can significantly increase your motivation to do it. Identify values or interests that align with the behaviour you want to change.
- Increase self-efficacy (page 121) and have the confidence that you can and will make the desired changes in your life.
- Develop positive feelings about the change. Changing your beliefs is a great start, but it's not enough on its own – you also have to feel good about the change you want to make.

---

Create positive reinforcement
by rewarding your changes.

---

## MAKING CHANGE STICK

Changing the way we act and think can be difficult; maintaining that change is even harder.

Often, we need to maintain a change for a long period of time in order for it to translate into tangible benefits. Flossing your teeth one time isn't going to lead to good oral health; smoking one less cigarette isn't going to improve your lung function; walking one time isn't going to increase your fitness. To get fit and strong, you need to move your body consistently – it needs to be a practice that you maintain over time. And it takes time before you start seeing the benefits of your hard work.

So how can we maintain behaviour change and make our new habits stick? What we don't want to do is rely on our willpower and intentional decision-making. Willpower is a wavering and exhaustible resource, and intentional decisions require willpower. If I want to eat a healthy breakfast, it's hard when the chocolate pops are sitting there battling it out with the dry oats. The chocolate pops will most likely win – because chocolate.

We must rely on environmental triggers; creating routines, rewards and incentives; and making the behaviour automatic – habitual. To do this, I'll put the chocolate pops at the back of the cupboard, then make my oats the night before and place them at eye level in the fridge. I'll also use a habit tracker to self-monitor my progress, and I'll take a moment to reflect on how good my body feels after eating a healthy breakfast.

Cue, routine, reward – that's how you make habit change stick.

# SUMMARY

» A multitude of factors influence our behaviour and the decisions we make. These can be broadly categorised into capability, opportunity and motivation (COM-B).

» The COM-B framework describes how every behaviour change requires us to have capability, opportunity and motivation. When change isn't happening, we're likely missing one of these factors.

» The first step towards behaviour change is performing a 'behavioural diagnosis' by considering why the behaviours are as they are and what needs to change for the desired or unwanted behaviours to occur or cease.

» To maintain behaviour change, we must rely on environmental triggers; creating routines, rewards and incentives; and making the behaviour automatic – habitual.

## ACTIVITY

# COM-B in practice

Let's apply the COM-B framework to help you make your desired behaviour changes. You can download this activity as a pdf through drginacleo.com/book so that you can print it out and work on more than one behaviour you would like to change. Alternatively, use your notebook or journal to write down your answers to each of the questions or prompts. Complete this activity for behaviours you would like to start as well as those you would like to stop.

Think of a behaviour you would like to either start or stop and write it down. Now, with regard to that behaviour, note your answers to each of the questions below using a scale of 0 to 10, where 0 is strongly disagree, 10 is strongly agree and 5 is neutral.[2] The idea is not to add up your answers to each question at the end, but to analyse your response to each question separately. A score of 0–3 indicates a low level of capability, opportunity or motivation, a score of 4–6 is a medium level and 7–10 a high level.

1. I have the *physical* opportunity to change my behaviour to develop or break my chosen habit. (In other words your environment provides the opportunity for you to engage in or stop the activity you've chosen, such as sufficient time, the necessary materials, reminders.)

2. I have the *social* opportunity to change my behaviour to develop or break my chosen habit. (In other words, your interpersonal influences, social cues and cultural norms allow you the opportunity to engage in the activity concerned, such as support from friends and family.)

3. I am *motivated* to change my behaviour to develop or break my chosen habit. (By motivation here, we mean conscious planning and evaluations, such as examining your own beliefs about what's good and bad. You might frame your motivation as 'I have the desire to ...' or 'I feel the need to ...')

4. Changing my behaviour to develop or break my chosen habit is something I do *automatically*. (In other words, you do it without thinking or consciously remembering to do it, or it's something you do before you realise you're doing it. It's unlikely at this stage of habit development that your response will be 10.)

5. I am *physically* able to change my behaviour to develop or break my chosen habit. (This means you have the physical skill, strength or stamina to engage in the activity concerned. If you strongly agree, you might frame this as 'I have sufficient physical stamina', 'I can overcome disability' or 'I have sufficient physical skills.')

6. I am *psychologically* able to change my behaviour to develop or break my chosen habit. (In other words, you have the knowledge and/or psychological skills, strength or stamina to engage in the necessary thought processes for the activity concerned, such as interpersonal skills, memory, attention and decision-making.)

Use your notebook or journal to examine each response and the reasons behind it in more depth. Make some notes on how you can increase the areas with low or medium scores in order to start or stop your chosen behaviour more effectively.

# Chapter 12

# Mastering motivation

WHAT DRIVES YOU TO SUCCEED, to persevere through challenges and to pursue your goals with determination? At the heart of this question lie the forces of motivation. Whether it's a desire for personal growth or career advancement, or simply to better your quality of life, motivation is a key and necessary ingredient in the pursuit of improvement. It's one of the most important reasons we choose to move forward and take action.

In this chapter, we'll look into the many facets of motivation, from the science behind what motivates us to the practical strategies we can use to enhance our own motivation. We'll also look at how our personal values, beliefs and experiences shape our drive to achieve.

But first, consider a simple question: What motivates you? Is it the desire for success, the thrill of accomplishment or the satisfaction of helping others? Take a moment to reflect on your own motivations and consider how they've influenced your choices and actions. As we embark on this exploration of motivation, keep in mind that understanding your own motivations is the first step towards harnessing their power to achieve your goals.

# WHAT IS MOTIVATION?

Motivation is a complex and multifaceted concept, with roots in both psychology and neuroscience. At its core, motivation involves activation of the brain's reward system, which releases chemicals such as dopamine and serotonin that create feelings of pleasure and satisfaction. These reward pathways are activated when we engage in behaviours that are associated with positive outcomes, such as achieving a goal or receiving recognition for an accomplishment. But the factors that influence our motivation are varied and complex, and can be influenced by everything from our genetics and upbringing to our social and cultural contexts.

Professor of psychology Douglas Mook defines motivation as the reason we initiate, choose or persist in specific actions in specific circumstances.[1] Simply put, motivation is the reason we act in a particular way.

## Components of motivational theories

The process of motivation can be divided into four key categories. These address the main themes in the theory of motivation, allowing a deeper understanding of motivation and how it is influenced:

1. **motivational priorities:** What motivates us.
2. **motivational processes:** How our motivational priorities come about and influence our behaviour.
3. **motivational change:** How our motivation develops over time and with experience.
4. **motivational differences:** How our motivation differs from other people's and at different times in our lives.

The table opposite briefly touches on what influences each component of motivation. Every one of these influencing factors can be broken down even further. For example, physiological factors can include breathing, thirst, hunger, libido, threat, pain and so on (turn to the Appendix for a more comprehensive breakdown). Instead of going into each of those now, I want us to focus on more practical tools for understanding and changing our levels of motivation. Later in this chapter, we'll outline the five key factors that influence our behaviour.

## COMPONENTS OF MOTIVATIONAL THEORIES

| Category | Focus | Influencing factors |
|---|---|---|
| 1. Motivational priorities | What motivates us | Physiological factors |
| | | Psychological factors |
| | | Social factors |
| 2. Motivational processes | How our priorities influence our motivation | Instinct |
| | | Habit |
| | | Drive |
| | | Choice |
| 3. Motivational change | How our motivation changes | Experience |
| | | Associative learning |
| | | Reasoning |
| | | Maturing |
| 4. Motivational differences | How we differ from each other | Priorities |
| | | Processes |
| | | Change |

## External versus internal forces

Motivation may be inspired by external or internal forces. External forces or extrinsic motivation refers to behaviour that is driven by external rewards or consequences, such as money, fame, recognition or praise. It's a type of motivation that comes from outside of ourselves.

In contrast, internal forces or intrinsic motivation is behaviour that is driven by internal rewards or personal satisfaction, such as a sense of accomplishment, enjoyment or fulfilment. It's a type of motivation that comes from within ourselves, and is typically driven by our own interests, passions or values.

While extrinsic motivation can be useful in some situations, such as when we need an incentive to do something we don't find all that interesting, intrinsic motivation is generally considered to be a more powerful and sustainable source of motivation. This is mainly because it's driven by personal satisfaction and is not dependent on external rewards or consequences. If you tell a child they will get a treat if they finish their homework, they will finish their homework to get the treat. If you no longer offer them a treat for doing their homework, then you've taken away their incentive, so they're not likely to want to do their homework without another kind of incentive.

A couple I know shared a story about the system of rewards they had set up for their son, which had produced much improved behaviour at the dinner table. 'He sits up straight and eats his peas and the Brussels sprouts and he's really very well behaved,' they said. Until, that is, the first time the family dined at a nice restaurant. The child looked around, picked up a crystal glass from the table and asked, 'How many points not to drop this?' A fabulously hilarious example of the unfavourable effects of overreliance on external rewards to shape children's behaviour.

Some great experiments with both children and adults have proven the theory that external rewards result in behaviour change until the rewards are no longer available. The experiment in children involved a classroom of kindergarten kids who were allowed to do any activity they wanted to in their free time – they could sing or draw, or play with blocks or other toys.[2] Through a one-way observational mirror, the researchers focused on the kids who showed a high level of interest in drawing – in other words, the children who were already intrinsically motivated to draw. They then introduced rewards by giving the kids a 'Good Player' certificate and affirming what a great job they had done. Naturally, the kids really liked that kind of reward and feedback.

Two weeks later, the researchers stopped giving the children rewards for their drawings and observed what percentage of their spare time they now spent drawing. As you would expect, they were significantly less interested in drawing – in fact, half as much – as they were before the study. The use of external rewards undermined the children's intrinsic interest, turning an attractive activity into something the children would only want to do if there was a payoff.

And this is the limitation of extrinsic motivation: once the incentive is gone, we find no real reason to keep performing the behaviour. But when we're intrinsically motivated, we tend to be more engaged, creative and persistent in our pursuits, which leads to greater achievements and fulfilment.

## Conscious versus unconscious forces

Motivation results from an interaction between conscious and unconscious factors. Conscious factors include our reflective processes, such as our conscious decisions and reasoning, while unconscious factors are our automatic processes, such as feelings, beliefs, past experiences and habits.

# WHAT DOES MOTIVATION FEEL LIKE?

Motivation can feel different for different people and in different situations. Generally speaking, motivation feels like a sense of excitement, enthusiasm and determination to take action.

When we feel motivated, we might feel a surge of energy or a sense of purpose that propels us forward. We might feel more focused,

---

Motivation feels like a sense of
excitement, enthusiasm and
determination to take action.

---

engaged and committed to the task at hand. We might also feel a sense of satisfaction or accomplishment as we make progress towards our goals.

On the flip side, when we lack motivation, we might feel bored, disengaged or apathetic about taking action. We might feel stuck or unsure as to how to move forward. We might also feel frustrated or disappointed with our lack of progress. Feelings of fear, depression and anxiety can turn off the motivation switch in our brain. You may have heard phrases like, 'debilitating fear', 'paralysing terror' or 'crippling anxiety'. Motivation moves us forward, but fear and anxiety can hold us still.

Ultimately, motivation is a positive emotional state that can help us change our habits and achieve our goals.

## THE GREAT MOTIVATION MYTH

Most of us know the habits we'd like to do less of – hello, procrastination and rumination, with a side order of impulse shopping, binge eating and social media scrolling. But the thing is, most of us want to be healthier and happier and live a more fulfilled life, which requires new habits. So why is it sometimes so hard to do the things we want to do?

There's a common misconception that we need to feel motivated in order to take action. 'I want to start a new hobby but I'm waiting to feel motivated.' 'I want to save more money, but I'll start when

I'm motivated to.' But the reality is, we get motivated as a result of taking action. Yes, that's right, action comes first and motivation follows. Action is a prerequisite to motivation, which means that if we want to make changes in our life, we'll often need to take action without feeling motivated to do so. When I read this in the scientific literature, my mind was blown. I was hoping that motivation would one day be presented in an easy-to-digest pill, so that I could live my best life without having to push myself, but it turns out that motivation is a resource we can tap into anytime. All we need to do is take the first step.

## Motivation isn't a lightning bolt that strikes us in January. You won't find it on Mondays, or on your birthday.

When I think of New Year's resolutions, I see this great motivation myth playing out. We can sometimes think that the start of a new year turns over this superpower of feeling motivated and energised to tackle our goals, but motivation isn't a lightning bolt that strikes us in January, or at any other time. You won't find it on Mondays, or on your birthday, or when you get back from your holiday. You'll find it in the process, the push, the action, the first steps.

I can't tell you how many times I didn't feel like going to the gym, but I did go, and as soon as I started moving my body, I got into my workout. I've never walked out of the gym and thought, 'Gosh, I wish I didn't do that.' Every time, I think how glad I am that I went, and that feeling motivates me to go again another time. Genius is not born; instead, mastery is made.

# PROCESS, STATE OR TRAIT?

Do you ever wonder why some people are more motivated than others? Well, it's not as simple as some people having a greater desire for change or more grit. Motivation can be understood in three different ways: as a process, a state or a trait.

## Motivation as a process

As we saw earlier in this chapter, motivation as a process is about the brain processes that energise and direct our behaviour. It's the conscious and unconscious factors that influence us to take action, whether driven by our thoughts or emotions. It's when we set a goal and take action towards achieving it. For example, a student might be motivated to study for an exam because they want to get a good grade. The process of motivation would involve the student setting this goal, feeling motivated to achieve it, and then taking action to study.

## Motivation as a state

Motivation as a state is a momentary feature we get, and it determines the priority a given action has over other possible actions. State motivation is influenced by our beliefs about the costs and benefits of performing a certain behaviour. It's also influenced by our intentions, rules, wants and needs, and our impulses and inhibitions. State motivation is present in the moment and can fluctuate from day to day and from moment to moment. For example, you could feel motivated to exercise on one day, but feel less motivated on another.

## Motivation as a trait

This is more about the enduring disposition of a person to prioritise one type of action over others. Trait motivation is influenced by our attitudes and values. It's seen as a relatively stable personality trait that characterises our general level of motivation in different situations and over time. For example, I have trait motivation to eat plenty of vegetables, it happens every day and I don't need to be in the mood for it. It's a regular part of my lifestyle because I value the benefits of vegetables (and I think they're delicious). I don't have trait motivation for meditating, I have state motivation for it. Meditation is something that comes in and out of my life, and I have to be really intentional about doing it for it to happen.

## FINDING INTRINSIC MOTIVATION

In Chapter 5 and earlier in this chapter, I described the importance and value of intrinsic motivation. So how do we get more of it?

Self-determination theory is a macro theory of human motivation and personality. It suggests that all humans have three basic psychological needs that underlie growth and development: autonomy, competence and relatedness. All three of these factors are required to make us feel intrinsically motivated to do something.

### Autonomy

You need to believe that you have a say and a choice in what you're doing. You need to frame your goals as being essential for you, for your own success. You need to choose how to achieve your goal rather than be told exactly how to do it by someone else.

For years, my friends had been encouraging me to take up a yoga practice, but for some reason I just wasn't into it. I can't tell you why. Maybe it was because if I was going to invest time into moving my body, I wanted to feel like I'd really worked out. I wanted to feel sore muscles and my heart beating faster than I can count. Then one day I wanted to do some stretches, so I put on a yoga video at home and boom, I now own three different yoga mats, I can tell you the difference between hatha and ashtanga, and I'm basically a yogini in the making (not really, but I do love yoga now). The only thing that changed was that I autonomously decided to try yoga. I made that decision for myself rather than doing it for someone else.

---

## You need to choose how to achieve your goal rather than be told exactly how to do it.

---

When I was working as a dietitian, I can't tell you how many times I saw people in my clinic who were only there because their doctor wanted them to come. They didn't want to be there, and they knew that and I knew that. It often felt like they were just seeing me to tick a box, to go back to their doctor and say, 'Yes, I saw the dietitian.' But they either weren't ready to make meaningful changes to their diet, or they didn't think seeing a dietitian was necessary. As a result, they were easily the least motivated people I've ever worked with, and I don't blame them. Although they weren't forced to come see me, they certainly weren't there because they wanted to be.

Do you feel like you have autonomy with your goals? Reflect on why creating your new habits is important to you.

### Relatedness

At our core, we all intrinsically need connection with the people around us to feel a sense of relatedness and oneness. Feeling like what we're doing is meaningful and valuable to other people can really boost our motivation, even when there is no physical reward for us.

There's a wonderful foundation where I live that organises a giant Christmas lunch for people who would otherwise not have Christmas: people who are homeless, victims of domestic violence, widows and widowers, pensioners who can't afford a fancy feast, and anyone else who doesn't have their own community or safe place. Last year we served lunch and wrapped presents for around 700 people. It was amazing. Hundreds of volunteers give up their Christmas Day to serve the community. An Elvis impersonator entertains the crowd; food is donated by restaurants, supermarkets and small businesses; and the meal is cooked by volunteer chefs. Presents are donated by everyday people in the weeks leading up to Christmas, each one carefully wrapped and labelled. Everyone goes home with a full stomach and a full heart. And when I say everyone, I mean both volunteers and guests. You see, if you asked me to work in a hot restaurant running food out to people for seven hours and not get paid for it, I'd look at you as though you were crazy. There's no way I would do that. But I volunteer at this soup kitchen every Christmas; it's one of the highlights of my year and I look forward to doing it because there's a beautiful sense of fulfilment in helping people and connecting with people who would otherwise spend a special day alone.

In motivational theory, relatedness refers to our willingness to interact, be connected to and experience caring for others. Not all our goals have to have relatedness – in fact, many of them won't – but you may just find that you have a greater level of motivation for any of your goals that you believe are meaningful or valuable to others. Running 10 kilometres (6 miles) to raise money to help someone out is much more motivating than running 10 kilometres just to get fit.

---

You may just find that you have a greater level of motivation for any of your goals that you believe are meaningful or valuable to others.

---

### Competence

The final factor in increasing intrinsic motivation is competence. Competence refers to experiencing mastery, but it starts with self-efficacy, which you now know to be the strongest predictor of success. With greater self-efficacy comes greater intrinsic motivation. The more you believe you can achieve something, the more motivated you'll be to give it a go. The more you believe you're getting better or are mastering something, the more motivated you will be to do it again. And the more you feel like you can master something, the more likely you are to remain focused on that thing.

When my training coach tells me my deadlifts are looking good, or Mitch tells me I make the best banana bread, it creates a positive feedback loop and fulfils my need for competence. It inspires me to want to do those things again.

Do you believe in your ability and your level of competence to achieve your goals? How can you measure your progress so that you can see you're getting better or getting closer to achieving your goal?

## FIVE WAYS MOTIVATION IS INFLUENCED

Motivation is a complex phenomenon that is influenced by a variety of things, but it's worth a look at these five key factors. Some may be more relevant to your situation than others.

### 1. Rewards and punishment

Reward pathways in our brain teach us that doing something will result in either a reward or a punishment. This is the essence of reinforcement learning, which helps motivate us to either increase or decrease behaviours based on the feedback we get.

Positive and negative reinforcement both help to increase a behaviour, while positive and negative punishment both help to decrease a behaviour.

## Increasing behaviour through reinforcement

- **positive reinforcement:** Here, the addition of something positive increases the behaviour, such as a reward, for example. If someone said, 'Every time you press this button, I'll give you $100, you'll stand there and press that button all day long. There's a reward in it for you. In the same way, when you start making healthy changes in your life and you notice changes in your body or mindset, that gives you positive reinforcement that what you're doing is paying off – and that increases your motivation to keep up those healthy behaviours.
- **negative reinforcement:** In the opposite way, negative reinforcement occurs when the removal of something negative increases the behaviour. Let's say you want to join a gym, for example, and for a limited time they are waiving the $200 joining fee. You're likely to feel more motivated to join because they've removed a potential barrier or something 'negative'.

## Decreasing behaviour through punishment

- **positive punishment:** This occurs when the addition of something negative decreases a behaviour. For example, if you've ever burnt yourself on a hot stove, you will be motivated to not touch the flame again. Some smokers report that developing a 'smoker's cough' motivates them to quit smoking.
- **negative punishment:** In this instance, the removal of something positive decreases a behaviour. If you're a parent, you may have said to your child something along the lines of, 'If you keep hitting your brother/sister, I'll take your toy away.' If an adult consistently drives over the speed limit, they'll lose their driver's licence. The reason I don't overeat

dark chocolate is that the caffeine in it impacts my sleep. Removing good sleep decreases how much dark chocolate I eat.

## 2. Variable-ratio reinforcement

One surprising finding from experimental studies has been that when a behaviour is rewarded only some of the time, it tends to be stronger and more persistent than when it's rewarded continuously. Gambling involves a variable-ratio reinforcement schedule, where not all pulls of the slot machine, for example, result in a win. Video games follow the same rule. The ping of your phone is enticing because there's an element of the unknown until you look at your phone and see who it is.

Here's an illustration. Say that every time you pulled the slot machine, you won – you're on a continuous and predictable winning streak. If you pulled it again and nothing happened, you'd probably think that the machine had run out of coins, and you'd stop playing.

But if you were playing on a slot machine and you won intermittently, then you'd think that if you pulled the machine and nothing happened, the win was still coming. You'd think that this was just a random break between rewards – so you'd hang around and play for longer, even though you weren't winning any more.

And that's how variable-ratio reinforcement works to increase our motivation to persist with a particular behaviour; it creates a sense of excitement and anticipation. It's most effective when the rewards are meaningful and the behaviour being reinforced is something we're intrinsically motivated to do.

There's no clear way of implementing variable-ratio reinforcement to increase our motivation, but it's an interesting aspect of the process.

## 3. Goals

Motivation is strongly influenced by our personal values and goals, which is why Chapter 14 is wholly dedicated to goal-setting. If we're working towards something we really care about, we're more likely to be motivated to put in the necessary effort to achieve it. Having goals can have a big impact on our motivation. This is because goals:

- direct our attention and focus
- give us energy to act and move forward (Research has shown that having a goal increases the level of effort we're willing to apply towards both physical and mental tasks.[3])
- support us in enduring longer in a specific task before giving up
- encourage us to find better solutions through intentions and strategies.

Goals can be made even more motivating when we create implementation intentions – where we plan specifically where and when we'll perform the action that will lead us towards our goal. We did this when we were creating new habits using 'When I … I will' and 'If … then' statements (see pages 80–1, 85).

## 4. Dopamine

This wouldn't be a book about habit change if we didn't dive into one of the main neurotransmitters released by our brain, dopamine, which plays a crucial role in our experience of motivation, reward, attention and pleasure. Understanding dopamine has helped us uncover so much about the inner workings of the human brain and even more about motivation. Neurotransmitters are chemicals that allow neurons to talk to one other. Like a key fitting into a lock, dopamine binds to receptors that make the neurons slightly more or less likely to fire.

For example, when we eat something really delicious, our brain releases dopamine in a region called the nucleus accumbens, which is part of the reward pathway. The dopamine creates a pleasurable sensation, a type of reward, which motivates us to repeat the behaviour so that we can experience the pleasure again.

Dopamine is often referred to as the pathway to pleasure. You may have heard of the 'dopamine rush' of drugs, gambling or addictive behaviour. This makes it sound as though dopamine is the chemical that makes you feel good. But it's more accurate to say that dopamine is involved in the drive or the experience of *wanting*. Dopamine is what makes us desire something, but not necessarily what makes us enjoy it. Dopamine is all about anticipation; it's about the drive towards future rewards. So it may make you desire chocolate, but it won't necessarily make you enjoy the taste of it.

---

## Dopamine is all about anticipation; it's about the drive towards future rewards.

---

In one really interesting study, the researchers put a group of smokers in a room and asked them to hand over their cigarettes. Half the group were told they could go outside and smoke after 20 minutes, the other half had to wait five hours for their first cigarette. The researchers measured the participants' brain activity and level of anticipation and found these gradually increased the closer they got to the time they were allowed to have their first cigarette, regardless of them having to wait 20 minutes or five hours. The group that had to wait longer didn't have the same spike in dopamine after the 20-minute mark because they knew they had to wait more than four and a half hours before it was their turn. That group sat calmly and their brain activity was normal. When they were approaching their turn to have a cigarette, the participants' brain activity was dancing on the graph as their brain was firing in anticipation of their cigarette. Dopamine helps us not just to notice rewards but to predict them. The participants started thinking about and looking at pictures of smoking and imagining what it was going to be like to draw in that first puff of smoke. It was the anticipation rather than actually having a cigarette that significantly heightened their dopamine levels.[4]

Our brains are constantly anticipating rewards and using that anticipation to guide our thoughts and behaviour. Things like being visually stimulated (such as with social media and video games), eating, achieving a goal, the anticipation of winning when feeling connected to others, gambling, engaging in a novel or exciting activity, sex or exercise (hello, runner's high), and learning new things, all give us a release of dopamine that reinforces the behaviour.

A study in Germany analysed MRI scans of more than 150 teenagers who were either occasional or frequent gamers.[5] The kids in the study were around 14 years old, meaning their brains were still developing and changes would be occurring in the way their brain made connections. The connections they made at this age would set them up for the rest of their lives, influencing the way they act and perhaps even their personality and temperament.

By playing rewarding video games, the kids were influencing the connections in their developing brains through the release of dopamine. Essentially, they were reinforcing certain networks in the brain that are sensitive and reactive to rewards. The pleasure of gaming is really derived through the uncertainties that occur continuously, such as who's going to win this time. Frequent gamers had a larger reward centre in their brain than those who played less often. This means that frequent gamers have to game even more to reach the same level of reward as their occasional gaming friends.

We know that anything that increases dopamine activity has the potential to be addictive. If the kids in the study only played video games and didn't find other activities rewarding, they started to become addicted to gaming, but if they played sport or music, or were involved in other social activities, then playing video games did not become a major problem. It goes back to balance and finding pleasure in a diverse range of activities.

But what goes up, must come down. You see, pain and pleasure sit on the same seesaw in the brain. The more we stimulate the dopamine system, which makes us feel euphoric, the more we dampen the whole system.

## Dopamine peaks and troughs

Dopamine levels are like a currency that determine our level of motivation, drive, reward and pleasure. When dopamine is at baseline, we feel a sense of calmness and contentment. When our dopamine levels are high, we feel energised and motivated, and we get an intensified sense of enjoyment or satisfaction from activities that are pleasurable or rewarding. On the other hand, when our dopamine levels are low, we feel tired, moody and unmotivated.

Our dopamine levels rise and fall, similar to water in a wave pool. If you've never seen a wave pool, it's basically a big concrete swimming pool with a mechanism that creates artificial waves, similar to those you see in the ocean. The waves can range from little ripples to big, crashing waves. To illustrate how dopamine levels rise and fall, imagine what happens to the water level in the pool when the waves are small compared to when they're big.

If the waves are small or sporadic, we can expect the level of water in the pool to remain the same. But if the waves are big and frequent, we can expect that some of the water is going to spill out and the baseline level of water that was originally in the pool is going to drop. If there is big wave after big wave, soon enough, the water level in the pool is going to drop. So for every big wave there's a decrease in the pool's water level. This is how dopamine works: when you have a big surge of dopamine circulating in your body, the seesaw effect takes place, and you get a drop in your baseline level. For every peak, there's a trough. For every experience of pleasure, we experience pain. You go from feeling energised and motivated to feeling tired and lacking the desire to move. To increase our dopamine levels again, we seek out the behaviours that help increase our dopamine levels so that we can feel calm and contented.

For example, when you get a notification on your phone – the ding of a text message – and you experience pleasure, your brain wants to bring the seesaw back into balance. This is called homeostasis. But instead of bringing you back to baseline or how you were feeling before you received the phone notification, you get a greater comedown and you feel a little bit worse than before; this is the pain balance. This is why when you get a phone notification you start anticipating the next one, or when you have the first bite of cake you're already thinking of the next bite.

Neuroscience professor Andrew Huberman gives a great example that I'll paraphrase here.[6] Let's say you're feeling hungry and you're craving a sandwich. Your anticipation of the sandwich is going to increase your dopamine levels. The seesaw effect then takes place and the spike in your dopamine results in a drop below baseline. Remember, for every peak, there's a trough. And it's in the trough – when your dopamine is low, and you're feeling tired and moody – that you begin craving something to make you feel better. This triggers your desire to go out and find that sandwich. It's in the pursuit of the sandwich that your dopamine levels increase again and you start to feel better. It sounds complicated, but it's quite simple. Your desire for things increases dopamine, but then your level of dopamine drops below baseline and it's that drop that triggers the drive to bring your dopamine level back up and makes you even more motivated to pursue the thing you wanted in the first place. It's an extremely clever system for desire and pursuit. Cravings trigger a peak in dopamine, a peak results in a trough, a trough makes you even more motivated to pursue a reward or desire. And it doesn't have to be a sandwich; it could be coffee, water a relationship, sex, music, a thrill, anything. The higher the peak, the deeper the trough.

## The pain–pleasure balance

This pain–pleasure balance is the reason we engage in certain behaviours in an attempt to make ourselves feel better when we're experiencing negative emotions. For example, if we're feeling bored or lonely or stressed, we might crave eating, or scroll on social media more than normal, or splurge on online shopping.

Over time, our brain can become desensitised to dopamine, so it starts to need more and more of the food, or gaming, or whatever behaviour gives us pleasure, to achieve the same level of reward. This is why when we do something that gives us a dopamine release, we want to do it over and over again.

Some things that increase our dopamine levels include:

- chocolate – × 1.5 times
- exercise that you enjoy – × 2 times
- the pursuit and the act of sex – × 2 times
- an ice bath or a very cold shower – × 2.5 times
- smoking nicotine – × 2.5 times
- cocaine – × 2.5 times
- amphetamine – × 10 times.

You can see why recreational drugs are so addictive. The dopamine peak is so high, and the euphoric pleasure so unnaturally elevated that it results in an even bigger dopamine drop and subsequent comedown. This feels like depression, and the only way to feel better again is to pursue another extreme spike in dopamine.

## Naturally restoring your baseline dopamine

Having low dopamine levels feels blah. You feel down and a bit blobby. It's natural to want to seek ways to increase your dopamine quickly so you can go back to feeling energised. But instead of chasing the dopamine dragon, all you need to do is sit and wait, because the trough *will* resolve itself. The baseline level of dopamine you were at before the peak will come back. You may have experienced craving something sweet but found that when nothing sweet was around for you to eat the craving went away.

Sitting with that blah feeling and waiting it out will empower you to become less reliant on unhelpful stimuli – texts, notifications, beeps, likes, comments, rings, sugar, meaningless sex, thrills – that accompany living in a modern world. It's okay to feel lonely or bored for a short period of time. Not taking your phone into the bath-room for entertainment isn't as hard as you think it will be. If you have a compulsive behaviour, pushing through the discomfort will help you to find pleasure in doing simpler and more natural activities so that you can gain control over your life. It will also create a much healthier dopamine balance than you would get by seeking quick hits of pleasure. If you feel you need to, I recommend working through your uncomfortable emotions with a trained psychologist.

Some evidence-based strategies for naturally restoring our base-line dopamine levels include:

- getting enough good-quality sleep. This is so important.
  Sleep deprivation reduces dopamine levels and adequate
  sleep restores those levels.[7] It's recommended that we get
  on average seven to nine hours of sleep a night. Make sleep
  a priority.

- engaging in non-sleep deep rest such as yoga nidra (drginacleo.com/book), a powerful relaxation practice that has been shown to increase baseline dopamine levels by a whopping 65 per cent.[8]
- viewing morning sunlight. If we do this for two to 10 minutes within zero to eight hours of waking, we can increase our dopamine levels by about 50 per cent.[9] The earlier you view sunlight after waking, the better.
- avoiding bright lights between 10 pm and 4 am, as they activate a brain region that radically reduces the amount of dopamine circulating in our system.[10] If you must view lights during these hours, try to make them as dim as possible.
- doing cardiovascular exercise. Moving our body in ways we enjoy and that increase our heart rate can help restore our baseline dopamine level.[11]
- eating foods that contain the amino acid tyrosine, which is found in cheese, soybeans, beef, lamb, pork, fish, chicken, nuts, eggs, beans and whole grains.[12] Tyrosine can be converted into dopamine, thus increasing its availability in the body.
- if you're up to it, taking a one- to three-minute cold shower, as cold as you can tolerate.[13] This is known to dramatically increase baseline dopamine for hours.
- drinking caffeine in the form of coffee or tea, which creates a mild increase in dopamine and increases the availability of dopamine receptors, so our body is more sensitive to circulating dopamine.[14] Make sure to avoid caffeine after 2 or 3 pm so that it doesn't impact your sleep.

## 5. Competing forces

We know that every habit follows the sequence of the habit loop – cue, routine and reward – meaning that every one of our habits gives us some kind of reward. Staying up too late impacts our sleep and health, but it gives us the reward of finishing that television series we've been dying to watch. The amount of motivation we have to do one action can be in competition with the amount of motivation we have to do something else. Some days we might be more motivated to sleep, whereas other days we might be more motivated to stay up and watch television. Different forces compete for our motivation.

I might find it harder to read a book in my spare time if I have easy access to free movies on television. This isn't because of a change in my desire to read books – I love reading – but watching movies provides a reward with less effort and less mental energy. In the same way, if I have cake in the fridge and I'm feeling peckish, I'm probably more likely to eat that than a piece of fruit, because in all honesty, I like cake more than I like fruit, especially if I'm feeling exhausted and ego depleted. In the head-to-head battle between reading and watching a movie, or eating cake versus fruit, the more appealing opponent will have a better chance of winning. That's unless you remain mindful and change your perspective on the options at hand.

## Spaghetti is worms, chocolate is mud and cheese is mucus

How much value you place on the options you have in front of you will have a significant impact on your motivation. As I said, my reward value for cake is higher than my reward value for fruit. If I try to resist the cake and eat the fruit instead, my self-control will deplete quickly because I'm depriving myself of what I really want. The only time the cake wouldn't impact my level of motivation would be if it was a cake I don't like, such as sponge cake. I'm not a huge fan of sponge cake. Give me a cheesecake any day. And that's where the way we frame things has a big impact on our motivation. If we change our perspective, we change our experience.

I was sitting on the grass outside my office, blissfully enjoying my lunch, when an elderly gentlemen pointed down at my bowl

If we change our perspective,
we change our experience.

and said, 'Are you enjoying those worms?' He couldn't possibly be referring to my mum's handmade spaghetti. I looked down at my bowl, puzzled by this man's comment. I thought he must have been losing his eyesight and maybe a few brain cells. Why would anyone shovel worms into their mouth? I looked up at his grinning face and slowly replied, 'Excuse me?', my tone betraying my utter confusion. Through his big smile, he said in a loud, confident voice, 'Spaghetti is worms, chocolate is mud and cheese is mucus, and that's how I lost 20 kilograms [44 pounds].' It sounded almost like a well-recited song: spaghetti is worms, chocolate is mud and cheese is mucus.

I thought, 'What is this man on about?' My face tells all – I would miserably fail at a game of poker – and he could clearly see that I was beyond perplexed. He stood next to me and explained that he had been carrying excess weight and that by reframing his thoughts about the foods he was prone to overindulge in, he no longer felt tempted by them. I replayed the sentence in my head: spaghetti is worms, chocolate is mud and cheese is mucus. Wow, not only was it pure wisdom, it was an invaluable lesson on perspective.

I thought about how I used to love Nutella – you couldn't leave a jar around me without guaranteeing I'd be elbow-deep in it. But then I read the ingredients breakdown of Nutella: 'sugar (56 per cent), vegetable fat ... emulsifier, flavouring'. None of that sounded very appealing. I no longer saw Nutella as delicious chocolatey goodness, and it stopped being a tempting food for me. Change your perspective and you change your experience.

## Other factors

Other factors that influence our motivation can include:

- **feedback:** We all love receiving positive feedback. We like hearing that we've done a good job or that our efforts have been noticed. Positive feedback can be a strong motivator, as it can help us feel good about our efforts and encourage us to continue. I use positive feedback with my husband to encourage him to do chores (one of the perks of being a behavioural scientist): 'You did such a great job in the garden, darling', 'I love that meal you made last night', 'Thank you for folding the washing.' It works like a charm.

- **environment:** The environment we're in can have a significant impact on our motivation. If we're in an environment that's supportive and conducive to our goals, we're more likely to be motivated to work towards them. But if we're in an environment that's hostile or unsupportive, our motivation may suffer.

- **past experiences:** Similar to reinforcement learning, our past experiences can shape our motivation in the present. If we've had positive experiences with a particular activity or task, we're more likely to be motivated to do it again in the future. On the other hand, if we've had negative experiences, we may be less motivated to engage in that activity.

- **emotions:** If we're feeling positive emotions such as excitement or enthusiasm, we're more likely to be motivated to take action. On the flip side, if we're feeling negative emotions such as anxiety or stress, our motivation will likely take a dive.

Just remember that these influencing factors can interact with each other in complex ways and that we're all motivated by different things. Understanding what motivates you as a unique individual can be the key to achieving your goals and finding fulfilment in the things you do.

## SUMMARY

» Motivation is defined as the reason for acting in a particular way.

» Motivation feels like a sense of excitement, enthusiasm and determination to take action.

» Intrinsic motivation requires autonomy, relatedness and competence.

» Many factors influence and alter our levels of motivation, and they can change from day to day or moment to moment.

» We feel motivated as a result of taking action. We shouldn't wait to feel motivated before taking action. Action is often a prerequisite to motivation.

## ACTIVITY 1

# What motivates you?

Take out your notebook or journal and respond to these prompts:

1. Think of something you do in your life that you're happy about – maybe an established healthy habit, such as exercising regularly, eating fruit and vegetables, having a good bedtime routine, reading regularly. What motivates you to do that thing?

2. Now think of a behaviour you want to establish in your life but you haven't started on yet. What has prevented you from feeling motivated to take action towards that thing? For example, perhaps it's a lot of effort, maybe you don't think you have the ability to achieve it, maybe it feels too big.

## ACTIVITY 2

# Making a motivation diagnosis

Use this activity to consider how motivated you are to initiate, maintain or cease a particular behaviour. Repeat the activity for each habit you want to change.

1. Do you think that the benefits of starting the habit outweigh the costs?
2. Are you willing to prioritise the habit over other habits if necessary?
3. Do you see the habit as normal/acceptable?
4. Do you have an effective plan for performing the habit?
5. Are you confident in your ability to perform the habit?

# Chapter 13

# Do something different

WE'VE EXPLORED THE NUANCES OF forming new habits and breaking old ones. Now we're going to investigate a different side to habits: what happens if we become too habitual and what can we do about it?

Is it possible be too habitual? The short answer is yes. Habits are incredibly powerful for creating structure and routine in our lives, but when we become too rigid or inflexible, we can limit our ability to adapt to changing circumstances and new experiences. Most of the time, what we do is what we do most of the time, and sometimes we do something different. We use the default internet browser on our computer, walk around the supermarket in the same sequence, park in the same spot, take the same routes, listen to the same music, watch the same new channel, eat the same food, and the list goes on.

Being too habitual puts us at risk of losing mindfulness in our day-to-day activities, and acting purely out of habit and not enough out of intention. This means we can be doing things that aren't serving us, but we continue to do them because they are automatic and subconscious.

For example, if someone has a habit of always eating the same foods or going to the same places, they may miss out on new and potentially rewarding experiences. Or if someone has a habit of always responding to stress in the same way, they may find it difficult to cope with new or unexpected stressors.

The ideal lifestyle is finding a balance between healthy habits and being flexible enough to adapt to new situations and experiences. And in this chapter, we'll see how to do just that.

## THE CONSEQUENCES OF HABITUATION

Let's start with what happens if we find ourselves doing what we've always done and playing out our habits day in, day out with very little variation. If we're not mindful, being too habitual creates tunnel vision and a disconnection between our values or intentions and our behaviour.

### Tunnel vision

Tunnel vision is basically a lack of attention to information. We can get stuck in our old ways, even if new, innovative or more efficient ways become available. This is common in big organisations, where they tend to continue using the same procedures and the same software systems, despite advancements in technology that can make their routine tasks much more efficient.

Do you do the same type of exercise or eat the same breakfast every day because it's serving you and you enjoy it, or could you be doing something else you might enjoy even more or could be even better for you?

As you know, I used to do powerlifting and I really loved it, but after a couple of years, when I asked myself what my training goals were, I realised that they weren't to keep getting stronger and stronger – which is one of the main elements of powerlifting.

My training goals included wanting to increase my mobility and flexibility and to train in a functional way. So powerlifting was no longer going to serve me with my newly recognised training goals. What's funny though is that I still catch myself sometimes apply powerlifting principles to my functional training, and Mitch reminds me that not every training session needs to involve lifting heavy weights.

## Disconnection

The second consequence of habituation is that we can develop a disconnection between our attitudes, values or intentions, and our behaviour. Our values or intentions might change, we might gain new knowledge or awareness of something, but our habits may remain the same.

For example, we might know that using a habit tracker is really important for creating new habits, but we might still not use a habit tracker regularly – unless we become conscious of that disconnection between our intentions and our behaviour. In the same way, we may know that scrolling on our phone just before bed is going to impact our quality of sleep, but we still continue to scroll out of habit.

Being too habitual is a display of behavioural inflexibility. This affects our ability to effectively solve problems, change perspective, improve the way we do things, maximise productivity, learn new skills and be creative or interact with others. Behavioural inflexibility dismisses innovation and keeps us operating in a context-dependent manner (with automatic habits), rather than a goal-directed manner (by acting on our knowledge and intentions). This, therefore, affects how we live our lives, how we treat ourselves, how we do relationships and how we work.

The good news is, we can combat tunnel vision and disconnection by practising behavioural flexibility. You can still have strong habits and be behaviourally flexible in other areas.

# BEHAVIOURAL FLEXIBILITY

Behavioural flexibility is the adaptive change in our behaviour in response to changes in our external or internal environment. It describes our ability to 'flex' our core behaviours and increase our behavioural repertoire so that we can respond to each circumstance in the most effective way rather than the way we've always done. It's essentially our level of adaptability.

The word 'repertoire' here means range, repository or collection of skills or types of behaviour that a person habitually uses. By increasing our behavioural repertoire we increase the spectrum of behaviours we naturally use.

For example, imagine you're working in a team with a diverse group of people who have a range of different communication styles. A behaviourally flexible person would be able to recognise and adapt to the various communication styles of their colleagues. They may use more direct language with some team members but a more indirect or polite approach with others. By doing so, they are able to effectively communicate and collaborate with all members of the team, despite the differences in communication styles.

Another example of behavioural flexibility is someone who can switch between tasks and work on multiple projects simultaneously, prioritising tasks and adjusting their approach to meet changing demands. This ability can be particularly useful in a fast-paced work environment where priorities can change frequently and workers must be able to adapt quickly to meet new challenges.

As an example of behavioural inflexibility, take a boss at work. In general they would be a very assertive leader who makes things happen, drives the business and wins the battles. Their assertiveness is great for the business, right up until a key team member comes to them with a personal problem. Barking a solution to the employee isn't going to work. It feels uncaring to the employee and creates an instant problem that could have been avoided with a less assertive response.

Or take someone who is quiet and dependable. Everything is well ordered and safe and accounted for, but deep down they are quite lonely. When this person goes out with a group of friends, there's someone they connect with, but they just can't quite find the courage to ask them out for a coffee – that's too far outside of their behavioural repertoire. A potential soulmate missed because they didn't want to take a risk.

Behavioural flexibility is about having both sides of the same behaviour – it's being open to new ways of creating solutions. So the assertive boss who is behaviourally flexible can see when to tone it down and try a less in-your-face approach to get better outcomes. And the wary person can take a controlled risk from time to time to experience more opportunities. Because after all, fear is temporary but regret is permanent.

Behavioural flexibility allows us to be more broad-minded and accepting of different situations. It lets us see things from different perspectives and essentially make better decisions.

## When was the last time you did something for the first time?

Increasing behavioural flexibility involves identifying aspects of your behaviour you rarely use – perhaps the opposite of how you would normally act in a certain situation. For example, if you're naturally a shy or reserved person, you may not speak up or initiate conversation. To change that, you simply do the opposite: you speak up, initiate conversation, share your opinion. Similarly, if you're naturally a more extroverted person, then to be more behaviourally flexible you could focus on listening more, being the quiet one in the room, observing what's happening around you rather than being in the centre of it.

I must warn you, this is easier said than done. You see, our natural tendencies and familiar environments and situations are comfortable. They provide us with a sense of security and predictability. When we encounter something new or different, it can trigger feelings of uncertainty, anxiety and even fear, which can of course be uncomfortable. After all, we're creatures of habit. Our brain is hard-wired to seek out familiar patterns and routines, and any deviation from those patterns can trigger a stress response. This is because our brain can see change as a threat to our sense of stability and security. When we're faced with new situations, we may not know how to act or what to expect. As a result, we don't often go out of our way to behave in different ways. Human beings experience a natural resistance to the unknown, because it's essentially the ultimate loss of control. This is true even if the unknown is benevolent or even beneficial to us.

Maybe you've lived your life thinking that a typical yearly salary of $50,000 from a reputable company is the highest you're capable of earning. Maybe you've spent so many years telling yourself that you're an anxious person that now you see it as part of your identity, adopting anxiety and fear into your belief system about who you truly are. Perhaps you were raised in a closed-minded social circle or an environment that reinforced your existing beliefs. Maybe you didn't know that you could challenge or reach new conclusions about politics or religion. Maybe you never thought that you were someone who could be tidy, have great fashion sense, feel content or even travel the world.

Doing something different can feel awkward and strange and out of character. But that's the whole point. As the old saying goes, if you always do what you've always done, you'll always get what you've always got. Feeling discomfort is a normal part of the process

---

If you always do what you've always done,
you'll always get what you've always got.

---

when trying something new or making changes in our lives. It can be helpful to acknowledge and accept these feelings, and to focus on the potential benefits of growth that can come from stepping outside our comfort zones. With practice, the uncomfortable feelings can become more manageable and eventually fade away.

As I write this, I'm reminded of a story of one of my study participants, Alex. The study was a clinical trial to determine if creating new habits or breaking old ones was more effective for long-term weight management and general wellbeing.[1] The participants in the breaking old habits group (called 'Do something different'), were sent text messages on random days of the week and at random times. The messages contained tasks for them to complete. They were things like 'Listen to a new radio station or genre of music today', 'Call a long-lost friend or relative', 'Drive a different way to work', 'Eat lunch in a different spot' – there was a long list of tasks that the participants were sent over a 12-week period.

When Alex came into the lab after the study to complete the post-intervention tests, I noticed that he was hobbling down the corridor on crutches. I asked him how he'd injured himself and he laughed as he shared his story. Alex was enjoying doing something different so much that he was doing a heap of extra tasks, like eating with his non-dominant hand, attending a salsa dancing class, and taking up music lessons. On one particular morning, Alex decided to put his jeans on right leg first rather than his usual left leg first. In doing this, he lost his balance, toppled to the floor and sprained his ankle – hence the crutches. He thought it was hilarious, and even mentioned that his injury didn't deter his housemates from doing something different with him – although they didn't attempt the jeans task.

I interviewed many other participants in the 'Do something different' intervention group to explore their experience on the program. Although some stated that early in the intervention doing something different was slightly uncomfortable, there was a general consensus that they really enjoyed being gently stretched out of their comfort zone. They said things like:

> 'The program made me think more and made me more aware of all the things that you do have to do to make a lifestyle change. I actually started looking for more things to do other than what you were texting. I would create little games that would get me out of my routine.'

> 'I'd think, "Yeah I can be into that", "I can do that" or "I can try that." It gave me confidence to think, "I can do a 10-kilometre [6-mile] walk." Before the program I wouldn't even think about it, I'd think, "Well, this won't happen."'

> 'I still try to do things differently. I'm still more aware of my eating and my exercise. I've changed the way I see things.'

> 'Doing something different moves you to think differently, not just consciously but unconsciously.'[2]

This was so exciting to hear, and even more exciting was seeing the participants' testimonies match their objective measures, which showed that on average, those who did something different significantly increased their sense of wellbeing, openness to change and healthy behaviour, and decreased their level of depression and anxiety.

One 'Do something different' participant baked cupcakes for her neighbour, they got chatting and now they're best friends. Another participant volunteered at a local soup kitchen where he met another fellow volunteer; they fell in love and three years later got married. Another participant discovered a love for gardening, another developed a passion for salsa dancing. Story after story, doing something different proved to be helping people feel like they were finally living.

## Why flex?

Most people have regrets, but we usually imagine that those regrets stem from the mistakes they feel they've made. That time they had too much to drink and embarrassed themselves. The toxic relationship they stayed in for too long. Losing their cool at their children. Having that second helping of ice cream and feeling sickly full. But new studies show that it's not necessarily the things we do in life that we regret, it's the things we don't do. It's the opportunity we didn't take, the job we didn't apply for, the person we didn't speak with, the trip we never went on, the investment we didn't make. Ultimately, we regret the chances we didn't take.

So this is a radical call-out to break out of your comfort zone and explore the different colours and shades within you. Doing something different won't necessarily help you break specific habits, but it's highly effective in helping you break general patterns of behaviour.

When we do something different, our brain goes through a series of changes that involve several regions and neural pathways. Firstly, the prefrontal cortex, which is responsible for planning and decision-making (our intentional brain), becomes more active as it tries to figure out the best way to approach the new tasks. Secondly, the brain's reward centre, the striatum, becomes activated as it anticipates the potential positive outcomes of successfully doing the new tasks. This can create a sense of excitement or motivation to continue trying. Additionally, the brain may also engage in a process called cognitive flexibility, which involves shifting between different ways of thinking of problem-solving strategies. This can help us adapt to the new task and come up with creative solutions. Overall, doing something different can lead to a range of brain changes as the brain works to adapt and learn new skills. These changes can feel challenging at first but can ultimately lead to increased cognitive flexibility and the development of new neural pathways.

Doing something different gets us out of our mundane routines and challenges us to do something out of the ordinary. That's really where life is experienced in its wonderful fullness. This is why doing something different has been proven to increase wellbeing, happiness and resilience, and reduce stress.[3] Being comfortable in uncertainty is a beautiful but rare resilience factor. People who tolerate uncertainty have much less anxiety and depression, and when stressful things happen they get over them quickly. Intolerance of uncertainty, on the other hand, strongly predicts anxiety and depression.

---

## Doing something different has been proven to increase wellbeing, happiness and resilience, and reduce stress.

---

Reframing uncertainty as the beauty of the mystery of life, and feeling the freedom of realising we don't control tomorrow, is a powerful mindset to have. There's true liberation in viewing things with curiosity and just going with the flow rather than trying to control the narrative.

I challenge you to try it for yourself. The activity at the end of this chapter will guide you to do three things differently this week. You can choose anything you'd like, whether that's from the list of suggestions or something you come up with yourself. This week I drove to work a different way, I went to the gym in the afternoon rather than my usual morning session, and I cooked using a new recipe. The idea is to gently reorganise your routine so that you can create more space for mindfulness, new experiences and, ultimately, a more exciting and fulfilled life.

# SUMMARY

» Habits are incredibly powerful for creating structure and routine in our lives, but when we become too rigid or inflexible we can limit our ability to adapt to changing circumstances and new experiences.

» The ideal lifestyle is finding a balance between healthy habits and being flexible enough to adapt to new situations and experiences.

» If we're not mindful, being too habitual creates tunnel vision and a disconnection between our values or intentions and our behaviour.

» Behavioural flexibility is adaptive change in our behaviour in response to changes in our external or internal environment. It describes our ability to 'flex' our core behaviours and increase our behavioural repertoire so that we respond to each circumstance in the most effective way rather than the way we've always done. It's essentially our level of adaptability.

» You can practise being more behaviourally flexible by gently reorganising your daily routines and general patterns, such as by trying a new food or listening to a new genre of music.

**ACTIVITY**

# Do something different

Increasing behavioural flexibility involves identifying aspects of your behaviour you rarely use – perhaps the opposite of how you would normally act in a certain situation. For example, if you tend to eat at the same cafés, pick a new café to go to. Or if you usually sit quietly in meetings, to increase your behavioural flexibility you might make an effort to share an idea or opinion. It's all about doing something different.

Use the list below to help you get creative with doing something different – or come up with your own idea. Write down your three choices in your notebook or journal and schedule them into your week.

## Example 'Do's'

- Newspaper: Change it or stop buying one.
- Magazine: Buy and read a different one.
- Radio/podcast: Change channels or start listening again.
- Food: Try something you've never eaten before. Be adventurous.
- Journey: Go somewhere new or take a different route to a familiar destination, such as work or your favourite seaside town.
- Public meeting: Go to the local town hall or somewhere else where there's a meeting.
- Sport: Why not try yoga, table tennis, cricket or swimming?
- Paint or draw: Use pens, pencils, paints or charcoal – whatever you wish.

- Watch a sports event live: Choose any event and go to watch it.
- Charity work: Choose any local group and go to help out.
- Domestic chores: Do something new. It doesn't matter whether it's the washing up or some DIY.
- Read: Choose something you wouldn't normally consider. It could be an obscure book or a trashy magazine.
- Write a story: Any subject, any length.
- Exercise: Do something different.
- Cinema: Go by yourself to watch a film.
- Contact: Call a long-lost friend or relation.
- Shop: Go somewhere different.

## Chapter 14

# Goal-setting essentials and pitfalls

I MUST ADMIT, I WOULD probably secretly roll my eyes and let out a silent sigh of indifference if I saw that there was a chapter on goals in a book I was reading. If I was at a conference and there was a session on goal-setting that was running at the same time as a session on watching paint dry, I'd be tempted to watch paint dry. I mean, it seems like such an elementary topic and we've all heard it so many times before. But changing habits starts with a desire to do something different for a change, and we achieve that through having a goal. So stay with me, because there are actually some very interesting and valuable nuances to goal-setting, and they can mean the difference between success and falling off the wagon.

Most of us set goals, but how many of those goals do we achieve and maintain? The majority of New Year's resolutions are forgotten by February. Goals are rolled over from one year to the next. So is there any point setting goals at all? The answer, of course, is yes. We don't necessarily need goals to sustain a change once it becomes habitual – more on that later in the chapter. But we do need goals to start a change, and without them it's easy to feel lost, aimless and unsure of what steps to take next.

In this chapter, we'll dive in with a few key evidence-based tips for effective goal-setting, so that you can set great goals and boost your chance of success whether it's for your career, relationships, health, finances, mindset or any other area of your life. We're going to run through the do's and don'ts of goal-setting – I call them 'goal-setting essentials' and 'goal-setting pitfalls'. When implemented effectively, goals act as a powerful motivator: they will inspire you and increase your focus and success.

So that we're on the same page, I want to start by defining what a goal is. The definition of a goal was conceptualised in the 1970s, and to this day researchers agree on the same definition: a goal is 'The object or aim of an action, for example, to attain a specific standard of proficiency, usually within a specified time limit.'[1]

---

Goals act as a powerful motivator:
they will inspire you and increase
your focus and success.

---

Some of our goals will have a finish line – perhaps a specific end point or outcome, such as completing a project or reaching a certain milestone. Other goals may be continuous or ongoing, such as personal growth or self-improvement goals like cultivating a daily meditation practice or developing better communication skills. These ongoing goals are more about making progress and continuing to improve over time than about reaching a specific end result. In a similar way, some of our goals may be about establishing and maintaining healthy habits over the long term, such as eating a balanced diet or exercising regularly. These types of goals are ongoing and don't necessarily have a clear finish line.

# WHY DO GOALS MATTER?

Goals are an essential element of success because they pave a clear path and help focus our attention on a specific task. We need goals to thrive and to feel motivated not only to start a new action but also to persist with that action over time. Without goals we run the risk of simply coasting through life without aspiring for or reaching greater heights.

---

Goals pave a clear path and
help focus our attention
on a specific task.

---

Goals affect our actions through several important mechanisms:

1. Goals serve a directive function: they direct our attention and effort towards goal-relevant activities and away from goal-irrelevant activities. This occurs on a cognitive and behavioural level. For example, researchers observed that people who were given feedback about multiple aspects of their performance on a driving task improved their performance in the areas for which they had goals but not in the other areas.[2]

2. Goals energise us mentally and physically, leading to greater levels of motivation.

3. Goals encourage us to persevere with our desired actions. Study participants who had a specific goal to complete a task persisted with the task much longer than participants who did not have that goal.[3] In the same way, goals can help us persevere when life throws a curve ball at us, because when we have an outcome in mind we will persist in our efforts longer to achieve that outcome.

4. Goals boost our experience of the reward and our sense of accomplishment. Say you successfully achieve a goal and you feel good, great and accomplished – that's a reward. If you achieved the same thing but it wasn't a goal, you won't necessarily feel accomplished. Say, for example, you set a goal to read a book chapter every week and you achieved that goal – you'd feel great for it. Compare that to reading through a book without necessarily setting out to achieve that. You may feel good for reading, but you won't have the same sense of achievement as when reading was a goal you achieved. By achieving something we set out to do, we build our self-confidence and self-efficacy, and increase our sense of reward – which we need in order to reinforce habits and rewire our brain.

A key indicator of whether a behaviour is habitual is if we keep doing it even in the absence of goals; we call this 'goal independence'. But in order to get to a place of goal independence, we first need to have goals and then be consistent enough for those goals to become automatic habits. Pablo Picasso once reputedly said, 'Our goals can only be reached through a vehicle of a plan, in which we must fervently believe, and upon which we must vigorously act. There is no other route to success.'

The three basic principles of goal-setting are:

1. A goal is better than no goal.
2. A specific goal is better than a broad goal.
3. A challenging (yet attainable) goal is better than an easy goal.

Keep these principles in mind as you work your way through the goal-setting essentials and pitfalls.

# GOAL-SETTING ESSENTIALS

You may have heard of SMART goals, which I'm completely in favour of. SMART goals are goals that are specific, measurable, achievable, relevant and time-bound. But I want to dig deeper and outline a few essential tools or skills we should implement when setting goals. These are tips I have curated from decades of research. We've covered some of them in previous chapters, so I'll just be touching on those ones here, but it's vital to package them in this section under the umbrella of effective goal-setting, to highlight their importance in this context.

As you read through each of these goal-setting essentials, you could reflect on your current goals and determine whether they fit with each of the tips or if they need refining.

## The decision

A goal starts with a *decision*. The English word 'decision' comes from the Latin *decidere*, where *de-* means 'off' and *caedere* means 'to cut' or 'to strike'. When we make a decision, we 'cut off' the other options and other courses of action.

To make a decision is to fix, establish, agree, conclude, determine, settle, make up one's mind. A decision binds us to a course of action: it's a *commitment*. The goal–performance relationship is strongest when we're committed to our goals, which means that when we're committed to our goals, we're much more likely to achieve them.

> A decision binds us to a course
> of action: it's a *commitment*.

The two key categories of factors that facilitate commitment to a goal won't come as a surprise:

1. how important the outcome or reward of the goal is to you
2. your belief that you can achieve the goal – your self-efficacy.

When we make a concrete decision, we can weaken our automaticity for habits we want to break and strengthen our automaticity for habits we want to create.

Have you made a concrete decision to achieve your goals?

## Feedback

We need to see some kind of progress in relation to the pursuit of our goals in order for that pursuit to be effective and sustainable. If you don't know how you're tracking, then it becomes difficult or even impossible to adjust your strategy to match what achieving the goal requires. For example, if the goal is to plant 40 trees in a day, you'll have no way to tell if you are on target unless you know how many trees have been planted.

When people realise they are below target, they usually either increase the amount of effort they put in to achieving their goal or change their strategy. Feedback acts like a moderator of goal effectiveness, because the combination of goals plus feedback is much more effective than goals alone.

Feedback can come in all shapes and sizes. It can be seeing progress on a habit tracker, tracking weight on a scale, seeing dollars in a bank account, receiving verbal affirmation from a friend or colleague, or even noticing changes in your mindset. When I was recovering from betrayal trauma and agoraphobia, I would make an effort to acknowledge the smallest wins: the first time I could walk through a shopping centre without panicking; the first time I was able to drive to my office; eating a nutritious breakfast seven days in a row. Years later, I still notice my progress and acknowledge that I've come a long way from the shell of a woman I once was. Doing this reminds me that I'm tracking in the right direction and that I've made progress. I did the same when I decided to quit dieting. I remember eating a bowl of oats with full-cream milk and being so chuffed with myself because dieting Gina wouldn't dare indulge in full-cream milk. Who you are today is not your potential; who you are today is just a point of reference.

However you choose to receive feedback in the pursuit of your goals, make it intentional and regular. Don't just look for when you've reached the finish line of your goal, but notice all the little steps, all the progress, all the small changes you're making towards reaching your goal. That positive reinforcement will do wonders for your perseverance, motivation, self-efficacy and, ultimately, success.

## Intrinsic motivation

We now know that motivation can be dichotomised into intrinsic and extrinsic motivation. Intrinsic motivation is driven by interest or enjoyment of the action and personal reward, whereas extrinsic motivation is driven by a desire to satisfy external demands by achieving external rewards such as money, recognition, pleasing others or avoiding punishment.

Intrinsic motivation isn't only essential for feeling motivated to achieve something. It's also essential for creating stronger intentions and more sustained changes in behaviour than extrinsic motivation. Extrinsically motivated behaviours represent a means to an end, and we're therefore less likely to engage in them.

Focus on the actions you need to take each day to achieve your goal. The achievement will come as you consistently perform the required actions. Keep your eyes on the rituals and routines you're creating and the result will take care of itself.

Are you intrinsically motivated to achieve your goals? What motivates you to want to achieve your goals?

## Self-efficacy

In Chapter 8, I described how self-efficacy is our belief in our own abilities, specifically our ability to meet the challenges ahead of us in completing a task successfully. Self-efficacy is the strongest predictor of success and is essential for goal-setting and goal commitment. You need to believe that you can and will achieve your goals, so be sure to adjust your goals to a level that you believe you can accomplish.

In addition to self-efficacy, an optimistic approach to goal-setting can boost success. Research shows that factors such as hope and optimism (which are fuelled by self-efficacy) have a significant impact on how we manage our goals.

In a study of 600 smokers, researchers found that self-efficacy guided the decision to quit smoking, so the participants who believed they could quit decided to quit.[4] The thing that guided the participants to persist with not smoking was satisfaction with the outcome of not smoking. So although we can be happy with an outcome of achieving a goal, we will likely only start attempting to accomplish the goal if we believe we can accomplish it.

I know that training to climb Mount Everest would do wonders for my cardiovascular health and fitness, but in all honesty, I get bad altitude sickness and I don't have the self-efficacy to climb 8849 metres (29,032 feet) above sea level. But I know that I can do a half-day hike in the mountain ranges near where I live on the Gold Coast. I wholeheartedly believe that I have the capacity to do that – I've done it before and can absolutely do it again. We must first believe in our ability to achieve a goal if we're to really commit to it.

Do you wholeheartedly believe that you have the ability to achieve your goals?

## Challenge

Goals must be challenging yet attainable. Think of how you feel when you've accomplished something challenging – you feel a sense of achievement and self-satisfaction, you become proud of yourself. Challenging goals also increase motivation because we can't coast our way to achieving them. We need to develop the skills and strategies to reach that goal, so we feel inspired and driven.

But if we take that too far and set a goal that's too challenging – perhaps one that's beyond our skill level or ability – and we don't achieve it, we can become dissatisfied, frustrated and self-defeated. So the challenge has to be at the sweet spot between too demanding and too easy.

In one study, researchers found that goals set at a specific difficulty consistently led to higher performance than encouraging someone to do their best.[5] They concluded that when people are asked to do their best, they tend not to do so. This is because the do-your-best goals have no external reference point and are therefore defined idiosyncratically. This allows for a wide range of acceptable performance levels, which is not the case when a goal level is specified. My best and your best might be different. Goal specificity doesn't necessarily lead to higher performance, because the specific difficulty of goals varies. But when we measure performance, we do find that goal specificity reduces variation in performance by reducing the ambiguity about what is to be achieved. We just need to know how much or how little challenge we should apply to our goals. My tip is start small and build the challenge of your goals while remaining at a level that you still believe is within your ability to accomplish.

We are motivated by *achievement* and the *anticipation of achievement*; this is what draws gamblers back to slot machines over and over again.

Are your goals challenging yet attainable?

## Complexity

The complexity of our goals goes hand in hand with their level of difficulty or challenge. Complex goals include actions that require a lot of skill and focus.

---

## We tend to procrastinate on attempting an action when the task is too complex.

---

Although it's essential for goals to offer a healthy dose of challenge, they should not be overly complex. Overly complex tasks can negatively impact our confidence, productivity and motivation. We tend to procrastinate on attempting an action when the task is too complex.

Even the most motivated people can become disillusioned if the goal's complexity is too great for their skill level. If possible, a complex goal should therefore be broken down into smaller, more achievable tasks. For example, if you've never rollerbladed before and you want to get good at rollerblading, your goal should be to practise rollerblading rather than doing fancy tricks. Or if you want to start cooking healthy meals, rather than trying to follow elaborate recipes, find simple, easy-to-make recipes.

Are your goals too complex?

## Count the cost

This is one of the most important tools you will learn in this book. Setting a goal is one thing, but actually taking the necessary steps to achieve that goal is another. Counting the cost involves considering what it will take to actually achieve the goal you've set yourself.

We're often guided by comfort. We stay close to what feels familiar and reject what doesn't, even if the uncomfortable thing is objectively better for us. Most people don't change their life until not changing it becomes the less comfortable option. Every change comes with a cost, a sacrifice, an adjustment.

Let's say, for example, that I set myself a goal of getting better sleep because I know it's one of the most important things I can do for my health and wellbeing. When considering the sacrifices I need to make in order to get a better sleep, I find that I need to:

- drink less caffeine
- avoid or reduce alcohol
- avoid screens for two hours before bed (including my phone, computer and television)
- set a bedtime routine where I go to bed and wake up at more or less the same time each day
- perhaps install new blockout curtains
- be ready for the effects on my social life.

I'm only likely to stick to my goal if I decide that those sacrifices are worth making. Nothing happens unless the pain of remaining the same outweighs the pain of change.

Your new life is going to cost you your old one. At a minimum, change will cost you your comfort zone, your sense of direction and your familiarity. It will cost you time and energy, perhaps even your social circles. At the heart of the matter, though, you are sacrificing what was built for a person you no longer are.

Reflecting on the sacrifices you may need to make to achieve your goals will help you anticipate the costs and stay realistic about the process.

What sacrifices do you need to make to achieve your goals? Are those sacrifices worth the outcome?

# AVOIDING GOAL-SETTING PITFALLS

When we set out to accomplish a goal, we want to reach the finish line. There's nothing more disheartening than having good intentions about achieving a desired outcome but feeling like we can never really get there. To help you to increase your success rate, here are some goal-setting pitfalls I commonly see and how to avoid them.

## Too big, too far, too many

The most common goal-setting pitfalls are setting goals that are too big or too far-fetched or setting too many goals. In this case, the list of goals resembles something more like Santa's Christmas list than a set of realistic, achievable aspirations. We know that our brains are only capable of making up to three changes at once, so by limiting the number of goals you set for yourself to three, you will significantly improve your chances of achieving those goals and won't overwhelm your brain.

The high achievers among us may not like hearing this. I certainly didn't, which is why I tried to cheat the system and set myself goals for five smallish habits. They weren't anything too outrageous; they were daily goals to drink two glasses of water before breakfast, meditate for five minutes, write down three things I'm grateful for, move my body for at least 30 minutes, and eat one piece of fruit. I thought that with my knowledge of neuroscience and habit change, I could totally achieve these five habits. I used a habit tracker to record my progress, but after about a week I noticed that I was only managing some of the habits every few days. You could definitely say that I was inconsistent at practising the five habits. I tried for another week, but the same inconsistency was happening.

If I was being honest with myself, doing five habits felt over-whelming and cognitively laboursome – something I didn't like admitting but couldn't deny. The plan clearly wasn't working, so I crossed out meditating for five minutes and scaled my habits back to only four. I thought, 'I can definitely handle four small changes.' But after another couple of weeks, I was still not performing all the habits every day and it was feeling like a chore to do them all. It wasn't a particularly enjoyable process, even though they were all things that would help my health and wellbeing. So I followed what the science says and scaled my habits back to only three a day. That was all I needed to do to consistently perform my new habits every day and see a full and colourful habit tracker. To this day, I've maintained those three habits. The lesson here is that even if you're someone with a fairly high capacity to process information and implement change, you just can't beat the science; our brain has the capacity to make no more than three changes at any one time.

So set yourself micro habits, start small and layer those micro habits as they become more habitual. Remember, simplicity changes behaviour. Even though it's very tempting to want to charge ahead, it's important not to rush into too much too soon. You're in this for the long haul, so give your brain and body time to rewire the new neural connections they need to make. With consistency, your new habits will become second nature and you will reach your goals.

## No trigger association

Setting a goal without associating it with a triggering cue requires ongoing memory, intention and willpower – which we know is a fleeting and exhaustible resource. Because we can't depend on our willpower or self-control in the long term, we must create cue–response associations so that the habits we want to create start to get triggered automatically when we encounter the cue. That's the only way we will continue to perform our habits even when we're down on self-control or tired. Cue, response, reward: that is how we create long-term, sustainable change.

## SUMMARY

» Goals create the motivation, perseverance and focus needed to achieve the desired outcome.

» Setting goals energises us mentally and physically, it encourages us to persevere with our desired actions, it motivates us, and it boosts our experience of reward and sense of accomplishment.

» Goal-setting essentials include making a binding decision, checking in with our progress, intrinsic motivation, self-efficacy, challenge, complexity and counting the cost.

» Goal pitfalls include setting goals that are too big, too far or too many; and not associating goals with a triggering cue (not creating cue–response associations).

## ACTIVITY 1

# Goal-setting essentials in practice

Now it's time to implement all the goal-setting essentials you just read about. This reflection activity will help you refine your goals if needed. It's also really motivating when you see that your goals are meaningful to you and that achieving them will help you to reach your highest potential.

Take out your notebook or journal. Working one at a time through each of your three goals, respond as fully as you can to these questions and prompts:

- Have you made a concrete decision to achieve this goal?
- How will you measure your progress? (i.e. How will you obtain feedback?)
- Are you intrinsically motivated to achieve this goal?
- Do you wholeheartedly believe that you can achieve this goal?
- Is this goal challenging yet attainable?
- Is this goal too complex?
- What sacrifices do you need to make to achieve this goal? Are those sacrifices worth the outcome?

**ACTIVITY 2**

# Are your goals REAL?

To help you stay motivated to achieve your goals, take out your notebook or journal and respond to the following four questions for each of your goals to see if they're REAL: *relevant, enriching, aligned* and *light you up*. Your answer to each question should be a clear yes. If it's not, you may need to revisit your goals so that they align with your overall desired outcome and your values.

- **Relevant:** Is this goal applicable and appropriate for the overall outcome you're trying to achieve?
- **Enriching:** Is this goal going to improve or enhance the quality of your life?
- **Aligned:** Is this goal aligned with your values and beliefs?
- **Light you up:** Does this goal inspire you? Are you excited by the idea of achieving it?

## Chapter 15

# Dealing with setbacks

SETBACKS ARE A PART OF LIFE. It's not a matter of *if*, it's a matter of *when*. So in this chapter let's talk about what to do when you hit those inevitable obstacles, and look at five key strategies that will get you back on track quickly.

## SUCCESS IS NOT A LINEAR PROCESS

Falling down is normal, natural and to be expected. Hiccups don't make you a failure; they make you human. The most successful people in the world have slip-ups and setbacks too. What makes them the most successful isn't their ability to avoid setbacks, it's their ability to persevere and get back on track.

You probably know the story of J.K. Rowling, the author of the *Harry Potter* series. After graduating from university, Rowling struggled to find success as a writer. She worked as a secretary and lived on welfare benefits while raising her young daughter as a single mother. Despite facing numerous rejections from publishers, Rowling never gave up on her dream of becoming a published author.

The year Rowling began writing her first book, *Harry Potter and the Philosopher's Stone*, her mother died after a long battle with multiple sclerosis. Rowling pushed through and continued writing over the next few years, but even after finding an agent, she still faced setbacks. Her first book was initially rejected by 12 publishers before being picked up by Bloomsbury.

Despite these tragedies and difficulties, Rowling didn't give up and her book became a massive success, earning critical acclaim and a dedicated fan base. She went on to publish six more books in the series, and the *Harry Potter* franchise has since become a cultural phenomenon, spawning movies, theme parks and merchandise.

Another story that comes to mind is that of Oprah Winfrey. Oprah was born into poverty in rural Mississippi and faced numerous obstacles throughout her childhood, including being raised in a dysfunctional family, experiencing sexual abuse, and struggling with other personal battles. Despite these challenges, Oprah developed a passion for journalism, and at the age of 22 she landed her first job as a news anchor in Baltimore. A few years later, however, Oprah was fired from her job due to being 'unfit for television'. Instead of giving up, Oprah used the experience as a learning opportunity and landed a job hosting a morning talk show in Chicago. The show was a hit, and Oprah's engaging personality and relatable storytelling style quickly made her a beloved figure in the world of daytime television.

Oprah faced another setback in the mid-1990s when she was sued by the beef industry after airing an episode about mad cow disease. The lawsuit lasted six years and cost Oprah millions of dollars, but she refused to back down and ultimately won the case in court. Despite these setbacks, Oprah continued to build her media empire and eventually launched her own television network. Today, she is one of the most successful and influential figures in talk show history.

Rowling's and Winfrey's stories are testaments to the power of resilience, perseverance and determination in the face of adversity.

---

> ## The best strategy isn't to avoid failure, it's to plan for it.

---

Changing your habits and reshaping parts of your daily life can be a process of two steps forward and one step back. The difference between success and going off course is if, when and how you get back up again. The best strategy isn't to avoid failure, it's to plan for it.

## FIVE KEY BOUNCE-BACK STRATEGIES

Let's have a thorough look at five key bounce-back strategies to get you back on track after a setback: resilience, scheduling, consistency, self-efficacy and self-compassion.

### 1. Resilience

Resilience is defined as the capacity to withstand or recover quickly from difficulties; it's a level of toughness. Being a resilient person doesn't mean you don't experience stress, emotional upheaval and distress. Rather, resilience involves the ability to adapt to and recover from setbacks.

If habit change happened in one easy attempt, we would all be living our best lives right now and we'd have the healthiest bodies and mindsets. We'd get enough sleep and nutrients and water, we'd all be meditating and reading regularly and never eating when we're not hungry. But change doesn't quite work that way.

A baby crawls before it walks, and we applaud it for taking that first crawl. There are many falls and tumbles as the baby learns to stand and take those first steps. But just because the baby successfully stood up or took a step, doesn't mean that every subsequent attempt to stand or walk will be successful. There will be more falls and more tumbles, because it's all part of the process and we expect these falls to happen.

This is how habit change works. As you start developing your new habit, you may be doing great for a little while, then have a tough period at work, or become unwell, and forget about your habit for a period of time and go back to your old patterns. Then you pick yourself back up and return to your new habit, this time spending a little bit more time performing it. And this cycle continues, because life will always present numerous challenges.

It may feel like you're starting from scratch every time you drop your new habit and pick it up again, but actually you're developing greater familiarity with your new habit, making it easier and easier the next time you do it. The more you perform a habit, the more automatic it becomes and the stronger your neural pathways become.

When Confucius reputedly said that our greatest glory is not in never falling but in rising every time we fall, he described the journey we all go through in life to succeed. He also highlighted the importance of resilience. Rising every time you fall and viewing any setbacks not as a sign that you won't succeed or that you've failed, but as opportunities to learn, grow and develop as a person, is the very essence of resilience.

Consider the inspiring story of Thomas Edison, who made 1000 unsuccessful attempts at inventing the light bulb. When a reporter asked, 'How did it feel to fail 1000 times?' Edison replied, 'I didn't fail 1000 times. The light bulb was an invention with 1000 steps.' Edison didn't see any of those unsuccessful attempts as failures, not even one of them. He saw each attempt as a stepping stone to success. This is an incredible example of resilience.

It can be tempting to view change in a binary way – success or failure. But having a lapse shouldn't be seen as a failure or used as a justification to give up. Instead, view a lapse as an opportunity to gain insight, reflecting as honestly as you can on why the lapse happened and how you could avoid or counteract it on your next attempt at change. Research has repeatedly shown that adopting this kind of mindset is crucial for changing ingrained habits – so much so that in the world of addiction, treatment is often referred to as 'relapse prevention', to acknowledge that treatment is as much about preventing the negative as it is emphasising the positive.[1]

To practise resilience, don't wait until tomorrow, or Monday, or next month to pick yourself back up after a setback. Pick yourself up as soon as possible, today, right now. If you overeat one meal, instead of thinking, 'I've ruined the day, may as well start again tomorrow,' think to yourself, 'I've just overeaten, but that's okay. That may happen from time to time. I've got the rest of the day to eat well and honour my body.' Mindset matters because it shapes physiology. Just as the impact of stress will depend on the narrative you place around it, the way you view each setback is a choice – is it a failure or an opportunity to learn how to succeed?

## 2. Scheduling

Some of us can be all-or-nothing thinkers. I was a chronic all-or-nothing thinker until I realised it wasn't serving me. I was terrible! I remember in my early twenties being on a diet plan. My mum offered me an apple and I ate it before realising that the apple was not part of my diet plan for that day. I spent the rest of the afternoon criticising myself for not sticking to the plan. I felt like a failure. Imagine if I'd eaten a muffin or a donut rather than an apple. I'm glad to say that I'm no longer an all-or-nothing thinker. Here's the logic that transformed me: it's not the individual impact of a setback that holds you back from achieving your goals. It's the cumulative impact of not getting back on track and not doing so quickly.

Staying up too late one night isn't going to have a huge impact on your health. Missing one planned workout isn't going to make you unfit. But if you're not getting enough sleep for extended periods of time and you stop moving your body altogether, then it's going to make reaching your health goals a lot more challenging.

This bounce-back strategy is all about finding ways to stick to your schedule, no matter how small the action is. I worked with a client I'll call Mia who had a really tight schedule. She worked long hours but wanted to prioritise her health more. On one particular day, Mia had planned to go out for a 30-minute run after work. But work got a little crazy, her meetings went overtime, and time started to get away from her. When Mia looked up at the clock, she realised that she had only 15 minutes to go for her planned run before needing to get ready for dinner with her friends.

At this point, Mia had two ways she could look at this scenario:

1. 'Fifteen minutes isn't enough time to go for my run.' She convinces herself that her time is better spent finishing off a bit more work.
2. 'Fifteen minutes isn't enough time to go for the run I'd hoped to do, but it's enough time to do some bodyweight exercises and still move my body.' She reduces the scope of her plan but still sticks to her schedule of moving her body after work.

If Mia chose to take on the attitude of the second option, she would be giving her mind and body a huge win. The benefit isn't necessarily doing bodyweight exercises, the benefit is sticking to her schedule and therefore reinforcing the habit of moving her body after work. Doing this will make it easier the next time she plans to move her body after work, because the neural pathways in her brain have been strengthened.

When I started powerlifting, my coach gave me a training schedule that included a morning gym session three days a week. I trained for a few weeks before getting a really bad head cold. I felt rubbish and knew my body needed rest, but I didn't want to lose my momentum of going to the gym in the mornings because this habit was still in the early development stages, and I knew that getting back into the rhythm would take a bit of effort. So I let my morning alarm go off at the time it usually would for training, I got dressed in my active wear, I got in the car, and I drove down to the gym, runny nose and all. I didn't get out of the car; after parking, I drove straight home and got back into bed. I couldn't powerlift but I could continue the schedule of getting ready and going to the gym. Once I felt better, the habit of getting to the gym was easy because I'd been reinforcing it by going each morning.

When you can't perform a full habit as planned, do the minimum you can do to stay on schedule. This will help you bounce back quicker than you would believe. It's valuable to think of some barriers you may encounter and make a plan for how you might still perform your habit. For example, if you want to make a healthy meal for dinner but you get stuck at work, what can you do to still eat a nutritious dinner? I personally have a few meals in the freezer for those days. I also have a healthy takeaway restaurant near my home that I can go to if I need. In the activity at the end of this chapter, you will have the opportunity to write a list of potential barriers to your goals and come up with solutions for those barriers so that you can stay on schedule.

## 3. Consistency

We've looked at the importance of consistency already (see Chapter 10), but we need to mention it here because it's the secret sauce to creating healthy habits. Consistency is by far the most important strategy for achieving long-term change.

Just stick at it. Do what you can, as often as you can. Keep doing it until it eventually feels like second nature. Keep going and go some more. Change the goalposts, make your micro habits even more

Just stick at it. Do what you can,
as often as you can.

micro if that's what you need to do. But instigating the habit and being consistent with it is what's going to build the neural pathways in your brain for your new habit.

Consistency, not intensity, is what will get you across the success line. So just keep on keeping on.

## 4. Self-efficacy

In Chapter 8, we highlighted that the strongest predictor of motivation and success is self-efficacy: the belief in our own ability to achieve the goals we set out for ourselves. Self-efficacy is confidence and assurance in your own personal ability; it's absolutely believing that you *can* and *will* achieve the goals you've set for yourself. The more you believe in yourself and in your ability achieve your goal, the more likely you are to achieve that goal.

I was at a seminar on implementation research a while ago where the premise was how to change health practitioners' behaviours. Out of all the different domains including knowledge, skills, intentions, social influence and so on, the strongest theme was self-efficacy. A surgeon who's been performing a certain surgery for a long time may know the latest research that shows a different technique is more effective, but unless they believe they can do it, they won't change the way they've always done things.

Having self-belief also gives you the freedom to make mistakes and allows you to cope with setbacks by seeing them for what they are – temporary hurdles. Every single day, focus on your goals, rewrite them and re-read them. In great detail, visualise yourself achieving them. Read empowering affirmations that are filled with positive messages that destroy limiting beliefs and build empowering beliefs. With time and consistency, your brain will start to rewire any old self-limiting beliefs and your new empowered beliefs will be your new normal. We become what we believe we can become.

Several years before starting my PhD, I went through what I would call a 'hippie' phase. I've been through a lot of phases in my life – the skater-girl phase, the R&B phase, the road-tripper phase, and then there was the hippie phase. During this hippie phase, I wore organic cotton, shopped at the local organic farmers' market, ate lentil burgers and drank only distilled water. I'd meet people who would say things like, 'Your thoughts and beliefs create your reality', 'Manifest it and it will happen' and 'You attract what you focus on.' I'd see vision boards and affirmations and self-declarations. To be honest, I palmed it all off as woo-woo. I believed in hard work, putting yourself out there and hustling for what you wanted in life. I believed in fate and destiny and didn't think for a minute that you could attract things into your life just by focusing on them. It made absolutely no sense to me. If you wanted something, you had to grind and earn it. Then there was a plot twist.

As I started developing a passion for neuroscience, I came across the reticular activating system (RAS). The RAS is a network of neurons located in the brainstem that plays a critical role in regulating arousal, attention and consciousness. It's roughly the size of your little finger, but its effects are incredibly imperative to your life. The RAS receives sensory information from various parts of the body and sends signals to the cerebral cortex, which is responsible for conscious awareness and decision-making. Among other functions, the RAS is involved in filtering out irrelevant or unnecessary information, allowing us to focus on important details. Just like a computer, our brain has a filter function. This filter function is programmed by what we focus on and, more importantly, what we identify with. It's the seat of what many people have referred to as the paradigms we maintain.

The RAS is the reason why, when you buy a new T-shirt, you suddenly see other people wearing that T-shirt too, even though you've never noticed it before. It's why, when you buy a new phone, you start noticing the same model of phone more often when you're out and about. And it's also why you can clearly hear your own name in a noisy room. Essentially, the RAS creates a filter for the things we're focused on, that we deem important, and that validate our identity and beliefs. It's endlessly working to filter the millions of bits of data that we receive every day in order to present you with only the things you find important.

So if you've had a previous experience that made you believe that you're inadequate, the RAS will filter every experience through that lens, and will seek out information that supports the idea that you're inadequate (even though that may not be the case at all). Your belief systems are strengthened and reinforced because of the way you've primed your RAS and the lens through which you view the world.

If you're a pessimist and default to thinking negative thoughts, it's because your RAS filter is programmed to present you negative pieces of data that support the belief that things will probably go wrong. In the same way, if you're an optimist and default to thinking positive thoughts, it's because your RAS presents you with a world of possibilities and opportunities rather than problems and roadblocks. If you prime your RAS to seek opportunities, solutions and reasons why you can achieve your goals, it will present you with the relevant pieces of data that confirm this belief.

So as it turns out, the science says that our thoughts and beliefs *can* shape our reality. The hippies were right. If you believe in your ability to achieve a goal, your brain will support this belief by highlighting all the reasons why you can and will succeed. This then motivates you to take steps that lead to that success. Consistent thoughts turn into beliefs, which lead to actions, which result in outcomes. So although the relationship between our thoughts, beliefs, identity, actions and outcomes is complex and multifaceted, we can conclude that our thoughts, beliefs and identity influence our behaviour and the choices we make, which in turn affect the outcomes we experience in our life. When we consistently think about something, it can become a belief that shapes our worldview and influences our actions. These actions then lead to the outcomes that reflect our beliefs and behaviours.

We can rewire and reshape our RAS through visualisation, affirmations and mindfulness. With persistence and practice, we can develop a more positive mindset and focus our attention on the reasons why we do indeed have the ability to achieve the goals we set for ourselves.

## Self-efficacy affirmations

Here are some examples of positive affirmations that can be helpful in shaping your RAS and increasing your self-efficacy:

- I am healthy.
- I am worthy.
- I am lovable.
- I am confident.
- I can do this.
- I eat food that is nourishing to my body.
- I am resilient.
- I look after my health.
- I am capable.
- I am strong.

The power of affirmations lies in repetition and belief. By consistently practising self-efficacy affirmations, we can rewire our mindset and strengthen our belief in ourselves and our capabilities.

This self-efficacy fuels commitment, stimulates action and persistence, and allows us the grace to carry on despite setbacks because it eliminates all-or-nothing thinking. To practise self-efficacy, adopt the belief and expectation that you can and will achieve your goals. It's a powerful mindset to have.

## 5. Self-compassion

The final setback strategy and one of my absolute favourites is self-compassion. Self-compassion is giving yourself the same kindness, gentleness and care you would give a friend. The biggest and most successful transformations come from a place of self-love and self-compassion, not self-loathing.

If I asked you to list all the things you loved, how long would it take for you to say yourself? Self-compassion is not self-indulgence like 'Oh, go on … snooze your alarm for another 15 minutes again today', and it's not self-pity. A parent who loves their child is not going to say, 'Yeah, do whatever you want.' That's not care and protection. A loving parent sets boundaries and rules, but they all come from a place of care.

Self-compassion is about recognising in ourselves that we are human, that we are naturally imperfect, and that we are all in this together. I've presented workshops and keynote speeches to a few big global organisations. When I'm speaking to high-end managers or people who are particularly skilled in their field, I like to create a shared human experience by asking everyone to stand at the very beginning of my talk. I then ask them to sit down if they've ever intended to do one thing but ended up doing something different, or if they wished they had more self-control, or if they have an unwanted habit they just haven't been able to kick. Every single time, 100 per cent of people resonate with at least one of those statements and sit down. We all fall, we all stumble, we all want to do better and be better.

In her book *Self-compassion*, Kristin Neff describes self-compassion as deeply valuing ourselves and caring for our own long-term wellbeing.[2] Eating one slice of cake needn't be self-indulgence but a form of self-care, but eating the whole cake stops us from reaching our full potential.

---

A moment of self-compassion can change your entire day; a collection of such moments can change the course of your life.

---

Self-compassion includes empathy, kindness, forgiveness, caring, tenderness and various other synonyms for acceptance and non-judgement. You don't have to achieve all your goals overnight. And you don't have to feel ashamed for being where you are now. All you have to focus on is one small thing you can do today that will get you closer to where you want to be. Slowly and gently, one step at a time, you can and will get there.

At the opposite end of the scale from self-compassion is self-criticism, which is strongly linked with feelings of unhappiness, dissatisfaction with life and self-sabotage. If you don't love something, you won't be motivated to treat it very well. If you tell yourself you're a failure, you will act in ways that align with those thoughts. If you tell yourself that setbacks are part of any success story, you will be empowered not only to cope with the stress of life, but to thrive in the face of it. Self-compassion feels good and gives you a sense of wanting to treat yourself well because you deserve to be treated well.

## Self-compassion versus self-criticism

| Self-compassion | Self-criticism |
|---|---|
| • Knowing we're all imperfect and mistakes are how we learn and grow<br>• Understanding that we are far more than our accomplishments<br>• Striving for fulfilment | • Viewing our mistakes as a failure and falling into cycles of negative self-talk<br>• Judging our self-worth by our performance and external success<br>• Striving for perfection |

Self-compassion is a practice of generosity. With self-compassion we mindfully accept that the moment is painful and embrace ourselves with kindness and care in response, remembering that imperfection is part of the shared human experience. A moment of self-compassion can change your entire day; a collection of such moments can change the course of your life.

# AIM FOR MOMENTUM

Try your best to let go of all-or-nothing thinking. Accepting you'll probably slip up a few times when trying to break a habit and coming up with a plan is one thing. Preventing feelings of frustration and failure when you do slip up is another.

---

### Slowly and gently, one step at a time, you can and will get there.

---

If you fall back into an old habit, you might wonder, 'Can I really do this?' You might begin to doubt yourself and feel inclined to give up. I want to encourage you to look at your successes instead. Maybe you're trying to stop drinking soft drink and you do that successfully for three days in a row. On the fourth day you have a soft drink and spend the rest of the day feeling like a failure. Having a soft drink after going a few days without one doesn't take away those past days. Remember, you can make a different choice moving forward.

Aim for momentum in a particular direction rather than perfection. Instead of focusing on your end goal and where you are in relation to that goal, remember that anything you do that's more of what you want is fantastic.

## SUMMARY

» Setbacks are a natural and expected part of life. It's not about avoiding them, it's about getting back up from them quickly.
» These five evidence-based bounce-back strategies will help you quickly get back on track and stay on track:
  1. resilience
  2. scheduling
  3. consistency
  4. self-efficacy
  5. self-compassion.
» Aim for momentum in a particular direction rather than perfection.

## ACTIVITY

# Your bounce-back plan

Think of potential barriers to you achieving your goals and write a list of possible solutions so that you can stick to your schedule and remain consistent with your new habits.

You can use implementation intentions ('If ... then' plans) as you did when you practised creating a new habit in Chapter 5: 'If [potential barrier], then [possible solution].' You can have multiple 'If ... then' plans for each goal, because you're likely to encounter multiple potential barriers along the way.

Using the example below and working in your notebook or journal, analyse the potential barriers to reaching each of your goals and write down your possible solutions.

**Example goal:** Eat a healthy dinner

| If [potential barriers] ... | ... then [possible solutions/ alternative actions] |
|---|---|
| If I get stuck at work and don't get time to cook a healthy dinner ... | ... then I will heat up one of the frozen home-cooked meals I prepared earlier. |

# Conclusion

As we come to the final pages of this book, I want to reflect on the journey that led us here. Throughout these chapters, we've explored the science of habits, why we have habits, and the practical strategies we can use to create new habits and break old ones. We've gained an understanding of the two forces that govern our behaviour: intention and habit, where intention is our reflective brain that makes deliberate decisions; and habit is our impulsive brain that represents our spontaneous, automatic, subconscious actions.

We've seen how habits shape our daily routines, our health, our productivity, our relationships and our identity. And we've learned that by understanding the mechanics and the neuroscience of habits, we can make deliberate choices that lead us to the outcomes we desire – living a life by design, not by default.

At the heart of this book is the appreciation that habits are not a destiny. We may be creatures of habit, but we are not powerless to change. Whether we want to lose weight, quit smoking, exercise more or be more productive, we can learn to create the habits that support our goals and aspirations. It may not be easy, but it is possible.

Every single habit you have right now can be changed. Success is not always a goal to reach or a finish line to cross, it's a system to create and a dynamic process to refine.

The secret sauce to creating new habits is consistency and context-dependent repetition. When we do something consistently, it becomes easier and more automatic over time; it embeds itself into our life and becomes second nature. This can work for us or against us, depending on the habits we cultivate. If we want to create positive habits, we need to start small – micro, in fact – focus on consistency, just show up, pick ourselves up with compassion when we have a setback, and be patient. It's futile to set big goals and hope for the best. We need to create a system of small wins that build momentum and reinforce our self-efficacy and commitment to change.

Another important takeaway is that habits are always triggered: they are context-dependent. Our environment, social norms and cultural values all influence the habits we create and maintain. If we want to change our habits, we need to become aware of the cues and rewards that drive our behaviour. We need to notice the triggers that lead us to engage in unhealthy or unproductive habits and implement strategies to disrupt those patterns. And we need to create environments that support our new habits and make them more likely to stick.

Perhaps the most powerful insight we've gained from studying habits is that we all share a common human experience: we are not alone in our battles. No matter what corner of the world we come from, we all have unwanted habits and habits that we want to create, and we all face challenges in trying to change them. I've committed my entire life and my career to the study and practice of habit change and yet I still have setbacks. I still experience intending to do something and ending up doing something else. Just like you, I'm still human. For too long we've been trying to use willpower and self-control, which we now know is an exhaustible resource and can't be depended on in the long term. So we must create habits for the behaviours that we want to maintain in our life, because habits don't need self-control to be actioned.

As I close this book, I want to leave you with a final thought. Habits are not just a means to an end; they are a reflection of who you are and what you value. Habits tell a story of your life. A single step towards creating your new life will change your present moment; a collection of such steps will change the course of your life. When you cultivate good habits, you're not just improving your health, your relationships or your productivity, you're becoming the person you have the potential to be. In the same way, when you break unhelpful habits, you are not just eliminating a negative behaviour, you are freeing yourself to live the life you want and deserve to live.

There is truly nothing more liberating than living a life filled with positive habits. My hope is that you now feel empowered to embrace the power of habits and use it to create your own habit revolution. Let's start small, be consistent and build our self-efficacy to do even greater things. Let's pay attention to the contexts and the triggers that drive our behaviour. And let's build a community of support that helps us stay on track. With these tools and a commitment to change, we can transform our lives, one habit at a time.

# Appendix

# The finer details of motivational theory

THE TABLES BELOW HIGHLIGHT THE factors that influence each component of motivation, whether that be what motivates us and determines our priorities; how our priorities influence our behaviour; how our motivation changes; or how motivation differs from person to person.

This information shows us that myriad factors influence our drive towards performing certain behaviours.

## 1. MOTIVATIONAL PRIORITIES
*What motivates us and determines our priorities?*

| Physiological | Psychological | Social |
|---|---|---|
| Breathing | Sensory pleasure | Belonging |
| Thirst | Comfort | Being respected |
| Hunger | Security | Status |
| Libido | Ownership | Being liked |
| Threat | Stimulation | Connectedness |
| Pain | Fulfilment | Power |
| Exploration | Relief | Reciprocity |
| Rest | Play | Justice |
| | Competency | Empathy |
| | Concordance | |

## 2. MOTIVATIONAL PROCESSES

*How do our priorities influence our behaviour?*

| Physiological | Psychological | Social |
|---|---|---|
| Neuronal activity<br>Synaptic activity<br>Hormonal activity | Thinking<br>Feeling<br>Associating<br>Comparing<br>Combining | Diffusion<br>Social influence<br>Communication<br>Imitation |

## 3. MOTIVATIONAL CHANGE

*How does our motivation change?*

| Physiological | Psychological | Social |
|---|---|---|
| Neuronal plasticity<br>Maturation<br>Structural change | Associative learning<br>Induction<br>Deduction<br>Analysis<br>Reducing cognitive<br>  dissonance<br>Habituation<br>Sensitisation<br>Identification | Cultural evolution<br>Group dynamics |

## 4. MOTIVATIONAL DIFFERENCE

*How does motivation differ from person to person?*

| Physiological | Psychological | Social |
|---|---|---|
| Genetics<br>Epigenetics<br>Maturation<br>Connectivity<br>Structural differences<br>Functional differences | Personality<br>Temperament<br>Identity<br>Personal rules<br>Attitudes<br>Desires<br>Goals<br>Values<br>Tastes<br>Habits | Connectivity<br>Norms<br>Culture |

# Acknowledgements

I AM GRATEFUL BEYOND WORDS to the many beautiful souls who have contributed to the creation of this book.

Firstly, to my beloved husband, Mitch, thank you for walking alongside me through every step of the writing process. Your endless support and encouragement have been my guiding lights. You have played every role in helping shape the pages of this book; you've been my biggest cheerleader, trusted critic, human test pilot, tireless confidant and dedicated editor. Your love and care have been constant sources of strength and inspiration.

To my parents, Rob and Nevine, I'm brought to tears when I think of the countless sacrifices you've made to make sure that I had every opportunity to excel in life. Your unconditional love and your unwavering belief in me have been the foundation of my every achievement, including this book. Thank you for encouraging me to stay curious and for fuelling my passion for learning. I am forever grateful for you and for your love and guidance.

To my bestest friends, Monica and Tenielle, as with every project or idea I pursue, you have journeyed through every mountain and valley with me along this creative journey. You, my Wonder Women, have provided solace during moments of doubt and celebration during moments of triumph. Thank you for always being there, for listening to my rambles, and for sharing your honest opinions. The way you passionately champion my aspirations, and your irrational unconditional support have been a life source in making this dream a reality.

To my agent, Simone, from the day we met, you believed that I had a book in me. Without you, this book would have remained as words floating around in my head. Thank you for believing in me, for your vision, your insight, and for gently pushing me to the very edges of my comfort. You are a queen.

To my editors, Nicola and Breanna, and my publisher, Murdoch Books publishing director and all-round guru Jane, thank you for your unwavering commitment to excellence. Your guidance and expertise have cohesively shaped the narrative into its best possible form. I am so appreciative of the invaluable perspective each one of you has brought to this project.

I would also like to extend my heartfelt appreciation to the researchers who came before me, whose pioneering work and dedication have paved the way for our understanding of habits and provided a solid framework for this book. Their names may not be known to all, but their collective efforts have had a profound impact on the knowledge and insights I have gained. I am indebted to their relentless pursuit of understanding human behaviour, and for their contributions to the study of habits.

It would be remiss of me not to take a moment to acknowledge you, the reader. Without your curiosity, passion and willingness to embark on this literary journey with me, this book would simply be words on a page. Thank you for giving my words a home and for breathing life into these pages. I hope this book has provided you with moments of enlightenment, reflection and inspiration. May it have challenged your assumptions, sparked your curiosity and deepened your understanding of your wonderful brain. Your engagement as a reader is an incredible gift, and I am truly humbled and grateful for your support.

Finally, to those who have played a part in this book behind the scenes, I extend my deepest appreciation. Your contributions, whether big or small, have played a vital role in bringing this book to the world.

With heartfelt gratitude,
Gina

# Notes

**Introduction: The power of habits**

1    G. Cleo, E. Beller, P. Glasziou, et al., 'Efficacy of habit-based weight loss interventions: a systematic review and meta-analysis', *Journal of Behavioral Medicine*, 2020, vol. 43, pp. 519–32, <link.springer.com/article/10.1007/s10865-019-00100-w>.

2    G. Cleo, 'Maintaining weight loss: a look at habits', PhD thesis, Bond University, 2018, <research.bond.edu.au/en/persons/gina-cleo/studentTheses>.

3    G. Cleo, P. Glasziou, E. Beller, et al., 'Habit-based interventions for weight loss maintenance in adults with overweight and obesity: a randomized controlled trial', *International Journal of Obesity*, 2019, vol. 43, pp. 374–83, <nature.com/articles/s41366-018-0067-4>.

4    G. Cleo, J. Hersch & R. Thomas, 'Participant experiences of two successful habit-based weight-loss interventions in Australia: a qualitative study', *BMJ Open*, 2018, vol. 8, no. e020146, <bmjopen.bmj.com/content/8/5/e020146>.

5    E. Perel, *The State of Affairs: Rethinking Infidelity*, New York: HarperCollins, 2017.

6   'A traumatic event is an incident that causes physical, emotional, spiritual, or psychological harm. The person experiencing the distressing event may feel physically threatened or extremely frightened as a result. That person will need support and time to recover from the traumatic event and regain emotional and mental stability.' J. Cafasso with M. Boland, 'Traumatic events', Healthline, 14 April 2023, <healthline.com/health/traumatic-events>.

7   'Post-traumatic stress disorder (PTSD), once called shell shock … is a serious condition that can develop after a person has experienced or witnessed a traumatic or terrifying event in which there was serious physical harm or threat. PTSD is a lasting consequence of traumatic ordeals that cause intense fear, helplessness, or horror.' S. Bhandari et al., 'Post-traumatic stress disorder', WebMD, 31 August 2022, <webmd.com/mental-health/post-traumatic-stress-disorder>.

**Chapter 1: What is a habit?**

1   W. James, *Talks to Teachers on Psychology and to Students on Some Insights of Life's Ideals*, Cambridge, Massachusetts: Harvard University Press, 1983 (first published 1916).

2   W. Wood, J.M. Quinn & D.A. Kashy, 'Habits in everyday life: thought, emotion, and action', *Journal of Personality and Social Psychology*, 2002, vol. 83, no. 6, pp. 1281–97, <pubmed.ncbi.nlm.nih.gov/12500811>; B. Veazie, 'Foundation principles: keys to success of a behavioural-based safety initiative', *Professional Safety*, 1999, vol. 44, no. 4, p. 24.

3   D.O. Hebb, *The Organization of Behavior: A Neuropsychological Theory*, New York: Wiley, 1949.

4   S. Orbell & B. Verplanken, 'The automatic component of habit in health behavior: habit as cue-contingent automaticity', *Health Psychology*, 2010, vol. 29, no. 4, 374–83, <pubmed.ncbi.nlm.nih.gov/20658824>.

5   S. Orbell & B. Verplanken, 'The strength of habit', *Health Psychology Review*, 2015, vol. 9, no. 3, pp. 311–17, <tandfonline.com/doi/abs/10.1080/17437199.2014.992031?journalCode=rhpr20>.

6    F.E. Linnebank, M. Kindt & S. de Wit, 'Investigating the balance between goal-directed and habitual control in experimental and real-life settings', *Learning and Behavior*, 2018, vol. 46, pp. 306–19, <link.springer.com/ article/10.3758/s13420-018-0313-6>.

7    B. Gardner, C. Abraham, P. Lally et al., 'Towards parsimony in habit measurement: testing the convergent and predictive validity of an automaticity subscale of the Self-Report Habit Index', *International Journal of Behavioral Nutrition and Physical Activity*, 2010, vol. 9, no. 102, <ijbnpa.biomedcentral.com/articles/10.1186/1479-5868-9-102>.

## Chapter 2: Why we form habits

1    R.W. Engle & M.J. Kane, 'Executive attention, working memory capacity, and a two-factor theory of cognitive control', *The Psychology of Learning and Motivation: Advances in Research and Theory*, 2004, vol. 44, pp. 145–99.

2    E.M. Krockow, ' How many decisions do we make each day?', *Psychology Today*, 27 September 2018, <psychologytoday.com/au/blog/stretching-theory/201809/how-many-decisions-do-we-make-each-day>.

3    L. Dumont, 'De l'habitude', *Revue Philosophique*, 1876, vol. 1, no. 1, pp. 321–66, translated in W. James, 'The Laws of Habit', *Popular Science Monthly*, February 1887, vol. 30, paraphrased in B. Verplanken, 'Introduction', in B. Verplanken (ed.), *The Psychology of Habit: Theory, Mechanisms, Change, and Contexts*, Cham, Switzerland: Springer, 2018, p. 2.

## Chapter 3: Habits versus intentions

1    R. Deutsch & F. Strack, 'Changing behavior using the reflective-impulsive model', in M.S. Hagger, L.D. Cameron, K. Hamilton et al. (eds), *The Handbook of Behavior Change*, Cambridge: Cambridge University Press, 2020, <cambridge.org/core/books/abs/handbook-of-behavior-change/changing-behavior-using-the-reflectiveimpulsive-model/A35DBA6BF0E784F491E936F2BE910FF7>.

2  See, for example, S. Potthoff, D. Kwasnicka, L. Avery et al., 'Changing healthcare professionals' non-reflective processes to improve the quality of care', *Social Science and Medicine*, 2022, vol. 298, no. 114840, <sciencedirect.com/science/article/pii/S0277953622001460>.

3  S. Danziger & J. Levav, 'Extraneous factors in judicial decisions', *Proceedings of the National Academy of Sciences*, 2011, vol. 108, no. 17, pp. 6889–92, <pnas.org/doi/full/10.1073/pnas.1018033108>.

4  F. Strack & R. Deutsch, 'Reflective and impulsive determinants of social behavior', *Personality and Social Psychology Review*, 2004, vol. 8, no. 3, pp. 220–47, <pubmed.ncbi.nlm.nih.gov/15454347>.

5  A. Kalis & D. Ometto, 'An Anscombean perspective on habitual action', *Topoi*, 2021, vol. 40, pp. 637–48, <link.springer.com/article/10.1007/s11245-019-09651-8>.

**Chapter 4: Habit triggers**

1  K.P. Smith & N.A. Christakis, 'Social networks and health', *Annual Review of Sociology*, 2008, vol. 34, no. 1, pp. 405–29, <annualreviews. org/doi/abs/10.1146/annurev.soc.34.040507.134601>; K. Wright, 'Social networks, interpersonal social support, and health outcomes: a health communication perspective', *Frontiers in Communication*, 2016, vol. 1, no. 10, <frontiersin.org/articles/10.3389/fcomm.2016.00010/full>.

2  S. Fujii & R. Kitamura, 'What does a one-month free bus ticket do to habitual drivers? An experimental analysis of habit and attitude change', *Transportation*, 2003, vol. 30, pp. 81–95, <link.springer.com/article/10.1023/A:1021234607980>.

**Chapter 5: How to create new habits**

1  Veazie, 'Foundation principles'.

2  S. Horowitz, 'Health benefits of meditation: what the newest research shows', *Alternative and Complementary Therapies*, 2010, vol. 16, no. 4, pp. 223–28, <www.liebertpub.com/doi/abs/10.1089/act.2010.16402>.

3   E.L. Deci & R.M. Ryan, *Handbook of Self-determination Research*, New York: University Rochester Press, 2002.

4   J. Jiang & A.-F. Cameron, 'IT-enabled self-monitoring for chronic disease self-management: an interdisciplinary review', *MIS Quarterly*, 2020, vol. 44, pp. 451–508, <misq.umn.edu/it-enabled-self-monitoring-for-chronic-disease-self-management-an-interdisciplinary-review.html>.

5   S. Compernolle, A. DeSmet, L. Poppe, G. Crombez et al., 'Effectiveness of interventions using self-monitoring to reduce sedentary behavior in adults: a systematic review and meta-analysis', *International Journal of Behavioral Nutrition and Physical Activity*, 2019, vol. 16, no. 1, no. 63, <pubmed.ncbi.nlm.nih.gov/31409357>.

**Chapter 6: How to break old habits**

1   B. Wiest, *The Mountain Is You: Transforming Self-sabotage Into Self-mastery*, New York: Thought Catalog, 2020, pp. 6–7.

2   W. Wood, L. Tam & M.G. Witt, 'Changing circumstances, disrupting habits', *Journal of Personality and Social Psychology*, 2005, vol. 88, no. 6, pp. 918–33, <pubmed.ncbi.nlm.nih.gov/15982113>; B. Verplanken & W. Wood, 'Interventions to break and create consumer habits', *Journal of Public Policy and Marketing*, 2006, vol. 25, no. 1, pp. 90–103, <journals.sagepub.com/doi/10.1509/jppm.25.1.90>.

3   S. Orbell & B. Verplanken, 'The automatic component of habit in health behavior: habit as cue-contingent automaticity', *Health Psychology*, 2010, vol. 29, no. 4, pp. 374–83, <pubmed.ncbi.nlm.nih.gov/20658824>.

4   W. Wood, L. Tam & M.G. Witt, 'Changing circumstances, disrupting habits', *Journal of Personality and Social Psychology*, 2005, vol. 88, no. 6, pp. 918–33, <doi.org/10.1037/0022-3514.88.6.918>.

5   H. Garavan & K. Weierstall, 'The neurobiology of reward and cognitive control systems and their role in incentivizing health behavior', *Preventive Medicine*, 2012, vol. 55, supplement, pp. S17–S23, <www.sciencedirect.com/science/article/abs/pii/S0091743512002186>; T. Beveridge, H. Smith, M. Nader & L.J. Porrino, 'Abstinence from chronic cocaine

self-administration alters striatal dopamine systems in rhesus monkeys', *Neuropsychopharmacology*, 2009, vol. 34, pp. 1162–71, <www.nature.com/articles/npp200813>.

6    A. Lembke, *Dopamine Nation*, New York: Dutton, 2021.

7    S.A. Brown & M.A. Schuckit, 'Changes in depression among abstinent alcoholics', *Journal of Studies on Alcohol and Drugs*, 1988, vol. 49, no. 5, pp. 412–17, <pubmed.ncbi.nlm.nih.gov/3216643>.

8    Lembke, *Dopamine Nation*.

**Chapter 7: The neuroscience of habits**

1    V. Balasubramanian, 'Brain power', *Proceedings of the National Academy of Sciences*, 2021, vol. 118, no. 32, no. e2107022118, <pnas.org/doi/full/10.1073/pnas.2107022118>.

2    M. Puderbaugh & P.D. Emmady, 'Neuroplasticity', in *StatPearls*, Treasure Island, Florida: StatPearls Publishing, 2023, <ncbi.nlm.nih.gov/books/NBK557811>.

3    C. Keysers & V. Gazzola, 'Hebbian learning and predictive mirror neurons for actions, sensations and emotions', *Philosophical Transactions of the Royal Society of London B Biological Sciences*, 2014, vol. 369, no. 1644, no. 20130175, <ncbi.nlm.nih.gov/pmc/articles/PMC4006178>.

4    'Cognitive dissonance', *Psychology Today*, <psychologytoday.com/au/basics/cognitive-dissonance>.

5    A. Huberman with A. Lembke, 'Understanding and treating addiction', *Huberman Lab* (podcast), <hubermanlab.com/dr-anna-lembke-understanding-and-treating-addiction>.

6    A.N. Gearhardt, C.M. Grilo, R.J. DiLeone et al., 'Can food be addictive? Public health and policy implications', *Addiction*, 2011, vol. 106, pp. 1208–12, <doi.org/10.1111/j.1360-0443.2010.03301.x>.

7    B. Lindström, M. Bellander, D.T. Schultner et al., 'A computational reward learning account of social media engagement', *Nature Communications*, 2021, vol. 12, no. 1311, <nature.com/articles/s41467-020-19607-x>.

## Chapter 8: Micro habits

1   J.R. Paxman, A.C. Hall, C.J. Harden et al., 'Weight loss is coupled with improvements to affective state in obese participants engaged in behavior change therapy based on incremental, self-selected "Small Changes"', *Nutrition Research*, 2011, vol. 31, no. 5, pp. 327–37, <sciencedirect.com/science/article/abs/pii/S0271531711000674>.

2   B. Gardner, P. Lally & J. Wardle, 'Making health habitual: the psychology of "habit-formation" and general practice', *British Journal of General Practice*, 2012, vol. 62, no. 605, pp. 664–66, <bjgp.org/content/62/605/664>.

3   N.D. Weinstein, P. Slovic & M.S. Ginger Gibson, 'Accuracy and optimism in smokers' beliefs about quitting', *Nicotine and Tobacco Research*, 2004, vol. 6, suppl. 3, pp. S375–S380, <academic.oup.com/ntr/article-abstract/6/Suppl_3/S375/1084740>.

4   A. Bandura, *Self-efficacy: The Exercise of Control*, New York: W.H. Freeman & Co., 1997, p. 101.

5   H. Ford, first published in *Reader's Digest*, September 1947, vol. 51.

6   B.J. Wright, P.D. O'Halloran & A.A. Stukas, 'Enhancing self-efficacy and performance: an experimental comparison of psychological techniques', *Research Quarterly for Exercise and Sport*, 2016, vol. 87, no. 1, pp. 36–46, <tandfonline.com/doi/abs/10.1080/02701367.2015.1093072>.

7   V. Van Gogh, letter to Theo van Gogh, 22 October 1882, letter no. 274, Van Gogh Museum of Amsterdam, <vangoghletters.org/vg/letters/let274/letter.html>.

8   E.A. Locke & G.P. Latham, 'Building a practically useful theory of goal setting and task motivation: a 35-year odyssey', *American Psychologist*, 2002, vol. 57, no. 9, pp. 705–17, <psycnet.apa.org/record/2002-15790-003>.

## Chapter 9: Where is our self-control?

1   S. Freud, *The Ego and the Id*, in J. Strachey (ed. and trans.), *The Standard Edition of the Complete Psychological Works of Sigmund Freud*, vol. 19, London: Hogarth Press, pp. 12–66 (original book first published 1923).

2   M.S. Hagger, C. Wood, C. Stiff & N.L. Chatzisarantis, 'Ego depletion and the strength model of self-control: a meta-analysis', *Psychological Bulletin*, 2010, vol. 136, no. 4, pp. 495–525, <pubmed.ncbi.nlm.nih.gov/20565167>.

3   R.F. Baumeister, E. Bratslavsky, M. Muraven & D.M. Tice, 'Ego depletion: is the active self a limited resource?', *Journal of Personality and Social Psychology*, 1998, vol. 74, no. 5, pp. 1252–65, <pubmed.ncbi.nlm.nih.gov/9599441>.

4   M. Muraven & R.F. Baumeister, 'Self-regulation and depletion of limited resources: does self-control resemble a muscle?', *Psychological Bulletin*, 2000, vol. 126, no. 2, pp. 247–59, <pubmed.ncbi.nlm.nih.gov/10748642>.

5   R. Newsom with H. Wright, 'The link between sleep and job performance', SleepFoundation.org, 28 April 2023, <sleepfoundation.org/sleep-hygiene/good-sleep-and-job-performance>.

6   M.S. Hagger, G. Panetta, C.M. Leung et al., 'Chronic inhibition, self-control and eating behavior: test of a "resource depletion" model', *PLoS One*, 2013, vol. 8, no. 10, no. e76888, <ncbi.nlm.nih.gov/pmc/articles/PMC3798321>.

7   L.S. Goldberg, 'Understanding self-control, motivation, and attention in the context of eating behavior', MA thesis, College of William and Mary, Williamsburg, Virginia, 2017, <scholarworks.wm.edu/cgi/viewcontent.cgi?article=1176&context=etd>.

8   L. Wang, T. Tao, C. Fan et al., 'The influence of chronic ego depletion on goal adherence: an experience sampling study', *PLoS One*, 2015, vol. 10. no. 11, no. e0142220, <ncbi.nlm.nih.gov/pmc/articles/PMC4642976>.

9   Hagger, Wood, Stiff & Chatzisarantis, 'Ego depletion and the strength model of self-control'.

10  F. Beute & Y.A.W. de Kort, 'Natural resistance: exposure to nature and self-regulation, mood, and physiology after ego-depletion', *Journal of Environmental Psychology*, vol. 40, 2014, pp. 167–78, <sciencedirect.com/science/article/abs/pii/S027249441400053X>.

11  A. Keller, K. Litzelman, L.E. Wisk et al., 'Does the perception that stress affects health matter? The association with health and mortality',

*Health Psychology*, 2012, vol. 31, no. 5, pp. 677–84, <pubmed.ncbi.
nlm.nih.gov/22201278>; J.P. Jamieson, M.K. Nock & W.B. Mendes,
'Mind over matter: reappraising arousal improves cardiovascular and
cognitive responses to stress', *Journal of Experimental Psychology: General*,
2012, vol. 141, no. 3, pp. 417–22, <ncbi.nlm.nih.gov/pmc/articles/
PMC3410434>.

12  M. Friese & W. Hofmann, 'State mindfulness, self-regulation, and
emotional experience in everyday life', *Motivation Science*, 2016, vol. 2, no. 1,
pp. 1–14, <psycnet.apa.org/doiLanding?doi=10.1037%2Fmot0000027>.

13  B. Khoury, M. Sharma, S.E. Rush & C. Fournier, 'Mindfulness-based
stress reduction for healthy individuals: a meta-analysis', *Journal of
Psychosomatic Research*, 2015, vol. 78, no. 6, pp. 519–28, <pubmed.ncbi.nlm.
nih.gov/25818837>.

14  M.K. Edwards & P.D. Loprinzi, 'Experimental effects of brief, single
bouts of walking and meditation on mood profile in young adults', *Health
Promotion Perspectives*, 2018, vol. 8, no. 3, pp. 171–78, <pubmed.ncbi.nlm.
nih.gov/30087839>.

**Chapter 10: How long it really takes to change a habit**

1  M. Maltz, *Psycho-Cybernetics*, excerpt, New York: Penguin Random House,
2015 (first published 1960), see <penguinrandomhouse.ca/books/318795/
psycho-cybernetics-by-maxwell-maltz-md-fics/9780399176135/excerpt>.

2  P. Lally, C.H.M. van Jaarsveld, H.W.W. Potts & J. Wardle, 'How are habits
formed: modelling habit formation in the real world', *European Journal of
Social Psychology*, 2010, vol. 40, pp. 998–1009, <onlinelibrary.wiley.com/
doi/10.1002/ejsp.674>.

3  Gardner, Lally & Wardle, 'Making health habitual'.

4  Lally, van Jaarsveld, Potts & Wardle, 'How are habits formed'.

5  Lally, van Jaarsveld, Potts & Wardle, 'How are habits formed'.

6  W. Schultz, 'Dopamine reward prediction error coding', *Dialogues in
Clinical Neuroscience*, vol. 18, no. 1, pp. 23–32, <tandfonline.com/doi/
full/10.31887/DCNS.2016.18.1/wschultz>.

7   'Mindful eating', The Nutrition Source, T.H. Chan School of Public
    Health, Harvard University, <hsph.harvard.edu/nutritionsource/
    mindful-eating>.

8   I.C.W. de Souza, V. Vargas de Barros, H.P. Gomide et al., 'Mindfulness-
    based interventions for the treatment of smoking: a systematic literature
    review', *Journal of Alternative and Complementary Medicine*, 2015, vol. 21, no. 3,
    pp. 129–40, <www.liebertpub.com/doi/abs/10.1089/acm.2013.0471>.

9   M. Picard & B.S. McEwen, 'Psychological stress and mitochondria:
    a systematic review', *Psychosomatic Medicine*, 2018, vol. 80, no. 2, pp. 141–53,
    <ncbi.nlm.nih.gov/pmc/articles/PMC5901654>.

10  E. Epel, *The Stress Prescription: Seven Days to More Joy and Ease*, New York:
    Penguin, 2022, see <elissaepel.com/the-stress-prescription>.

11  J.P. Jamieson, W.B. Mendes, E. Blackstock & T. Schmader, 'Turning
    the knots in your stomach into bows: reappraising arousal improves
    performance on the GRE', *Journal of Experimental Social Psychology*, 2010,
    vol. 46, pp. 208–12, <pubmed.ncbi.nlm.nih.gov/20161454>.

12  M. Chaiton, L. Diemert, J.E. Cohen et al., 'Estimating the number of
    quit attempts it takes to quit smoking successfully in a longitudinal cohort
    of smokers', *BMJ Open*, 2016, vol. 6, no. e011045, <bmjopen.bmj.com/
    content/6/6/e011045>.

13  H.C. Becker, 'Alcohol dependence, withdrawal, and relapse', *Alcohol
    Research and Health*, 2008, vol. 31, no. 4, pp. 348–61, <psycnet.apa.org/
    record/2010-16227-005>.

14  A.E. Mason, K. Jhaveri, M. Cohn & J.A. Brewer, 'Testing a mobile mindful
    eating intervention targeting craving-related eating: feasibility and proof
    of concept', *Journal of Behavioral Medicine*, 2018, vol. 41, no. 2, pp. 160–73,
    <ncbi.nlm.nih.gov/pmc/articles/PMC5844778>.

15  B. Hathaway, 'Addicts' cravings have different roots in men and women',
    *Yale News*, 30 January 2012, <news.yale.edu/2012/01/30/addicts-cravings-
    have-different-roots-men-and-women>.

16  J.F. Sallis, M.F. Hovell & C.R. Hofstetter, 'Predictors of adoption and
    maintenance of vigorous physical activity in men and women', *Preventive*

*Medicine*, 1992, vol. 21, no. 2, pp. 237–51, <pubmed.ncbi.nlm.nih.gov/1579558>.

**Chapter 11: The recipe for change**

1   S. Michie, M.M. van Stralen & R. West, 'The behaviour change wheel: a new method for characterising and designing behaviour change interventions', *Implementation Science*, 2011, vol. 6, no. 42, <implementationscience.biomedcentral.com/articles/10.1186/1748-5908-6-42>.

2   C. Keyworth, T. Epton, J. Goldthorpe, et al., 'Acceptability, reliability, and validity of a brief measure of capabilities, opportunities, and motivations ("COM-B")', *British Journal of Health Psychology*, 2020, vol. 25, pp. 474–501, <bpspsychub.onlinelibrary.wiley.com/doi/10.1111/bjhp.12417>.

**Chapter 12: Mastering motivation**

1   D. Mook, *Motivation: The Organization of Action*, New York: W.W. Norton & Co., 1996, p. 4.

2   C. VanDeVelde Luskin, 'Mark Lepper: intrinsic motivation, extrinsic motivation and the process of learning', *The Bing Times*, Bing Nursery School, Stanford University, 1 September 2003, <bingschool.stanford.edu/news/mark-lepper-intrinsic-motivation-extrinsic-motivation-and-process-learning>.

3   Locke & Latham, 'Building a practically useful theory of goal setting'.

4   D.E. Bradford, J.J. Curtin & M.E. Piper, 'Anticipation of smoking sufficiently dampens stress reactivity in nicotine deprived smokers', *Journal of Abnormal Psychology*, 2015, vol. 124, no. 1, pp. 128–36, <ncbi.nlm.nih.gov/pmc/articles/PMC4332561>.

5   S. Kühn, A. Romanowski, C. Schilling et al., 'The neural basis of video gaming', *Translational Psychiatry*, 2011, vol. 1, no. e53, <nature.com/articles/tp201153>.

6   A. Huberman, 'Leverage dopamine to overcome procrastination and optimize effort', *Huberman Lab* (podcast), <hubermanlab.com/leverage-dopamine-to-overcome-procrastination-and-optimize-effort>.

7   A.J. Kesner & D.M. Lovinger, 'Wake up and smell the dopamine: new mechanisms mediating dopamine activity fluctuations related to sleep and psychostimulant sensitivity', *Neuropsychopharmacology*, 2021, vol. 46, pp. 683–84, <nature.com/articles/s41386-020-00903-5>.

8   T.W. Kjaer, C. Bertelsen, P. Piccini et al., 'Increased dopamine tone during meditation-induced change of consciousness', *Cognitive Brain Research*, 2002, vol. 13, no. 2, pp. 255–59, <pubmed.ncbi.nlm.nih.gov/11958969>.

9   A. Huberman, 'Andrew Huberman's light and sun exposure guide', Medium, 30 April 2022, <medium.com/@podclips/andrew-hubermans-light-sun-exposure-guide-dd62a43314df>.

10  D.C. Fernandez, P.M. Fogerson, L. Lazzerini Ospri et al., 'Light affects mood and learning through distinct retina-brain pathways', *Cell*, 2018, vol. 175, pp. 71–84, <pubmed.ncbi.nlm.nih.gov/30173913>; L. De Nike, 'Study links exposure to light at night to depression, learning issues', Hub, 15 November 2012, <hub.jhu.edu/2012/11/14/light-exposure-depression>.

11  T.E. Foley & M. Fleshner, 'Neuroplasticity of dopamine circuits after exercise: implications for central fatigue', *Neuromolecular Medicine*, 2008, vol. 10, pp. 67–80, <link.springer.com/article/10.1007/s12017-008-8032-3>; S. Heijnen, B. Hommel, A. Kibele & L.S. Colzato, 'Neuromodulation of aerobic exercise – a review', *Frontiers in Psychology*, 2016, vol. 6, no. 1890, <ncbi.nlm.nih.gov/pmc/articles/PMC4703784>.

12  S. Kühn, S. Düzel, L. Colzato et al., 'Food for thought: association between dietary tyrosine and cognitive performance in younger and older adults', *Psychological Research*, 2019, vol. 83, pp. 1097–1106, <link.springer.com/article/10.1007/s00426-017-0957-4>.

13  A. Yankouskaya, R. Williamson, C. Stacey et al., 'Short-term head-out whole-body cold-water immersion facilitates positive affect and increases interaction between large-scale brain networks', *Biology*, 2023, vol. 12, no. 211, <mdpi.com/2079-7737/12/2/211>.

14  A.H. Nall, I. Shakhmantsir, K. Cichewicz et al., 'Caffeine promotes wakefulness via dopamine signaling in *Drosophila*', *Scientific Reports*, 2016, vol. 6, no. 20938, <link.springer.com/content/pdf/10.1038/srep20938.pdf>.

# Notes

## Chapter 13: Do something different

1   Cleo, Glasziou, Beller et al., 'Habit-based interventions for weight loss maintenance in adults with overweight and obesity'.

2   Cleo, Hersch & Thomas, 'Participant experiences of two successful habit-based weight-loss interventions in Australia'.

3   B. Fletcher & K.J. Pine, *Flex: Do Something Different*, Hatfield, Hertfordshire: University of Hertfordshire Press, 2012; Cleo, Glasziou, Beller et al., 'Habit-based interventions for weight loss maintenance in adults with overweight and obesity'.

## Chapter 14: Goal-setting essentials and pitfalls

1   Locke & Latham, 'Building a practically useful theory of goal setting'.

2   Locke & Latham, 'Building a practically useful theory of goal setting'.

3   E.A. Locke, 'Motivation through conscious goal setting', *Applied and Preventive Psychology*, 1996, vol. 5, no. 2, pp. 117–24, <sciencedirect.com/science/article/abs/pii/S0962184996800059>.

4   T. Boardman, D. Catley, M.S. Mayo & J.S. Ahluwalia, 'Self-efficacy and motivation to quit during participation in a smoking cessation program', *International Journal of Behavioral Medicine*, 2005, vol. 12, pp. 266–72, <link.springer.com/article/10.1207/s15327558ijbm1204_7>.

5   E.A. Locke & G.P. Latham, *A Theory of Goal Setting and Task Performance*, Englewood Cliffs, New Jersey: Prentice Hall, 1990.

## Chapter 15: Dealing with setbacks

1   S.M. Melemis, 'Relapse prevention and the five rules of recovery', *Yale Journal of Biology and Medicine*, 2015, vol. 8, no. 3, pp. 325–32, <ncbi.nlm.nih.gov/pmc/articles/PMC4553654>.

2   K. Neff, *Self-compassion: The Proven Power of Being Kind to Yourself*, New York: HarperCollins, 2011.

# Index

**A**

abstinence 99–101

activities

applying the COM-B
framework 188–9

creating a new habit, five steps
for 85–6

doing something different 230–1

identifying goal scenarios and
solutions goals 264

identifying micro habits 132–3

identifying wanted and unwanted
habits 36

identifying your cues 70–1

identifying your habit triggers 69

mapping unwanted habits 102–4

measuring habit strength 32–3

reflecting on goals 247–8

reflecting on micro habit
goals 133–4

reflecting on motivations 217–18

reflecting on unwanted habits 178

replenishing your self-control 153

addictions 33–4

abstinence and 99–101

alcohol 99

dopamine and addiction 210–11

food 112–13

gaming 100, 207–8

gender differences 175–6

affirmations 259–60

alcohol

abstinence from 99

addiction, gender differences
in 175–6

ego depletion and 143, 144

as unwanted habit 90, 93, 94

all-or-nothing thinking 262

anti-Hebbian learning 94

    *See also* Hebbian learning

anxiety, treating with curiosity and

    kindness 172–5

automaticity 23–6, 29–30, 38

    *See also* time required to form,

        change and break habits,

        factors affecting

autonomy 199–200

**B**

behaviour. *See also* behaviour

    change. *See also* intention. *See*

    *also* forming and changing habits

    definition 16

    intention compared with

        habit 46–51

    laziness versus exhaustion 142–3

    reflective–impulsive model 51–4

    values alignment and 111–14

behaviour change. *See also* behaviour.

    *See also* forming and changing

    habits

    behavioural flexibility 222–8

    capability 179–80, 183–4

    COM-B analysis 182–3

    COM-B framework 179–82

    maintaining the change 185–6

    motivation 180, 184–5

    *See also main entry*: motivation

opportunity 180, 184

benefits of habits 1–2, 12–13, 23,

    73–5

efficiency 42

energy preservation 39–40

evolutionary benefits 38

natural flow 40–1

blood sugar levels 146

brain, human

    brain versus mind 105–6

    brain's role in habits 109–11

    characteristics 106–7

    impulsive brain system 48–51

    neuroplasticity 107–9

    reflective brain system 48

    reflective–impulsive model 51–4

    reticular activating system 257–9

    systems overview 45–8

breathing, deep 150

**C**

changing habits. *See* forming and

    changing habits

chocolate 57, 99

chronic pain, ego depletion and 144

cognitive dissonance 112

comfort zone, getting out of.

    *See* behaviour change.

    *See* forming and changing habits

competence 202

consistency 255–6

    *See also* scheduling

**D**

disconnection, between intentions
    and behaviour 221
    *See also* cognitive dissonance
dopamine 205–12
    abstinence and 99
    in addiction context 34
    in habit versus addiction context 34
    role in reward prediction
        error 165–6

**E**

eating habits. *See also* weight loss
    attempts
    abstinence from specific foods 99
    author's personal experience 164–5,
        239
    autonomy, role of 200
    cravings, managing 149–50
    dessert as a habit 90
    ego depletion and 143, 144
    food addiction 112–13
    habit loops 92
    highly processed foods 113, 163–4
    micro habits 119
    momentum, maintaining 262–3
    restructuring 95, 96–7
    reward prediction error 163–5
    rewards, paying attention to 172–3
    self-control 135, 138–9
    trait versus state motivation 199
    triggers 57–8, 61–2, 64

ego depletion 138–45, 167
    *See also* self-control
execution habits 129–31
exercise, benefits of 150–1
exercise habits
    author's personal experience 197
    changing habits as goals
        change 220–21
    cue–response association 96
    ego depletion and 143
    falling out of the habit 90
    frozen habits 98
    gender differences 176
    illness, dealing with 254–5
    micro habits 119, 120, 124–5, 126
    relatedness as motivation 201
    restructuring 97
    self-efficacy and goal-setting 240
    setbacks, dealing with 254
    triggers 64
exposure therapy 149

**F**

fear, as overarousal symptom 129
flow, natural 40–1
food habits. *See* eating habits.
    *See* weight loss attempts
forbidden fruit effect 141
forces of behaviour. *See* intention.
    *See* habits. *See* goal-setting
forming and changing habits 19–20,
    21–3

# Index

*See also* behaviour change.

    *See also* exercise habits.

    *See also* weight loss attempts.

brain activity during 109–11

breaking old habits 87–8

breaking unwanted habits, four
    steps for 98

creating new habits, five steps
    for 79–84

curiosity and kindness, using as
    strategies 172–5

forming new habits 75–9

gender differences 175–6

good and bad habits, differences
    between 176–7

habit-formation framework 75–9

micro habits, importance of.

    *See* micro habits

myths about 155

reprogramming 92–5

restructuring 95–8

simplicity, significance of 118–19

time required for. *See* time required
    to form, change and break
    habits, factors affecting

frozen habits 98


**G**

gaming

    brain changes in gamers 207–8

    gaming addiction 100

gender and habits 175–6

goal-setting

    challenging goals, setting 241

    commitment to goals 237–8

    cues, creating 245

    definition of 'goal' 234

    effects of on actions 235–6

    feedback on progress 238–9

    intention and habit, roles of 47

    intrinsic motivation and 239–40

    motivation and right-size
        goal-setting 127–8

    pitfalls 244–5

    principles 236

    sacrifices required 242–3

    self-efficacy affirmations 259–60

    simple versus complex goals 242

gratitude practice 162, 167


**H**

Habit Change Institute 12

habits

    addictions compared to habits 33–4

    author's research and
        experience 4–7

    automaticity. *See* automaticity

    being too habitual 219–20, 220–1

        *See also* new things, trying

    benefits. *See* benefits of habits

    brain's role in. *See* brain, human

    changing habits. *See* forming and
        changing habits

    characteristics 27–31

definition 15–16

forming habits. *See* forming and
    changing habits

gender differences 175–6

habit chains 10, 62–3

habit loop, the 17–18

identifying 31–2

intention compared with habit.
    *See* intention

micro habits. *See* micro habits

motivation to form, change or break
    habits. *See* motivation

self-control versus habit.
    *See* self-control

strength of habits, measuring 32–3

time required to break habits.
    *See* time required to form,
    change and break habits,
    factors affecting

values alignment and
    habits 111–14

Hebbian learning 21–2, 93–4
    *See also* anti-Hebbian learning


**I**

impulsive brain 45–6, 48–54

instigation habits 129–31

intention
    brain processes and 45–6, 48–51
    habit compared with 45–6
    intention–behaviour gap 46–8
    reflective–impulsive model 51–4


**L**

language learning 122

laziness versus exhaustion 142–3


**M**

'manifestations', neuroscience
    of 257–9

meditation habits
    COM-B framework and 181
    trait versus state motivation 199

micro habits
    goal-setting and 245
    instigation versus execution
        habits 129–31
    reward pathways and easy wins 121
    self-efficacy, effectiveness in
        boosting 121–4
    success rates 119–20
    trajectory versus speed 121

mind, compared with brain 105–6

mindset, reticular activating system
    and 257–9

motivation
    action as prerequisite to 196–7
    competing motivational
        forces 212–13
    definition 180, 192–3
    emotions and past experiences,
        effects of, on 215
    environmental factors 215
    extrinsic versus intrinsic
        motivation 193–5

factors influencing 268–9

goals as motivating forces.
*See* goal-setting

intrinsic motivation, prerequisites
to 199–202

maximising 184–5

motivational theories, components
of 192–3

positive feedback 215

as process 198

rewards and punishment 194–5,
202–4

setting right-size goals 127–8

sport and motivation 127–8

as state 198

as trait 198–9

variable-ratio reinforcement 204

what lack of motivation feels
like 196

what motivation feels like 195–6

movement, benefits of 150–1

**N**

natural flow 41

nature, role of in stress
reduction 146

neurogenesis 109–10

neuroplasticity 107–9
*See also* brain, human

new things, trying 222–8

New Year's resolutions 197, 233

**P**

perspective 147, 213–14

post-traumatic stress disorder 9–11,
12

powerlifting 53–4, 220–1, 254–5

**R**

radical acceptance 167–8

reflective brain. *See* intention

relatedness 200–1

repetition, as characteristic of
habits 27–8

research into habits, author's
experience and findings 4–7

resilience, practising 251–3

reticular activating system 257–9

rewards and punishment 194–5,
202–4

**S**

scheduling 253–5

self-compassion 260–2

self-control
behavioural and social problems
stemming from lack of 136
benefits 145
definition 135
ego depletion 138–45
forbidden fruit effect 141
habits versus self-control 151
nature of 136–8
replenishing 145–8

self-criticism 262

self-efficacy 121–4

  affirmations 259–60

  competence, intrinsic motivation
    and self-efficacy 202

  deficit of 122–3

  goal-setting and 240

  maintaining through
    setbacks 256–60

senses, as perception aids 37

setbacks, dealing with 249–51

  consistency and scheduling 253–6

  momentum 262–3

  resilience 251–3

  self-compassion 260–2

  self-efficacy 256–60

sleep

  dopamine and sleep 211

  sleep deficit, effects of 142

smoking habit and cessation attempts

  anticipation, effect of 206–7

  anticipatory anxiety 172

  ego depletion and 143, 144

  marketing and 112

  restructuring 95

  reward prediction error 164

  self-efficacy 240

  studies 25–6, 31

  triggers for smoking 58

social media habits

  ego depletion and 144

  habit reprogramming 94–5

manipulation by developers 113–14

  micro habits 121

  triggers 61

sport

  exercise as habit. *See* exercise habits

  natural flow and 41

  powerlifting 53–4

stress

  effects 148

  managing, through
    movement 150–1

  managing, with deep
    breathing 150

  practising awareness of 149–50

  reframing 168–9

  role in habit formation 166–9

synaptic pruning 110

synaptic strengthening 110

**T**

time required to form, change
  and break habits, factors
  affecting 155, 156, 169–72

  complexity of behaviour 161

  consistency 159–0

  habitual nature 157–9

  inconsistency 160

  reward prediction error 162–6

  reward value 161–2

  stress 166–9

trauma 9–11, 12

  exposure therapy 149

# Index

triggers of habits

  categories 59

  common triggers 65

  definition 58–9

  emotions 63–4

  location 60–2

  preceding events and actions 62–3

  qualities of effective triggers 66–8

  social situations 64–5

  time 60

tunnel vision 220–21

## U

unwanted habits, why we have 88–91

## V

values, alignment between habits
  and 111–14

video gaming. *See* gaming

## W

weight loss attempts. *See also* eating
  habits

  author's observations as
    dietician 3–4

  author's observations as habit
    researcher 4–7

  author's personal experience 29–30,
    140–1, 239

  micro habits 120, 124–5, 126

  perspective, significance of 213–14

  self-control 137, 140–1

  setbacks, dealing with 253

  trying something new, effects
    of 225–6

willpower. *See* self-control

worrying, as habit 173–5